RYA Knots Ropework Handbook

by Gordon Perry & Steve Judkins

Illustrations by Steve Lucas

2008

© RYA 2008
© Gordon Perry & Steve Judkins
First Published 2008
The Royal Yachting Association
RYA House, Ensign Way, Hamble
Southampton SO31 4YA
Tel: 0845 345 0400
Fax: 0845 345 0329
Email: publications@rya.org.uk
Web: www.rya.org.uk
ISBN: 978-1-905104-75-8
RYA Order Code: G63

All rights reserved. No part of this publication or cd-rom may be stored in a retrieval system, or transmitted, in any form or by any means, electronic, mechanical, photocopying, recording or otherwise, without the prior permission in writing of the publishers.

A CIP record of this book is available from the British Library.

Note: While all reasonable care had been taken in the preparation of this book, the publisher takes no responsibility for the use of the methods or products or contracts described in the book.

Acknowledgements: Ken Nelson, for his narrowboat ropework contribution, Jenny and her horse-drawn narrowboat "IONA", Master rigger, Brion Toss for his contributions on the Brummel Splice and fellow members of the International Guild of Knot Tyers. Finally to Marlow Ropes for their kind help in providing the rope which was used in making the knots, splices and ropework for the illustrations.
Cover Design: Creativebyte
Typeset: Creativebyte
Proofreading and indexing: Alan Thatcher
Printed in China through World Print

Introduction

Although this book has been written and illustrated specifically with the boating fraternity in mind; the content is nevertheless applicable to a much wider readership.

The book is structured around three main steps in knotting and ropework; the first "Learning the Ropes" provides for those beginning to learn about rope, knots and handling lines, with chapters on rope materials and construction, its care and use, the terminology used and the tools of the trade, culminating in a brief on belays, blocks and tackles. Then for the beginner learning to tie knots there is a gradual progression from elementary knot structures through to learning to tie the most essential knots used afloat.

The next part is devoted to a selection of knots, bends, hitches, loops and splicing, which have many and varied uses afloat; aimed at revising and enhancing the reader's knowledge of useful knots with a comprehensive chapter on Splicing, Seizing and Serving.

The final part of the book can be classed as "Advanced Knotting" featuring the Turk's Head, Star Knot, and 'how to make' some of those practical projects in rope and line that you wished you knew how to do, including lanyards, rope mats, fenders, a boat lead line and a selection of decorative and traditional boat ropework.

Watch out for the "Bosun" too, he has many a worthwhile tip to help you on your way.

ACKNOWLEDGEMENTS

No book on knots, splicing and ropework is the work of one man and although my name appears on the cover, this book is compiled using the knowledge and help gleaned from many other authors and fellow members of the International Guild of Knot Tyers from around the world.

My right hand man, without whom this book would not have been written, is Yachtmaster and fellow IGKT Member, Steve Judkins, who should rightly share in any credit, particularly for the enthusiasm, practical knowledge and facilities he was able to provide. The illustrator, Steve Lucas, I am sure you will agree, has produced some stunning illustrations to add to your pleasure of owning and using this book; this is largely because he has shown a keen interest in the subject and great attention to detail. The final member of the 'team', deserving of a bouquet, for her patience, tolerance and design ideas, is Lauren Wood of Creativebyte Ltd.

My thanks also go to Ken Nelson, for his Narrowboat ropework contribution, and to Jenny and her horse drawn narrowboat 'IONA', to Master Rigger, Brion Toss of Port Townsend, USA for his contributions of the Brummel Splice and the St Mary's Hitching. Finally we have Marlow Ropes Ltd for providing the rope with which most of the knots and splices in the illustrations were tied.

Learning The Ropes — 7

Materials – Natural Fibres	9
Materials – Man-made Fibres	10
Stranded Ropes	11
Multiplait Ropes	11
Braided Ropes	12
Rope Markings	13
Shock Cord & Tape	13
Care & Maintenance	14
Hand Coiling Stranded Ropes	17
Hand Coiling Braided Ropes	18
Deck Coiling Ropes	19
Terminology	20
Tools	21

Blocks & Tackles — 23

Blocks	24
Tackles	25
Tricing	25
Runner	25
Gun Tackle	26
Handy Billy	26
Luff Tackle	26
Double Luff	26
Light Gyn	27
Parbuckle	27
Spanish Windlass	28

Belays — 29

Single Bollard	30
Double Bollard	30
Staghorn	31
T Bar	31
Cleat	32
Belaying Pin	33
Ground Stake	34
Ring	35
Winches	36

Progressive Knot Tying · 37

End & Stopper Knots	39
Bends	44
Binding Knots	46
Hitches	48
Loops	55

Rope End & Stopper Knots · 59

Overhand & Figure of Eight Knots	60
Heaving Line Knot	61
Monkey's Fist	62
Matthew Walker Knot	64
Manrope Knot	66
Common Whipping	67
Sailmaker's Whipping	68
Palm & Needle Whipping	69

Bends · 71

Sheet Bend – Variants	73
Sheet Bend – Double	74
Sheet Bend – One Way	75
Heaving Line Bend	76
Racking Bend	77
Seizing Bend	78
Alpine Butterfly Bend	80
Ashley's Bend	81
Rigger's Bend	82
Fisherman's Knot	84
Fisherman's Eight Knot	85
Harness Bend	86
Blood Knot Bend	88
Carrick Bend	90
Bowline Bend	92

Hitches · 93

Half Hitches	95
Cow Hitches	96
Clove Hitch	97

Prusik Hitch	98
Blake's Hitch	99
High Post Hitch	100
Pile Hitch	101
Icicle Hitch	102
Anchor Bend	103
Timber Hitch and Killick Hitch	104
Scaffold Hitch	105
Buntline Hitch	106
Guyline Hitch	107
Halyard Knot	108

Loops & Nooses 109

Overhand Loop	111
Double Overhand Loop	111
Artilleryman's Knot	112
Alpine Butterfly Loop	113
Bowline	114
Common	114
Climber's method	115
Tucked	116
On a Bight	117
Water	118
Running	119
Figure of Eight Loop	120
Packer's Knot	121
Bottle Knot	122
Double Fisherman's Loop	123
Jury Mast Knot	124

Lashings & Bindings 125

Mousing Hooks	128
Mousing a Shackle	129
Half Hitch Lashing	130
Marling Hitching	131
Chain Hitching	132
Trucker's Hitch	134
Square Lashing	136
Diagonal Lashing	138
Transom Knot	140
Rope Stopper	141
Chain Stopper	142

Splicing, Serving & Seizing — 143

Three Strand Backsplice	146
Three Strand to Chain Splice	147
Three Strand Eye Splice	148
Three Strand Short Splice	150
Three Strand Long Splice	152
Multiplait Eye Splice	154
Multiplait Short Splice	156
Multiplait Rope to Chain Splice	158
Halyard Becket or Backsplice	160
Braid on Braid Eye Splice	161
Braid with Core Eye Splice	164
Reduction Splice	166
Hollow Braid Eye Splice	168
Yachtsman's Roll Splice	170
Rope to Wire Splice	172
Three Strand Rope Grommet	175
Serving	177
Seizing	179

Marlinespike Ropework — 181

Turk's Head Knots	183
Star Knot	190
Decorative Coverings	192
King-Spoke Turk's Head	194
Two Short Lanyards	196
Knife Lanyard	199
Binoculars Lanyard	200
Spectacles Lanyard	202
Thump Mat	204
Mast Dropper	205
Cabin Strings	206
Ocean Plait Mat	208
Square Mat	210
Side Fender	212
Disc Fender	214
Bell Rope	218
Baggy Wrinkle	222
Lead Line	226

CHAPTER 1:

LEARNING THE ROPES

MATERIALS - NATURAL FIBRES
MATERIALS - MAN-MADE FIBRES
STRANDED ROPES
MULTIPLAIT ROPES
BRAIDED ROPES
ROPE MARKINGS
SHOCK CORD & TAPE
CARE & MAINTENANCE
HAND COILING STRANDED ROPE
HAND COILING BRAID ON BRAID
DECK COILING ROPES
TERMINOLOGY
TOOLS

Introduction: Learning the Ropes

To master the practical aspects of knotting and ropework, it is important to learn a little about the materials, tools and terminology used. By taking time to study this chapter first, you will achieve a better understanding of the text and subsequently be able to converse with others about knots and rope with confidence. Starting with brief notes on the materials used for making both natural and man-made fibre ropes, the chapter goes on to explain how stranded, braided and plaited ropes, shock cord and tape, are made up and marked.

The care and maintenance of rope is covered next, including the different methods of spooling, coiling and hanking rope and twine, tips on handling new line and a table of Do's and Don'ts.

The chapter concludes with a comprehensively illustrated section devoted to the tools and terminology used in explaining knots, splicing and marlinespike ropework, which, in order to understand the subject is a 'must read'.

Rope Construction - Materials

NATURAL FIBRES

Cotton: From the seed boll of *Gossypium*. White/off-white in colour. Nice to handle but very little strength.

Coir/bass: From the fibre enveloping the coconut, fruit of *Cocos nucifera*. Dark tan colour. This rope will float until it becomes waterlogged.

Jute: From bast fibres of *Corchorus capsularis or olitorius* – Used to make small woven ropes (sash cord) or garden twine.

Flax: From bast fibres of *Linum usitatissimum* - Used mainly for textiles – much of the old canvas was a mixture of cotton and flax. Now used mainly to make a 'hemp like' rope and some small stuff, like household string.

Hemp: From bast fibres of *Cannabis sativa*. Almost all rope, until about 100 years ago was hemp. Pale in colour, with good handling qualities.

Sisal: From the leaf fibres of the cactus-like plant – *Agave sisalana* – pale golden colour. General purpose ropes and binder twine.

Manila: From the leaf fibres of the Abaca (wild banana) plant. Straw coloured. A general purpose rope, which has largely replaced hemp. The quality of manila rope today varies considerably, from good quality smooth rope with regular fibres, to rough rope made from fibres which vary in thickness - take care handling this rope as you are likely to get splinters from it.

MAN-MADE FIBRES

Polyamide (Pa) (Nylon)
Discovered in the 30s by the Du Pont company. A very strong, smooth white rope that has the ability to stretch. Prone to going hard with age, Nylon ropes need UV protection and lose a little strength when wet. Uses: Mooring lines, safety lines etc.

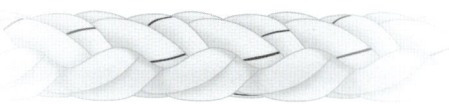

Polyester (PES/PET) (Dacron™, Terylene™, Vectran™)
White fibres, retains its strength when wet and does not stretch like Nylon – particularly if pre-stretched. Hard wearing. Uses: Halyards, static lines, control lines, general purpose.

Polypropylene (PP) (Hardy Hemp™ – Marstron™)
Used to make inexpensive ropes, and to make mock natural fibre ropes! Also made up from split-film (blue) – It floats and can be brightly coloured. Uses: Water ski-ropes and lifelines.

Polyethylene (PE)
Made from white or coloured coarse fibres. Also floats. Polythene development has also resulted in ropes being manufactured from High Modulus Polyethylene (HMPE), which is size for size as strong as steel wire rope. Light weight, water resistant and low stretch properties make it popular for use in sailing dinghies and high performance yachts, but beware, HMPE is weakened considerably by knots!

Polybenzoxazole (PBO) – (Zylon™)
PBO has an extremely high tensile strength and can be used for standing rigging. Like HMPE, knots reduce the strength considerably, resulting in the need to terminate the ends in either swages or around deadeyes.

Rope Construction - Stranded

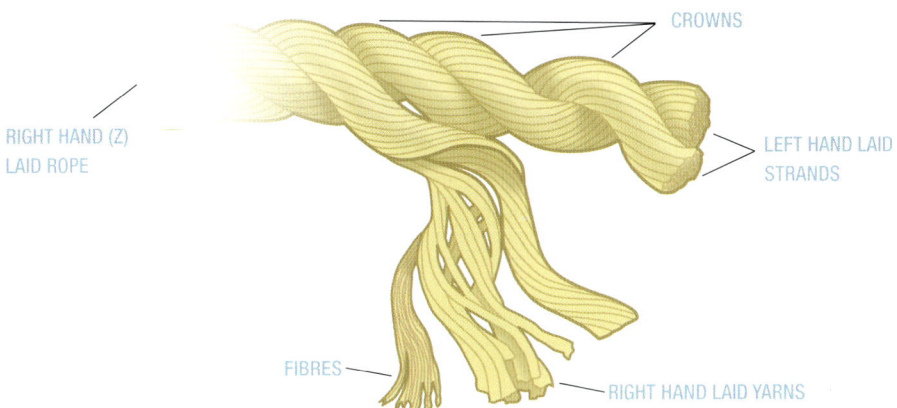

VARIATIONS

Left Hand Laid
The strands are laid twisting to the left, sometimes referred to as 'S' laid.

Hard Laid
The strands are wound very tightly together making the rope very stiff.

Soft Laid
The strands are wound loosely together, making the rope soft and supple.

4 Strand Rope
Sometimes referred to as shroud laid rope, more common on the Continent than in the UK – has 4 strands and a single small strand core.

Cable Laid Rope
9 strands made up of 3 x 3 strand ropes and can be either right or left hand laid.

Rope Construction - Multiplait

Multiplait rope (8 or 12 strand) consists of 2 or 3 pairs of right hand laid strands, plaited with 2 or 3 pairs of left hand laid strands. Sometimes referred to as 8 plait, but not to be confused with 8 plait hollow braid ropes.

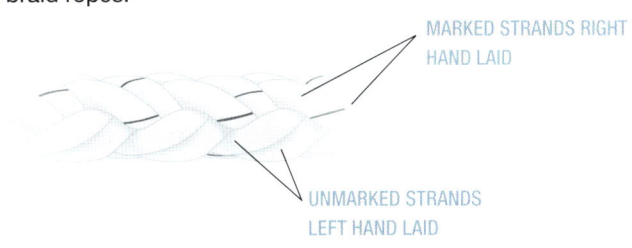

Rope Construction - Braided

BRAID WITH LOOSELY TWISTED CORE

MATT BRAID WITH 3 STRAND CORE

BRAID ON BRAID

BRAID WITH DYNEEMA™ CORE

Rope Markings

Rogue's Yarn
The Rogue's Yarn is rarely seen these days. The Admiralty used a single coloured thread in one strand of their ropes as an identification mark: the ropemasters at Chatham still use a yellow yarn. Commercial rope makers used black, which is now used by Marlow Ropes Ltd. Rope identification today is quite complex, with each manufacturer having their own system of markings, details of which can be found on the Internet or their brochures.

Standard Material Markers
Man-made fibre ropes have an ISO and British Standards colour code for identification, similar to the Rogue's Yarn, these (when used) consist of a single yarn in a strand or woven into the braid.

Green - Polyamide (Nylon) (PA)
Blue - Polyester (PES/PET)
Orange - Polyethylene (PE) and (HMPE)
Red - Polypropylene (PP)

Unfortunately some manufacturers use the same colours to identify their brand, so care should be taken when using these yarns to identify material.

Another, more reliable method of identifying some ropes is the 'Identification Tape'; unfortunately the rope has to be pulled apart to find it. This is a thin film tape buried in one strand or the core, which gives the manufacturer's name, material (Specification Number) and year of manufacture.

CE Marking of ropes and splices is becoming increasingly more common and essential for Personal Protection Equipment ropes and lines. The CE Mark will be around the outer cover of the rope covered with a transparent shrink-wrap.

Shock (bungee) Cord and Tape

Shock, or 'bungee' cord consists of a bundle of rubber strips packed tightly together inside a flexible cover. Most shock cord is designed to be used at a maximum stretch of one third its natural length.

SHOCK CORD

WEBBING TAPE

Care and Maintenance

HANDLING COILS AND INSPECTING ROPES

Care and Maintenance of Cordage
New rope, cord and line is carefully coiled, hanked, spooled or made into a ball appropriate to its type and construction. When you buy new cordage it will come in one of the following forms, so here are a few pointers on how best to handle them.

Hanks
A hank of rope is no more than a coil held by turns around its girth – these range from a few to a complete 'typical clothes line hank'. To keep rope, especially natural fibre ropes, entrapped like this for a long period of time is not good for the rope, as the turns 'settle' and make future use quite difficult. Hanks should be a temporary measure and unwound, coiled naturally and left to settle before use.

Ball
Small stuff can be rolled into a ball, especially if you are sorting out a 'birds nest' of line that has tied itself in all sorts of tangles. Once formed it should be placed in a cloth or net bag which is tied at the neck with the end of the line protruding from it. Pull the line from the bag and as the ball gets smaller, reduce the size of the bag by moving the neck tie down a little. This also applies to the hollow balls, often used with garden twine – except that you should take the twine from the centre of the ball, as you would a coil of rope.

Spool or Bobbin

Another popular method of supplying small stuff is the spool or bobbin – these are intricately wound on a hollow tube while it is spinning; the line should be taken off the same way, by spinning the tube and not taken off the end as this is likely to cause kinking. Spools like this are best used suspended on a horizontal rod.

Reels or Drums

Reels or drums are a convenient way of transporting and dispensing rope - no doubt you have seen the rows of reel racks in your local chandlery. Smaller reels are commonly used for small line like whipping twine and cord up to about 3mm (.0098ft). The rope or line is again wound on a rotating reel, therefore the correct way to take rope off is to rotate the reel and pull the rope off the way it went on - you may not have a rack like the chandler, but a broom handle or boat hook through the reel will do the same job. With the reels, hold the centre each side between your thumb and forefinger then pull the line off.

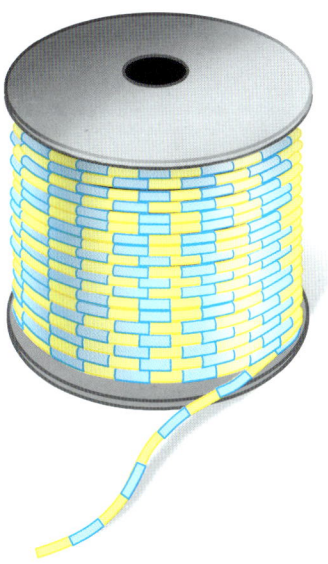
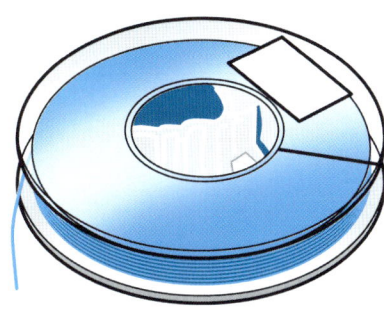

Coil

Ropes that do not come on a reel are usually coiled. The coils are wound on a collapsible spool arrangement which rotates to wind the rope onto it. When the coil is complete it is tied with pre-positioned stops then removed from the spool and is sometimes bagged. Removing rope from a coil can be done in two ways – either suspend the coil on a turntable which will rotate and allow you to pull the rope from the outside of the coil, or better still, pull the end of the rope from the centre of the coil. However, there is a right way and a wrong way to do this, so – place the coil on its edge, untie the stops and pull the end of the rope out, if it kinks put it back and turn the coil over and take the end from the other side. When you have removed sufficient rope, re-tie the stops.

Rope Care

Ropes and lines will serve you well, provided they are properly cared for; not just when they are being used but before and after use too. Someone's life, your boat and equipment, to say nothing of your personal pride all depend on how well you care for the ropes you use.

The following list of Do's and Don'ts are here as a reminder; most are common sense and the list is not exhaustive.

Do:
- Use the right rope for the job
- Check for damage regularly
- Remove kinks and tangles before use
- Remove rope from new reels or coils with care
- Keep rope clean
- Remove knots when not in use
- End for end ropes subjected to wear at one point
- Stow dry or hang wet ropes properly coiled

Don't:
- Subject ropes to chemicals, sand, grit or oil
- Subject ropes to excessive friction on fittings or winches
- Overload ropes - especially shock-cord
- Stand on ropes
- Leave untreated man-made fibre ropes exposed to UV too long

Inspecting Rope

Rope should be inspected at every stage of its life and at every opportunity (especially halyards and rigging that are out of sight or above eye level). Inspect new rope before use, regularly check pinch points around deck fittings and sheaves, check sheets or gantlines at the first available opportunity if they have had an excessive jerk. Above all, if a person's life depends on the support of a rope it MUST be inspected before use and if in regular support use, like a designated gantline, it should be CE marked.

CARE & MAINTENANCE

Stranded Rope – Make a visual check for:
- Kinks
- Permanent splices, whipping or seizings showing signs of movement
- Surface wear or friction burns that have broken any yarns
- Open the lay and check for friction damage and stretch which will be shiny, or rot which will show as powder in natural fibre rope.
- Chemical, oil or grit damage
- UV deterioration (fibres breaking and lifting from the yarns)

Braided Ropes – Check for:
- Visual - damaged cover - abrasion or strands that have been caught and lifted. (Both of these need consideration as to how much of the strength of the safe working load will be affected)
- Visual - chemical, oil or grit damage
- By Feel - run the rope through the hand feeling for:
    - Hard spots (possible friction damage)
    - Reduction in core diameter - (possible break or damage from pinching)
    - Core and cover balanced - (cut the sealed/whipped end off and milk the cover from the other end, occasionally cut both together and re seal/whip).

Hand Coiling Stranded Rope
Coil with the lay of the rope twisting the line a little by turning the right fist towards the left palm. Near the end, pass a bight through the coil under the left hand, back over the top of the coil down to the turns, then pull on the end to tighten. Suspend by the end or on a peg or hook.

Learning the Ropes

Hand Coiling Braid on Braid

Because braid cores have no 'lay', to avoid kinks the rope must be coiled in a figure eight pattern. Hold the coil over the palm of one hand, extend the other hand allowing the rope to pass through the fist, then bring the fist back to the other hand palm to palm – the rope will form figure eight loops quite naturally. Near the end, take a few turns around the coil, pass a bight through the coil, over the top and back to the turns. Suspend by the end.

Stowing Stiff or Awkward Ropes - Chain Shortening Hank

Some ropes, no matter how hard you try will not coil neatly. One way to overcome this is to lay the rope out doubled, double that again then put a slipped overhand in the end with the two bights, then bring all four parts through the knot as a bight, forming chain shortening. Pull the end through the last bight and suspend by the two bights.

CARE & MAINTENANCE | 19

Deck Coiling Ropes

Rope that is too long or too large to coil in the hand is coiled on the deck – using a clockwise circular motion for right hand laid stranded ropes, or braid with a right hand twist or parallel core or an anti-clockwise circular motion for left hand laid stranded ropes. Braid on braid ropes can be coiled either way, or coiled to the right with an occasional left hand under-turn laid into the coil.

COIL

CHEESE

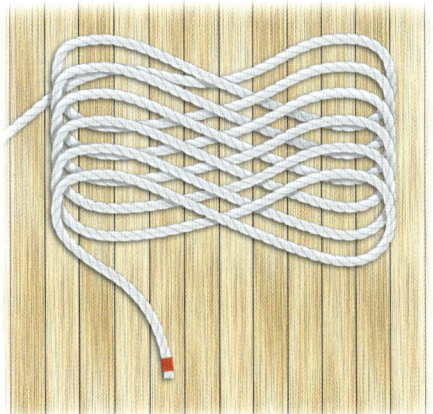

FLAKE (OR FAKE)

TIP FROM THE
BOSUN'S LOCKER

If you are going to rinse your ropes in a washing machine, coil your ropes using the chain shortening method to avoid tangles, hang up to dry then pull the end to undo the hank.

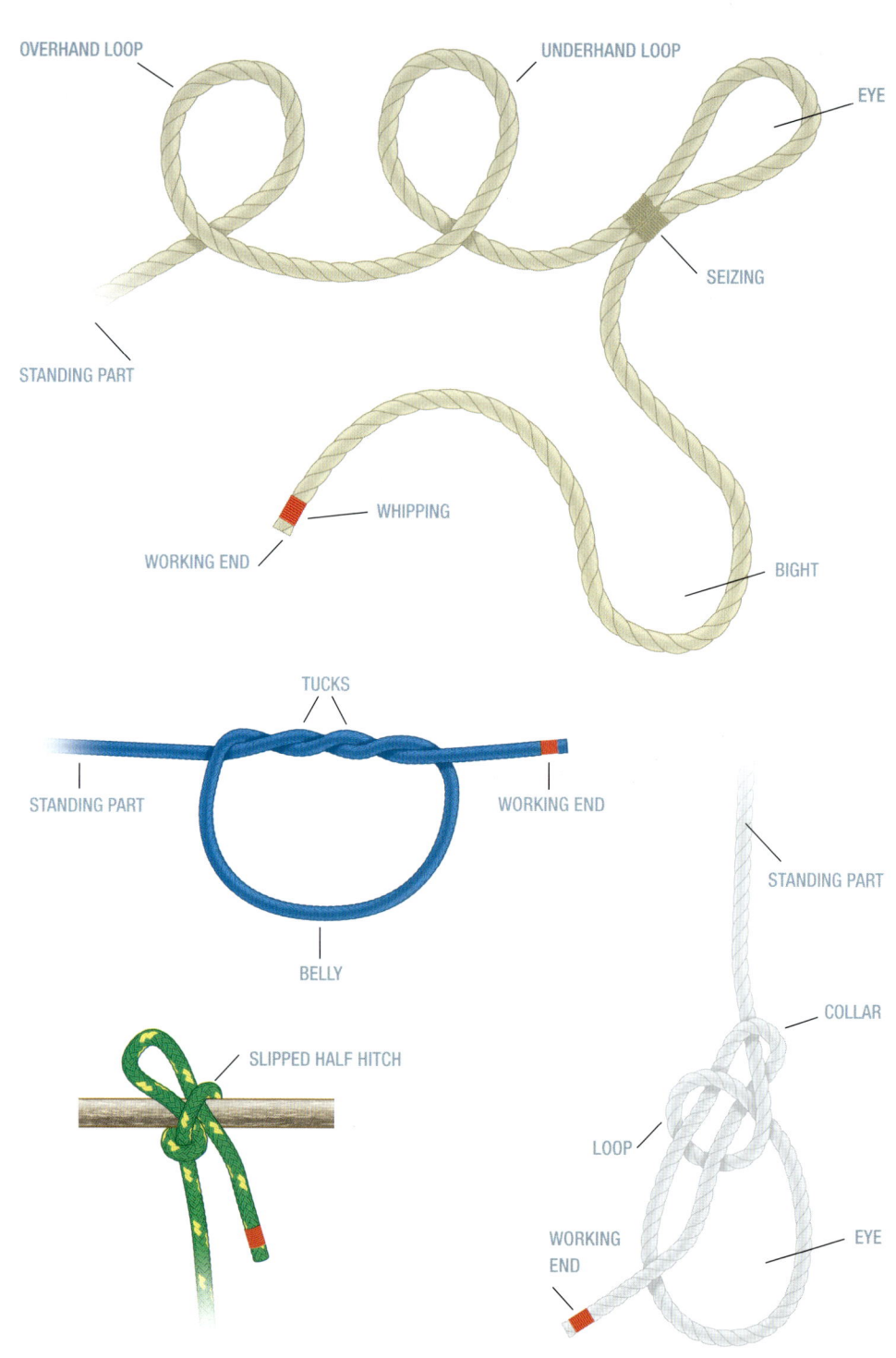

Tools

Like any other trade, rigging, sailmaking and ropework have a selection of specialist tools that have been developed over the years, to make working various materials more efficient. Although the knife and spike are the foundation tools of the trade, there are many others which the boater with an interest in knot work will accumulate over the years; some of these are shown here.

SAILMAKER'S TOOLS

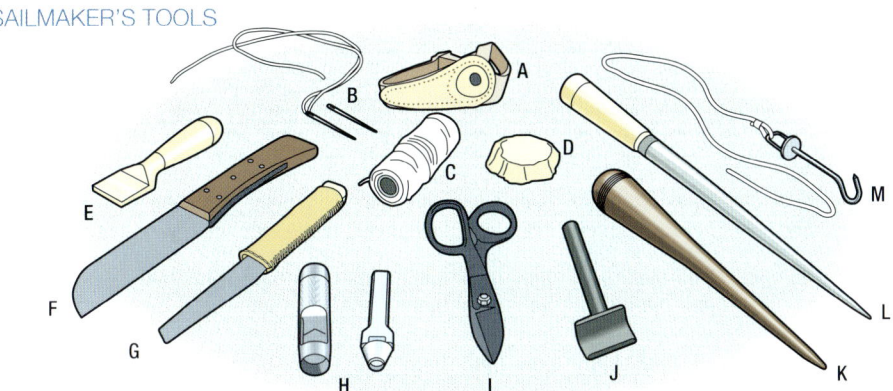

- A. Sailmaker's Palm
- B. Needles
- C. Sailmaker's Twine
- D. Bees Wax
- E. Seam Rubber
- F. Rigger's Knife
- G. Shoemaker's Knife
- H. Wad punches
- I. Scissors
- J. Serving Tool
- K. Wooden Fid
- L. Pricker
- M. Sail Hook

SPLICING TOOLS

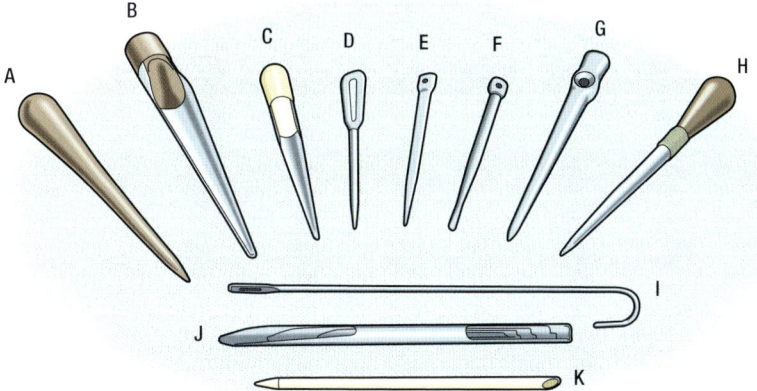

- A. Wooden Fid
- B. Swedish Fid (Large)
- C. Swedish Fid (Small)
- D. Marling Spike & Shackle Key
- E. Marling Spike (Tapered point)
- F. Marling Spike (Duckbill point)
- G. Heavy Marling Spike
- H. Wire splicing spike
- I. Splicing Needle (Marlow)
- J. Hollow metal splicing fids
- K. Hollow plastic splicing fid

GENERAL PURPOSE TOOLS

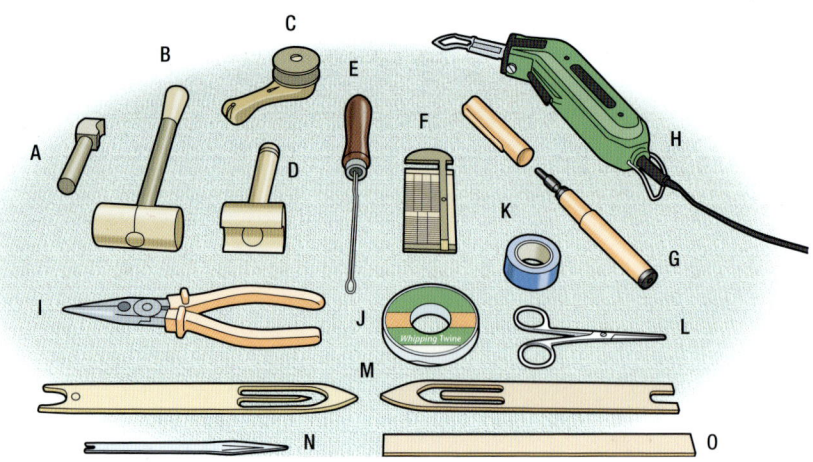

- A. Serving tool
- D. Serving Mallet
- G. Portable Hot Knife
- J. Whipping Twine
- M. Netting Needles
- B. Heaving Mallet
- E. Wire loop
- H. Electric Hot Knife
- K. Tape
- N. Small Netting Needle
- C. Serving board & Reel
- F. Rope Gauge
- I. Pliers
- L. Forceps
- O. Mesh Gauge or Stick

SEAMING PALM AND NEEDLE IN USE

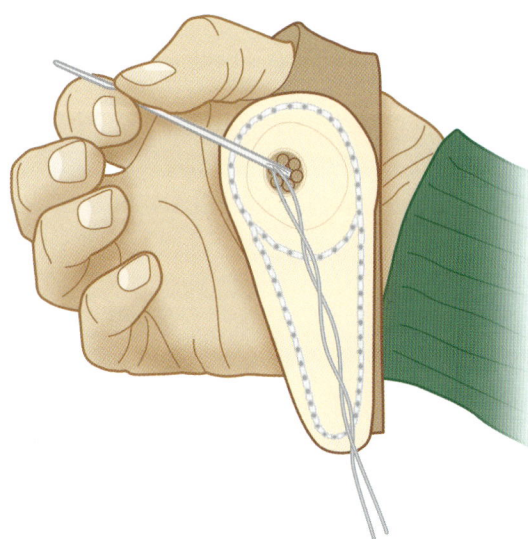

CHAPTER 2:

BLOCKS & TACKLES

BLOCKS

TACKLES

TRICING

RUNNER

GUN TACKLE

HANDY BILLY

LUFF TACKLE

DOUBLE LUFF

LIGHT GYN

PARBUCKLE

SPANISH WINDLASS

Introduction: Blocks and Tackles

Tackles (Tay-calls) are made up of blocks and rope (fibre or wire) in order to reduce the effort required to move a load. The 'mechanical advantage' provided by a tackle is determined by the number of sheaves, the way the 'fall' (standing part, runner and hauling part) is rove through the blocks, whether the standing part of the fall is fixed to the standing or moving block and of course friction. The 'fall', which has to be in a suitable position to heave on, will largely determine whether the tackle is rigged to 'Advantage' or 'Disadvantage'. It might seem strange that you would want to rig a tackle to disadvantage, but in many situations afloat a horizontal pull is the only practical way to rig a tackle, and that might mean rigging to 'Disadvantage'.

As well as Tackles, Parbuckling and the Spanish Windlass also provide the sailor with mechanical assistance using ropes – both are included in this chapter.

BLOCKS

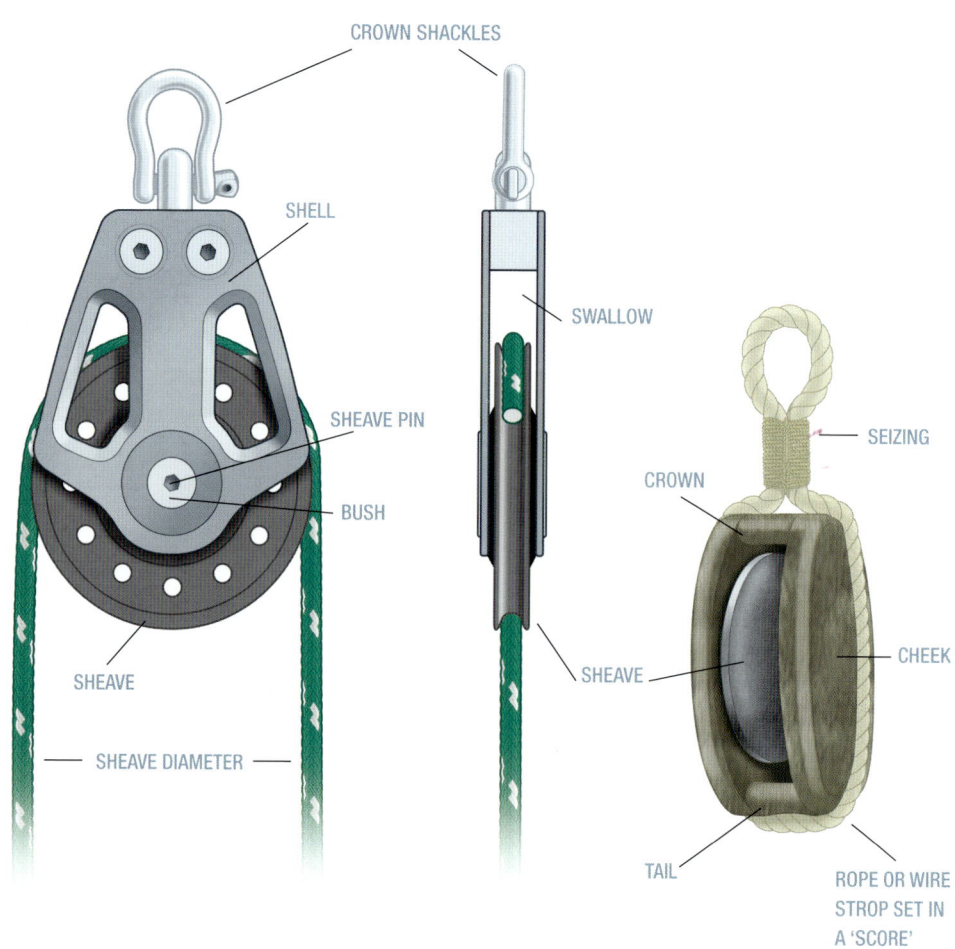

TACKLES

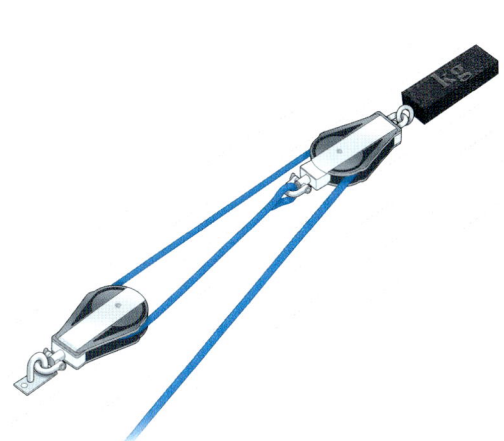

Tackle rigged to ADVANTAGE.
The fall emerges from the moving block.

Tackle rigged to DISADVANTAGE.
The fall emerges from the standing block.

TRICING

RUNNER

A Single Whip with the 'fall' attached to the load and run through a standing single sheave block. This arrangement does not provide any saving of effort and is mostly used as a halyard or as a 'lead block' through which a fall is rove to a convenient plane for handling.

A Single Whip used to advantage. The standing part of the 'fall' is secured to a deck fitting - where it can, if necessary, be run through a lead block to provide horizontal haul.

GUN TACKLE

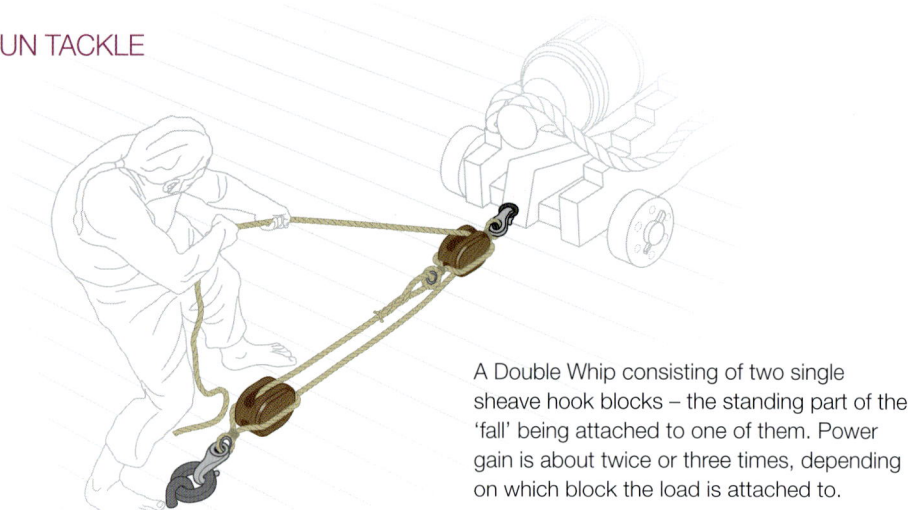

A Double Whip consisting of two single sheave hook blocks – the standing part of the 'fall' being attached to one of them. Power gain is about twice or three times, depending on which block the load is attached to.

HANDY BILLY

Also normally a Double Whip, but as its name implies it really is a 'come in handy' tackle for those times afloat when you need a helping hand. The standing part of the 'fall' is attached to the single sheave hook block then rove to disadvantage using a double block that becomes the standing block. Power gain is about three times.

LUFF TACKLE OR JIGGER

Like the Handy Billy, a Luff Tackle is rove through a single and double block, but this time they are both hook blocks, which means that it can be rigged with the load on either end. Power gain is about three or four times.

DOUBLE LUFF

A typical main sheet rig with the moving block attached to the boom. Two double blocks with a power gain of four or five times.

LIGHT GYN

Used for lifting heavy items off the deck. The Gyn tackle is made up of a three sheave standing block and a two sheave moving block.

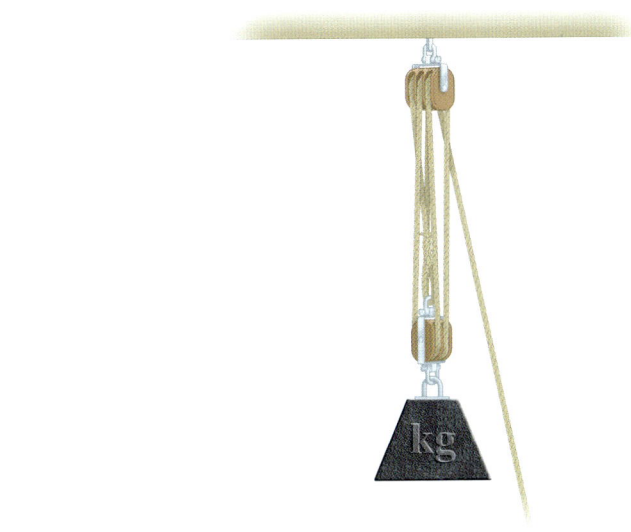

PARBUCKLE

By securing one end of two, or three lines, passing the bights around an object then hauling on the free end, a load can be raised up to the level of the secured ends with less effort than a direct pull. Hence it is possible to lift a load (or person) from the water to deck level using this method; using halyards and winches to haul on the free ends will give even more lifting power.

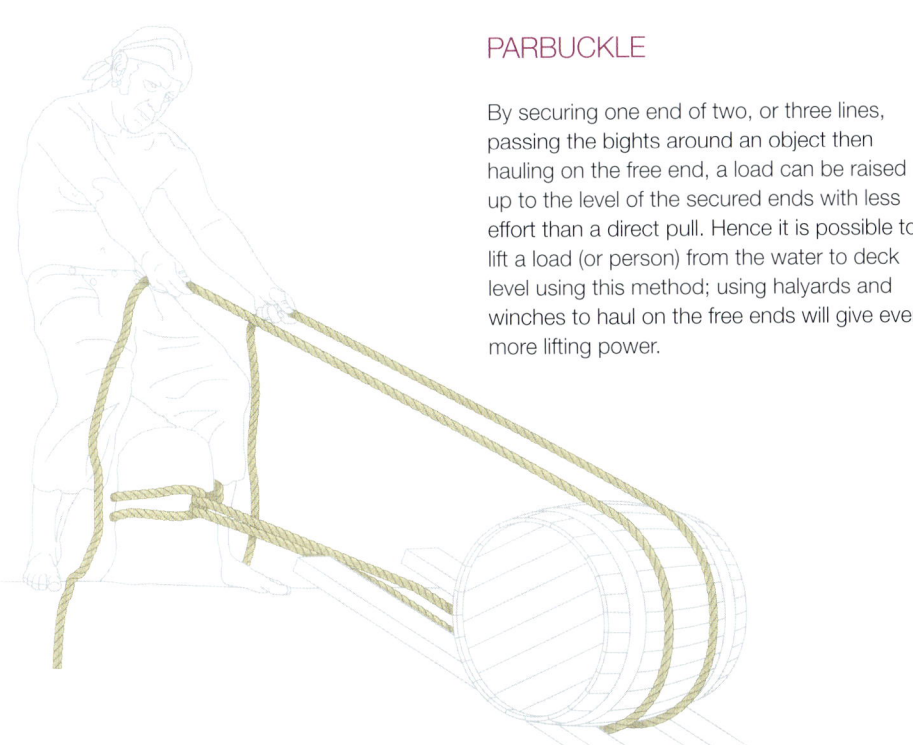

SPANISH WINDLASS

A simple but effective device for hauling a rope taut for serving, tightening seizings or for 'marrying' ropes under tension. Use with CAUTION – rope under tension is like a spring, so if the end of the tommy bar/marling spike is released it will flick back with considerable force. Also take care not to distort or damage the rope by over-tightening.

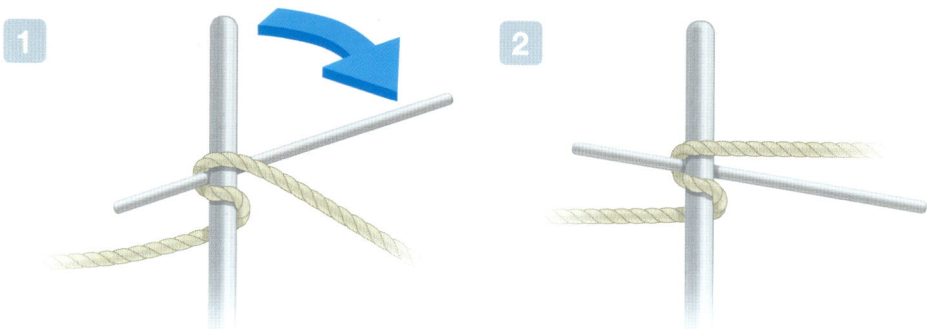

Two rotating steel rods in a rigger's bench is the ideal situation for applying the Spanish Windlass, but that is not likely to be a situation available to most people – so we have to improvise and use a stout stanchion, handrail or other cylindrical fitting. Secure both ends of the rope so that there is some slack in it. Bring a small bight in front of the upright and insert a tommy bar or marling spike into the bight as shown in diagram 1. Now rotate the bar in the direction shown, which should now be putting a little tightness into the rope.

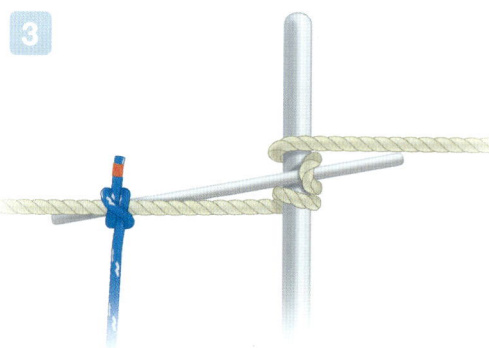

Rotate the tommy bar around the upright until sufficient tension is applied to the rope, taking care to keep hold of the bar. To secure the tommy bar, tuck the bar behind the rope and SECURE it (a Clove Hitch will suffice) or tie it off to another point with a lanyard.

CHAPTER 3:

BELAYS

SINGLE BOLLARD
DOUBLE BOLLARD
STAGHORN
T-BAR
CLEAT
BELAYING PIN
GROUND STAKE
RING
WINCHES

Introduction: Belays

To 'Belay' is to bring to a bollard, pin, cleat, or other fixed fitting a rope or wire in such a fashion that it can be hauled in, checked, surged, veered, let go and more importantly be secured to that fitting in a safe and secure manner.

Single Bollard

Used for securing berthing ropes/warps or any line requiring firm holding. Also known as a Bit, especially if holding cable/chain gear. When using a single bollard on the quayside, be considerate of other users – who may want to leave before you.

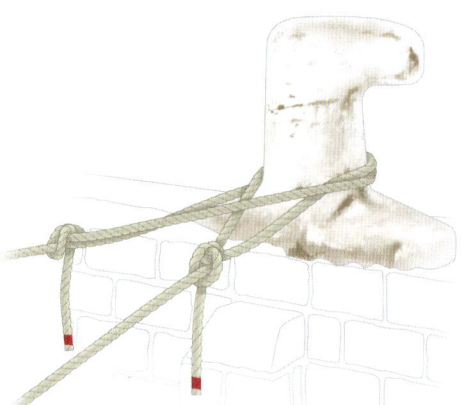

Belaying to a single bollard can be achieved with a simple eye either tied with a bowline or spliced. When using an eye or loop remember to 'dip the eye' of your rope through any existing loops, so that any one can be lifted off without having to move the others. When using the bight of a rope then the Lighterman's or Mooring Hitch is appropriate. Wire ropes without loops on the end should be secured with at least three turns and a Racking Seizing applied across the standing part and the working end.

Double Bollard

Double bollards are more likely to be found on the deck of larger vessels. Two turns around the leading bollard will provide adequate control when veering or holding.

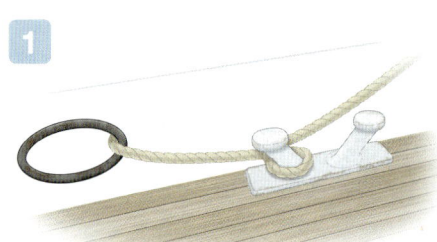

Take one or two turns around the leading bollard to adjust the tension then secure using figure of eight turns over both bollards. Secure with a Racking Seizing if necessary.

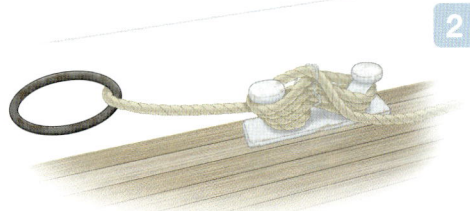

Staghorn

The Staghorn Bollard is another common ships' deck fitting – its main advantage being that it provides a much better means of control when paying out lines. It can also be used to accommodate more than one line.

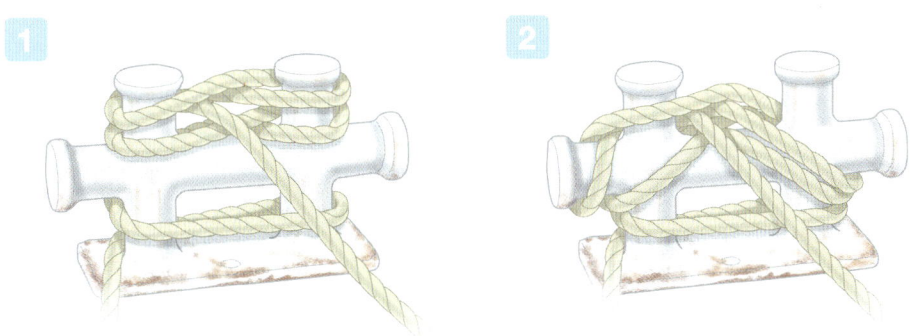

T-Bar

Used as a deck fitting on smaller vessels, especially the bow of a narrowboat.

Take one full round turn around the stem. Take a second turn around one bar and complete with a figure eight turn.

Secure by applying more eights or with a half hitch over one bar.

Cleat

Found in various forms and sizes made from wood or metal in all vessels, it is used for securing light ropes.

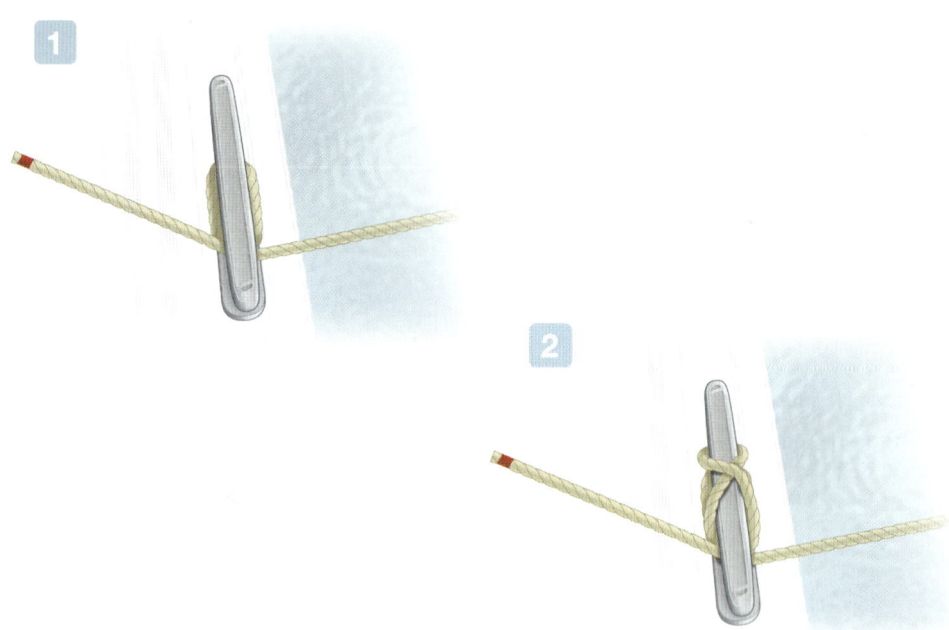

Take one complete turn around the cleat, under the horns. Make the second turn in the form of an eight over the top of the two horns.

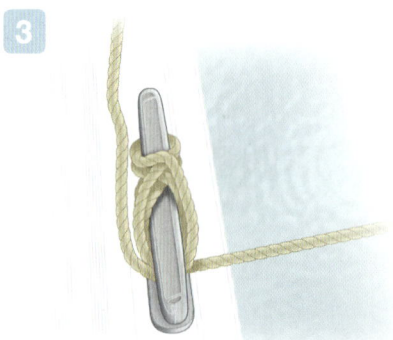

Secure with sufficient turns, there is no need to tie off with a half hitch.

Belaying Pin

The belaying pin is the forerunner of the cleat, and is used in the same manner, mainly on traditional craft and large sailing vessels of the 'tall ships' classes.

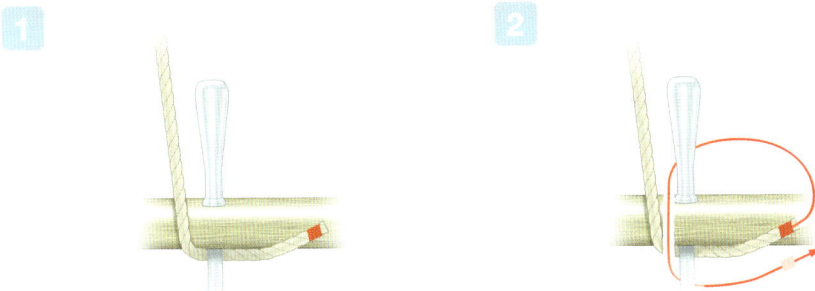

Ensure the 'lead' of the rope to the pin is such that it is in front of the rail and is passed around the lower or furthest part of the pin first. Note that not all pins go through rails; some are mounted in blocks or even through masts or bollards. Make a complete turn around both halves of the pin.

Follow up with a series of figure eight turns around both halves of the pin.

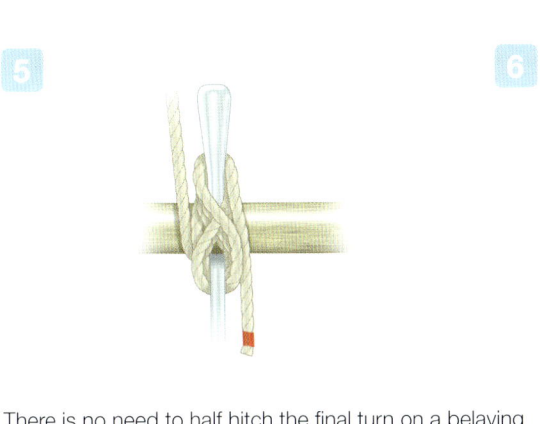

There is no need to half hitch the final turn on a belaying pin, but it may be necessary on other types of pin.

Ground Stake

Ground stakes are commonly used on canal, river or lake banks and on beaches.

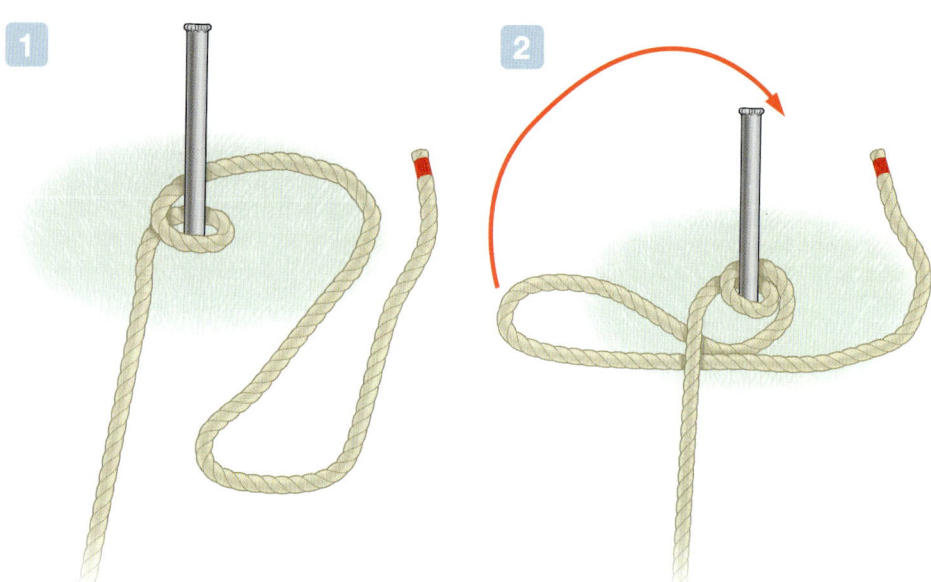

Belaying to a pin or stake like this is best achieved by using the Lighterman's Hitch or Mooring Hitch. It is simple to execute and will not jam. Taking a very long end, commence with a round turn on the pin, and then pass a bight under the standing part and over the pin.

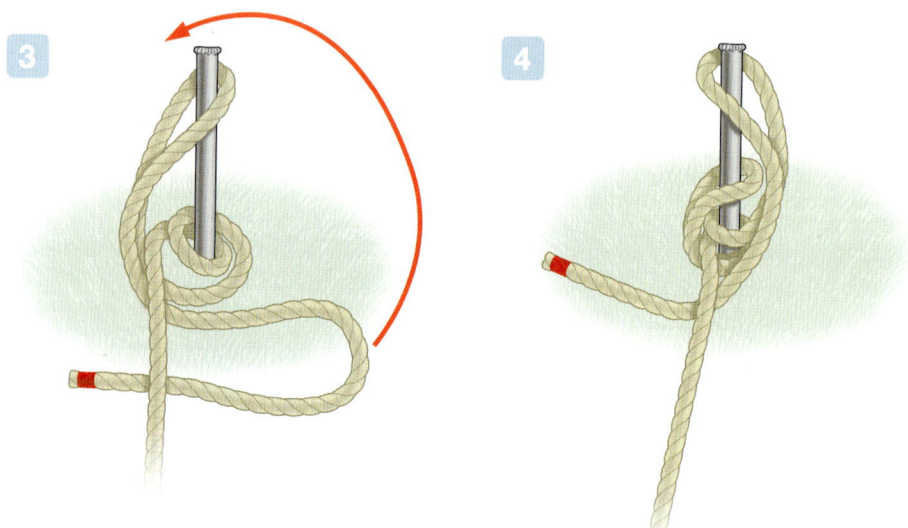

Pass another bight in the opposite direction and place that over the pin. If necessary a third bight can be used, but two should be sufficient and there is no need to tie it off.

Ring

Rings are another quayside fixing, popular on marina sponsons and jetties, not forgetting that most small dinghies have a ring to attach a painter to the stem post. Two knots are appropriate for belaying to a ring – the Round Turn and Two Half Hitches and the Fisherman's or Anchor Bend.

The Round Turn and Two Half Hitches is shown in diagram 1. The Fisherman's Bend starts with a round turn then the working end is passed between the turns and the ring…

before being secured with a half hitch around the standing part. If this belay is to be under any excess movement, the working end should be seized to the standing part.

Winches

A winch or windlass can be mechanically or hand powered and is used as an aid to hauling and veering ropes and cable. Although it is not a primary belaying fitting, it is often used to belay a line which is held in the hand or sometimes left made up ready for use and the rope tail secured to a primary belaying fitting.

1

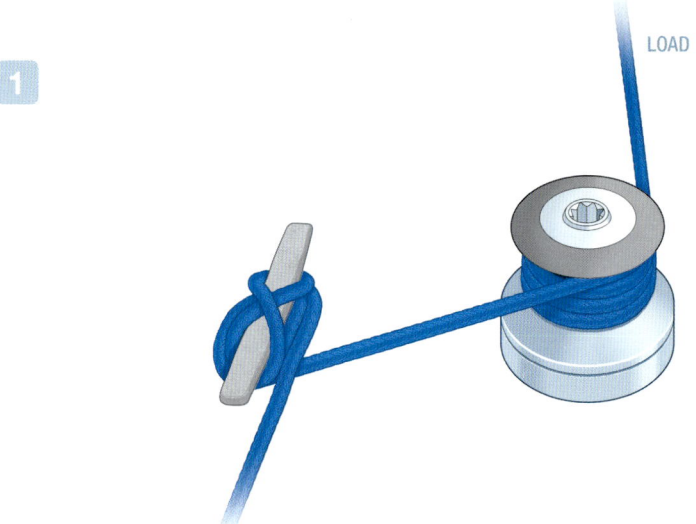

A hand powered winch requires at least three turns which are started from the bottom of the winch drum. The rope end can then either be hand held or secured to a cleat, as shown. Ensure that the standing part, bearing the load, does not ride up over the turns as it will be impossible to veer the line.

2

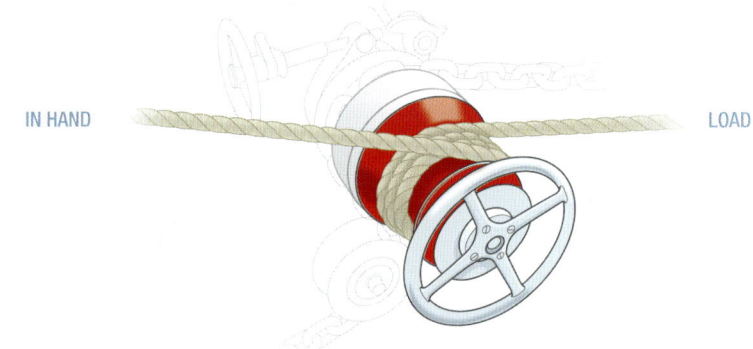

The mechanically powered windlass shown above requires at least three turns, laid on, in the direction of the turn, from inside to outside of the drum. The rope is backed up by hand then subsequently transferred to a primary belay fitting like a bollard or cleat.

CHAPTER 4:

PROGRESSIVE KNOT TYING

END OR STOPPER KNOTS

BENDS

BINDING KNOTS

HITCHES

LOOPS

Introduction: Progressive Knot Tying

BASIC KNOTS FOR BOAT USERS

The knots in this chapter are considered to be those most used and those that should be known by all boaters. When underway, at sea, on the river, canal or lake a skipper can give verbal orders to carry out any seamanship evolution that he requires you to do; what he cannot do, especially when under pressure, is to talk you through or tie knots for you. Therefore it is fundamental that any person acting as crew is able to tie the basic knots unaided.

For the beginner, this chapter is set out in stages; starting from the very basics to gradually build up a sound knowledge of knotting, which can be carried forward into the more complicated knots in this book. It is also hoped that you will not just learn, and practise these knots on a regular basis, but also think about what makes them the right knot for the job, why they are secure or not, how they work in some lines and not in others, etc. And for those of you who are revising your knotting skills – be sure to read the text as well as following the diagrams; you might just pick up a tip that will be useful one day.

To practise the knots in this section you will need three pieces of line, ideally about 1.5 metres long, one with a diameter of 1 to 4 mm and two between 8 and 12 mm in diameter.

End and Stopper Knots

Tied by fish and birds, man and monkey, the Overhand Knot is the foundation of knotting and the basis on which well over 30 other knots are tied. A thorough understanding of the characteristics and methods of tying the five different Overhand Knot variations shown here, will make the more complex knots, included in this book, very much easier to learn.

SINGLE OVERHAND KNOT

Sometimes known as a 'Thumb Knot' the Overhand Knot is used as a temporary stopper knot in the end of small stuff – sewing thread, whipping twine and small lines, primarily to stop them from fraying at the ends. A pair of these knots also forms the basis of the Fisherman's Knot, as you will see later in the chapter.

Form an overhand crossing loop then tuck the working end through the loop from back to front – pulling on the standing part and the working end to tighten the knot. Be aware that, if pulled up really tight, this knot can be difficult to untie in fine lines and threads.

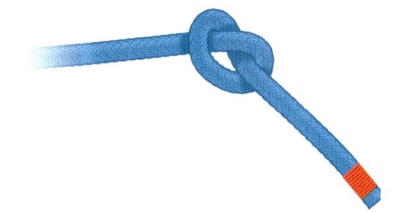

SLIPPED OVERHAND KNOT

This knot is an ideal introduction to forming knots that can be 'slipped' – in other words they can be untied by pulling on the working end, just like you can a shoelace. Because the Overhand Knot can be difficult to untie in some lines, it may be necessary to form one that can be 'slipped' easily. An example of this is when using sewing twines; the Slipped Overhand Knot makes a better stopper knot to prevent the end coming through the material, but then when you want to tie it off, the knot can be slipped to leave a long enough end to secure it with. This knot also has a large part to play in the forming of many other useful knots – even a Bowline.

Tie as you would the Overhand Knot but instead of passing the working end through the loop, pass a bight in the working end through instead. Pull the standing part and the bight to tighten the knot (ensuring that the working end is not pulled through). To untie, or 'slip' the knot, pull on the working end.

END AND STOPPER KNOTS

DOUBLE OVERHAND KNOT

The Double Overhand Knot is larger, more secure and does not reduce the strength of a line as much as the Single Overhand. Its primary use is to form a stopper knot in the end of a line or cord; some even favour this knot over the Figure of Eight in the ends of halyards and sheets. Become very familiar with this knot as it forms the basis of many other knots you will find later in this book.

1

Form an overhand crossing loop then tuck the working end through the loop from back to front twice.

2

To tighten, pull on the standing part and the working end. When first tying this knot, use your thin line and pull the ends slowly, observing how the belly of the loop wraps itself on the outside of the knot.

3

Having tied it in your thin line, now try it in a thick one – much more difficult to pull up and you will find that you have to massage the knot in place. The lesson here is that not all knots suit all ropes.

OVERHAND LOOP

The Overhand Loop provides a quick and easy way of forming a fixed loop in the bight of a line. It is the weakest of all fixed loops and when not under load, it can easily shake undone, so do not use it in place of any of the Bowlines – more as a 'handy loop'.

To tie, make a long bight in the line then use the bight as you would a single working end – form an overhand crossing loop then tuck the end of the bight through it as shown in the diagrams.

OVERHAND NOOSE

Study the form of this knot carefully and note the difference between this and the Slipped Overhand Knot. The Overhand Noose is an Overhand Knot tied in the working end around the standing part so that it slides along that standing part. The Slipped Overhand Knot, on the other hand does not slide.

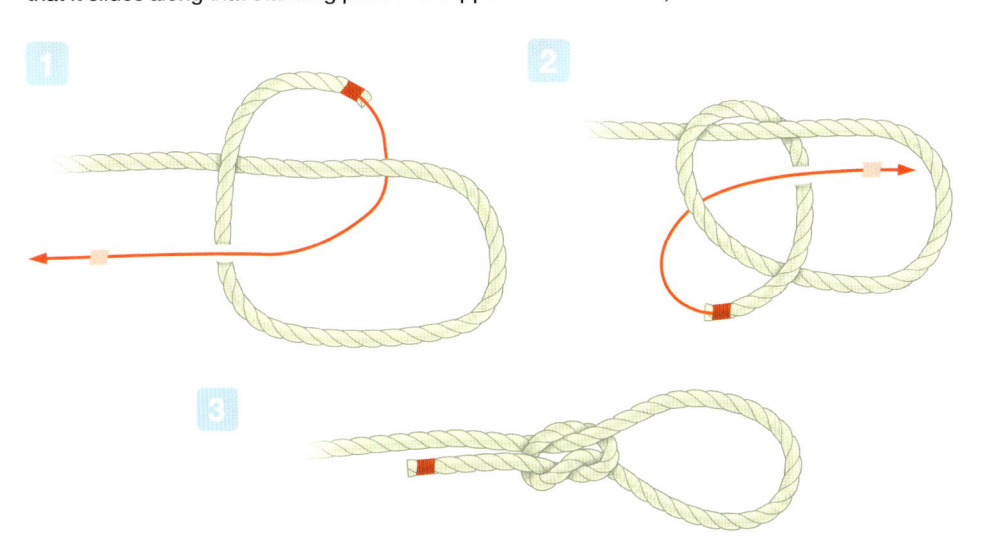

Form an overhand crossing loop, pass the working end behind the standing part and up through the loop. Complete the overhand knot in the working end.

FIGURE OF EIGHT KNOT

The Figure of Eight Knot is the classic end of rope stopper knot used by sailors in halyards and sheets, to prevent the end of a rope running out of a block or fairlead. Easy to tie and remember, the Figure of Eight Knot is a very versatile knot that can be applied as a bend, hitch, loop and noose, as you will see later in the book. One word of caution; this knot easily comes undone if subjected to constant flailing; remember to leave a long end.

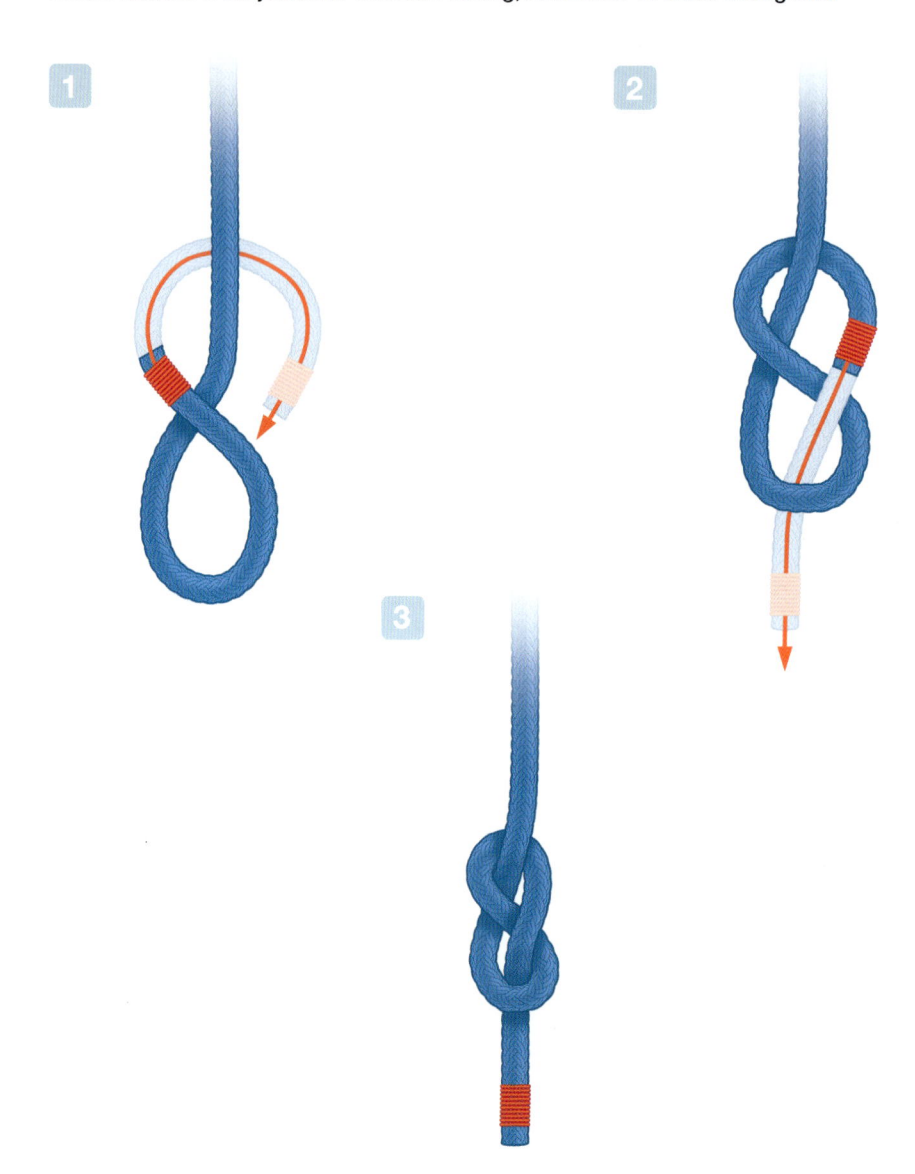

Form an overhand crossing loop, with a long working end. Pass the working end behind the standing part then from front to rear through the loop.

END AND STOPPER KNOTS | 43

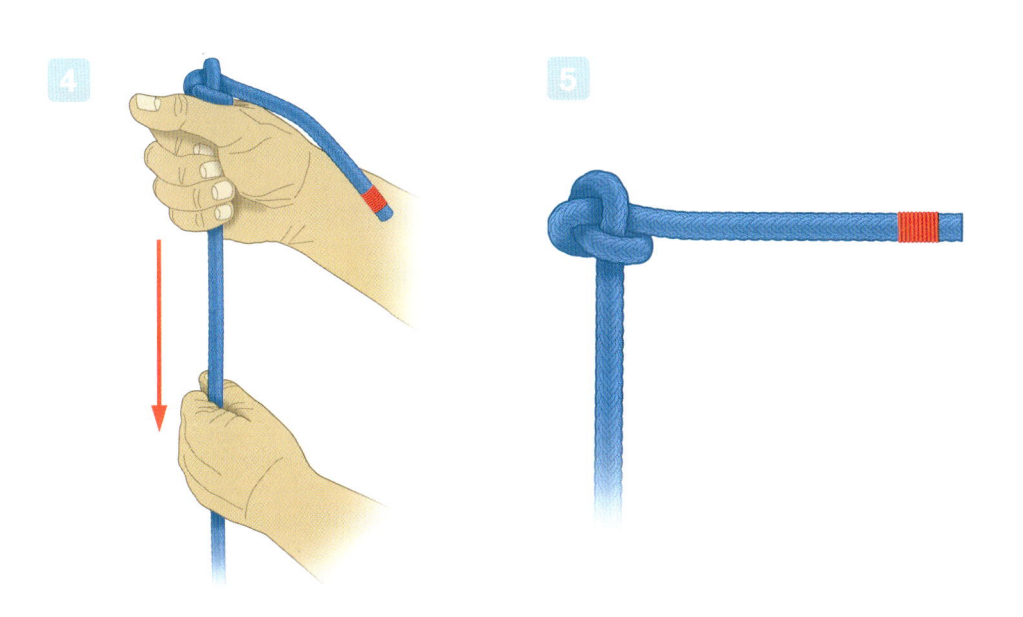

To tighten: pull the knot up with the standing part and the working end then hold the standing part cupped through one hand, as shown in diagram 4, then pull down on the standing part with the other hand to form the knot as shown, leaving a long end.

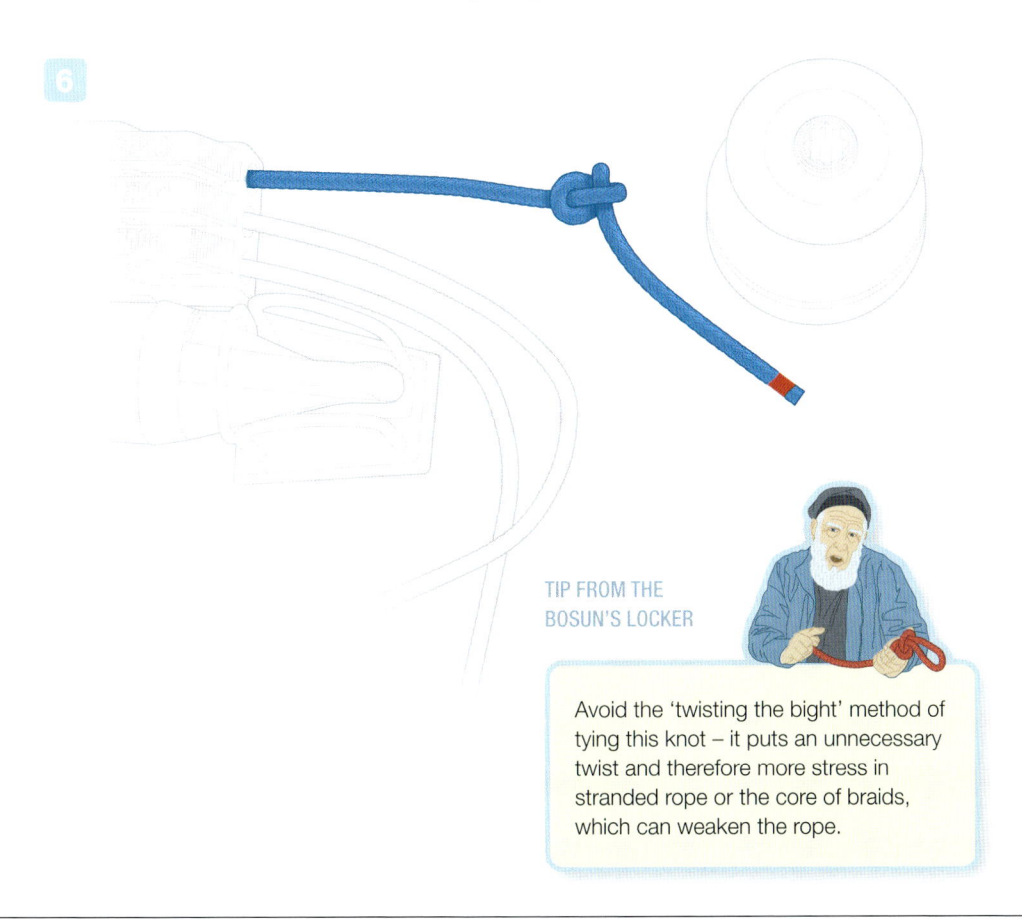

Progressive Knot Tying

TIP FROM THE BOSUN'S LOCKER

Avoid the 'twisting the bight' method of tying this knot – it puts an unnecessary twist and therefore more stress in stranded rope or the core of braids, which can weaken the rope.

Bends

FISHERMAN'S KNOT

A 'Knot' among Bends – the reason is that there is also a Fisherman's Bend (or Anchor Bend) and as this particular method of joining two ropes' ends employs the Overhand Knot, the name has stuck. The single Overhand Knot variant of the knot is one of the most efficient ways of tying two lines together. A useful knot for joining ropes that are used for climbing or working aloft.

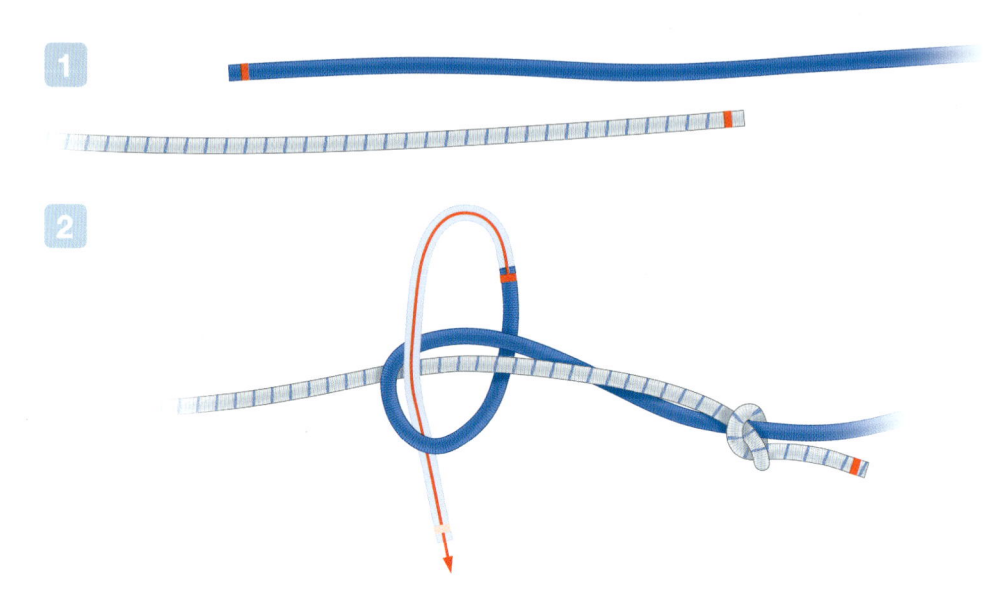

1

2

Lay the two lines parallel with the two working ends overlapping. Form an overhand knot with the end of one line around the standing part of the other line as shown in diagram 2.

3

Repeat with the working end of the second line around the standing part of the first one – note that the working end of each Overhand Knot is on the outside of the knot.

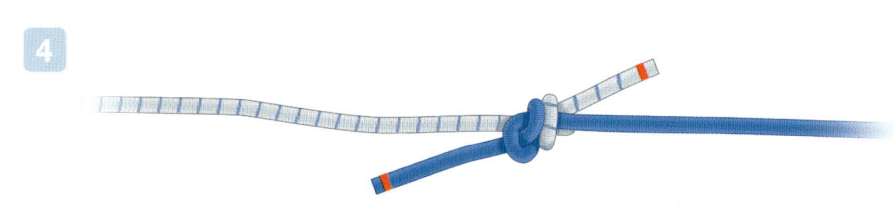

4

Pull on both standing parts to draw the two Overhand Knots together until they are snug.

BENDS | 45

SHEET BEND

The Sheet Bend can be used to join two ropes that are of slightly differing thickness – but with caution. This is one of those knots which, unless it is under load, can come undone very easily; which is probably why it is not now used to secure sheets to sails!

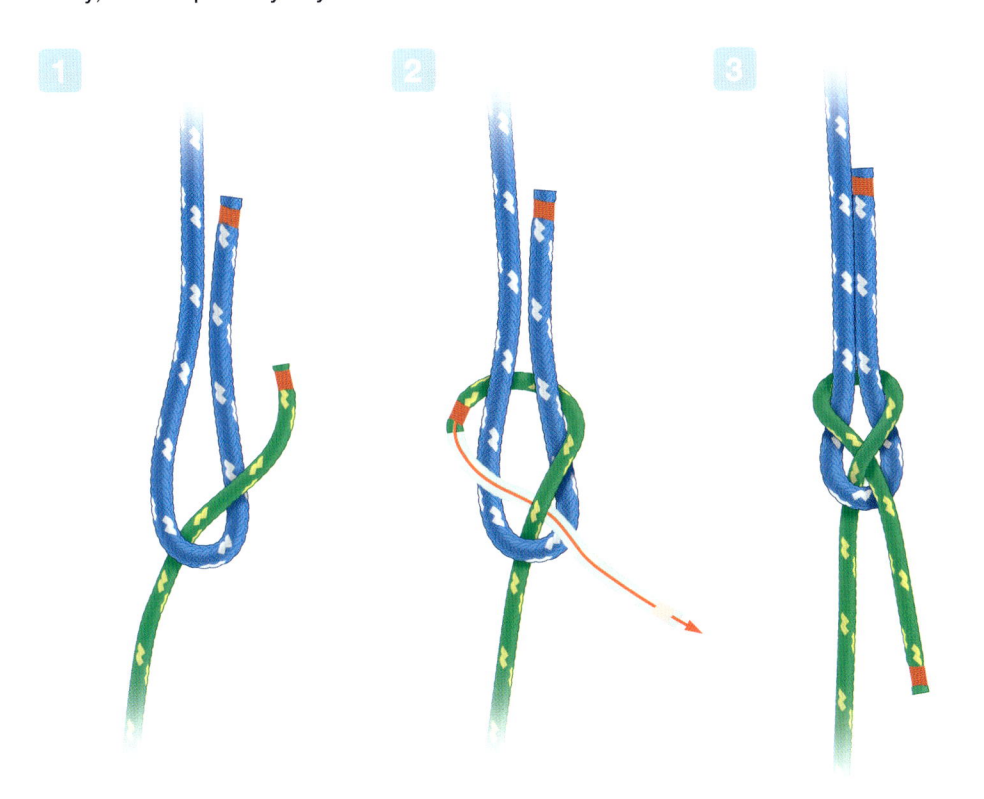

Make a closed bight in the end of the thicker line. Pass the smaller diameter line from back to front up through the bight of the first line, then around behind both parts of the first line, in the direction shown (under the short end first). Now bring the working end across the front of the closed bight tucking it under its own standing part on top of the bight. Dress the knot by pulling on both standing parts.

TIP FROM THE BOSUN'S LOCKER

Ensure that both working ends emerge from the knot on the same side or it will be unstable.

Progressive Knot Tying

Binding Knots

HALF KNOT

The Half Knot is technically an Overhand Knot, but instead of being tied in the end of a line it is tied using two ends of the same line; probably the first knot we learned as a child for tying our shoe laces. It is also one of those knots which will not stand alone without being secured in some way, normally by adding another Half Knot of the opposite handedness forming the Reef Knot.

Take the two ends of a line, one in each hand. Cross the right hand working end over the left hand working end, tuck it under and out to the left. Pull the two working ends to tighten or adjust to size.

REEF KNOT AND GRANNY KNOT

The Reef Knot is a 'binding' knot, which is why it is used in traditional reef points (gaskets) of sails, tying bandages, bows and other bindings. Easy to tie, and equally easy to untie, by capsizing the knot, the Reef Knot has for many years been one of the staple 'handy' knots. Although the Reef Knot has been considered in some circles to be a 'bend' it is NOT recommended; mainly because it is so easy to capsize and come undone. The Granny Knot has little use, but is included here so that the reader can recognise it and be aware of its limitations.

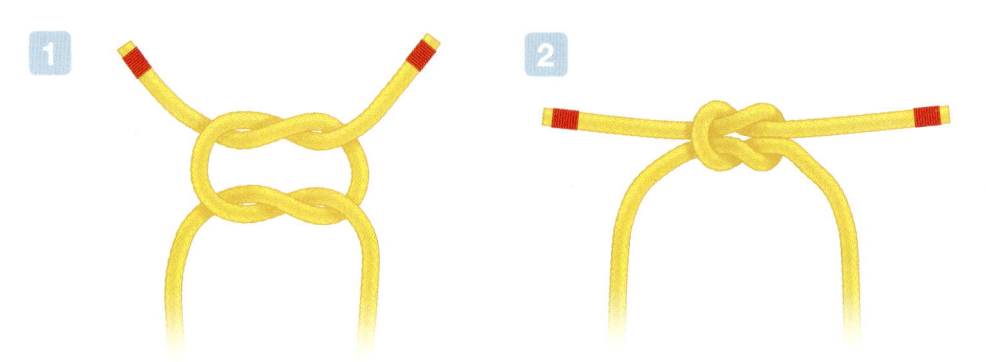

Form a Half Knot; pull it up as tight as necessary to form a suitable binding around the object. Now form another Half Knot on top of the first one, taking care to start by crossing the now left hand working end over the right before tucking and pulling up tight. "Right over left, then left over right" – or the other way round, it makes no difference. Note how you now have two interlocking bights, with the working ends and standing parts emerging beside each other and the knot laying flat. To untie, especially if it is wet and has been under load, give the working end and the standing part of one end a sharp pull apart to capsize the knot; the result will be that line going straight and the other forming a 'Lark's Head Knot' around it, which can easily be slipped off; hence the reason to avoid using it as a bend.

REEF BOW

The knot most of us learned to tie our shoe laces with, can be equally useful where a slipped Reef Knot is needed; for example, tying bundles with line or tape, where they will be safe with a slipped knot yet easy to untie. Having learned to tie this knot using a 'Right over left, left over right' Reef Knot sequence – try it the Granny Knot way (see below) – you will notice that the Reef Bow lays across the standing parts horizontally, but the Granny Bow lays at 90 degrees to them.

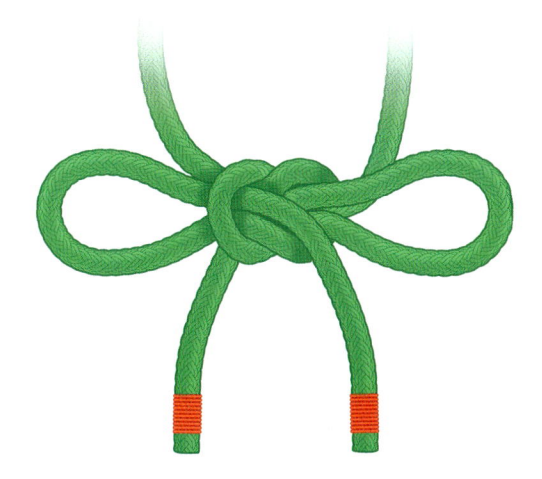

GRANNY KNOT

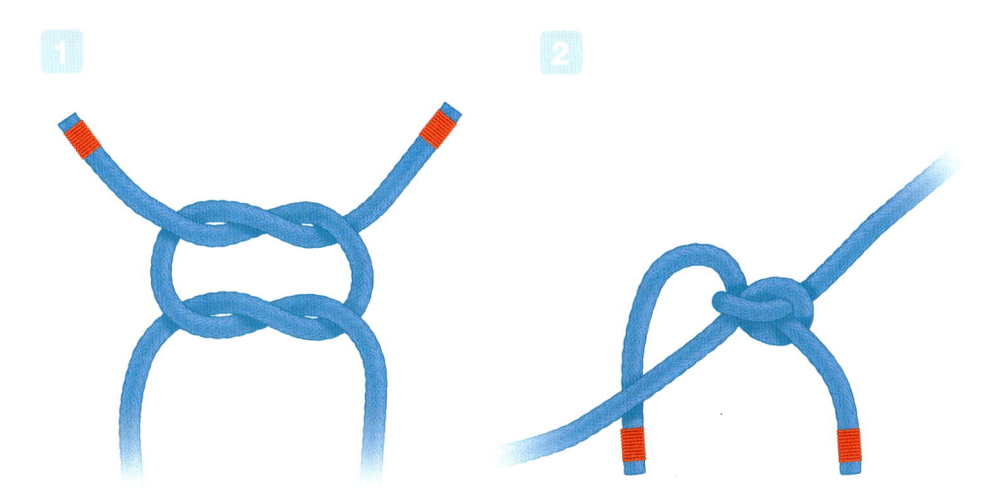

Form a Half Knot, passing the right working end over the left, pull up; now form a second Half Knot by passing the right working end over the left again, before pulling up tight. Note how the standing part and working end of each line now emerge from different sides of the bight. To demonstrate the insecurity of this knot, tie it so that it is just snug – now pull on both standing parts and the knot will take on a different form with the two working ends emerging at right angles. Give the two standing parts a few sharp jerks and watch how the two working ends get shorter, eventually, especially in slippery line, the knot will of course come apart.

Hitches

HALF HITCH

The Half Hitch is only used as part of another knot or lashing, it will not stand alone (unless held or under certain load conditions) and will come undone if not secured. Nevertheless it is an important part of many knot structures and tie-off procedures, so it needs to be understood.

Pass the working end around a spar, rail, rope or other object and cross it under the standing part. Note that it is only the standing part bearing on the working end that holds this knot in place.

MARLING HITCH

The Marling Hitch is also one of those knots that is used in conjunction with another knot, or lashing. However, unlike the Half Hitch, the Marling Hitch, because it is an Overhand Knot (with its ends at right angles to the wrap), it does have slightly better holding properties, which why it is used for lashing up bundles and hammocks, etc.

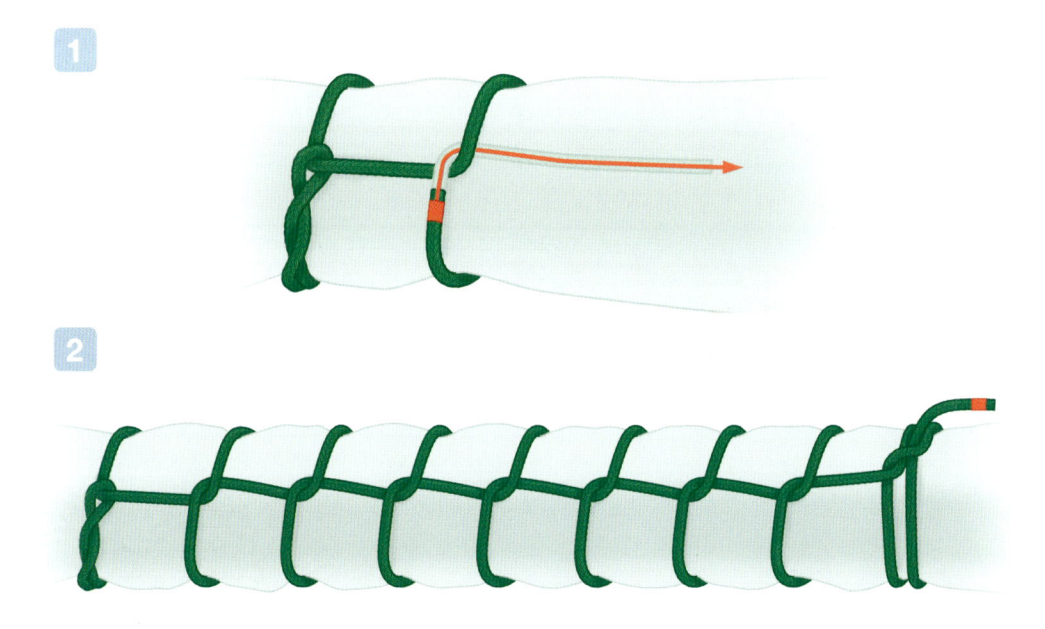

Secure the standing part (e.g. with a Clove Hitch or Timber Hitch). Take the working end around the object(s) to be lashed, back over the standing part then tuck it under itself, pull tight and adjust the lead of the working end at 90 degrees to the wrap, ready to commence the next turn. When sufficient wraps have been made, secure the lashing with two half hitches in the form of a Clove Hitch.

CLOVE HITCH

Quick and easy to tie, the Clove Hitch is useful for securing fender lines to guardrails and ropes around posts or stakes, especially where the load on the line is roughly at right angles to the object, or as a general purpose knot for such things as: tying off the end of a line that has been used for lashing, seizing or binding, as well as securing a tiller when not in use and rigging a temporary guardrail. Structurally, the Clove Hitch is two Half Hitches, which allows it to be tied in several different ways. When making a temporary hitch to a rail (for example a fender line that you know you are going to move or take in hand at some stage), the second Half Hitch can be tied as a 'Slipped Half Hitch' making release and moving much easier and quicker. Always leave a long working end when tying Clove Hitches, because the knot can rotate and the working end slip back into the knot, releasing it.

CLOVE HITCH TO RAIL OR RING

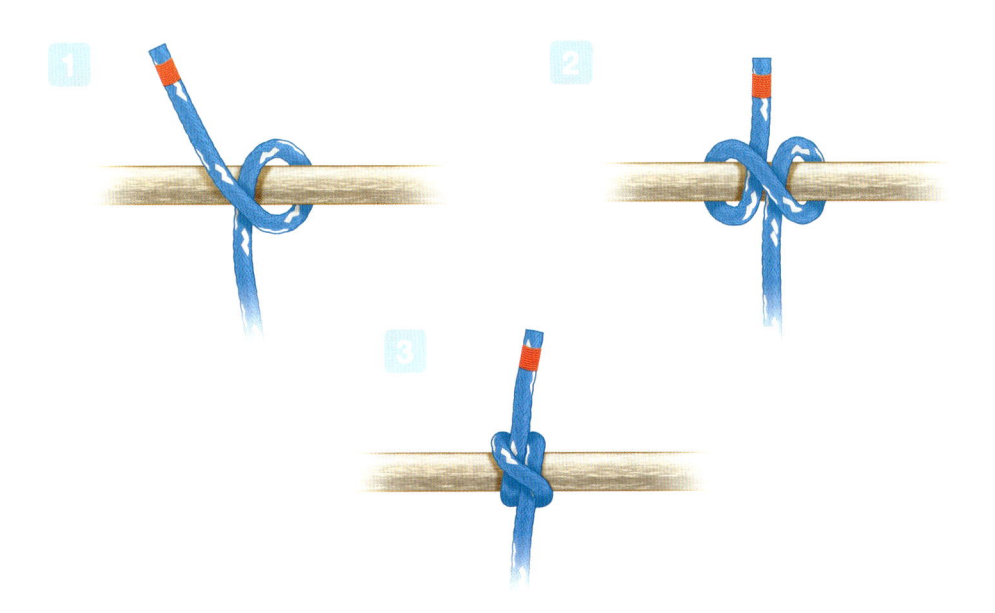

Pass the working end over the rail, then make a crossing turn over itself – this can be right to left or left to right of the standing part, depending on the handedness of the tyer. Continue to make another complete turn around the rail then tuck the working end under its own part, to lie alongside the standing part.

TIP FROM THE BOSUN'S LOCKER

When tying to a ring, keep the protruding crossover of the knot away from the wall, deck or other fixing point, to prevent chafing.

SLIPPED CLOVE HITCH

Tie the knot as you would over a rail or through a ring, but instead of completing the second Half Hitch with the working end, pass a bight formed in the working end to form a 'Slipped Half Hitch'. Make sure you leave a fairly long end and remember that this knot is not as secure as a standard Clove Hitch.

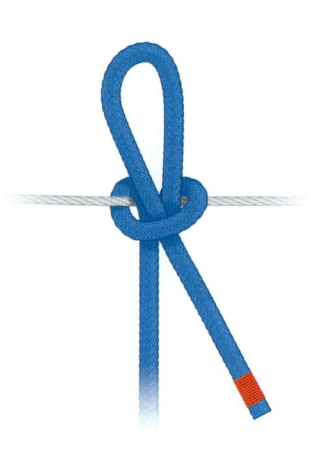

CLOVE HITCH OVER A POST

When the end of a post, bollard or spar is exposed, the Clove Hitch can be applied by forming two Half Hitches, either one at a time, as you would with large rope, or, in light lines, by forming them in the hand and dropping the knot over the object.

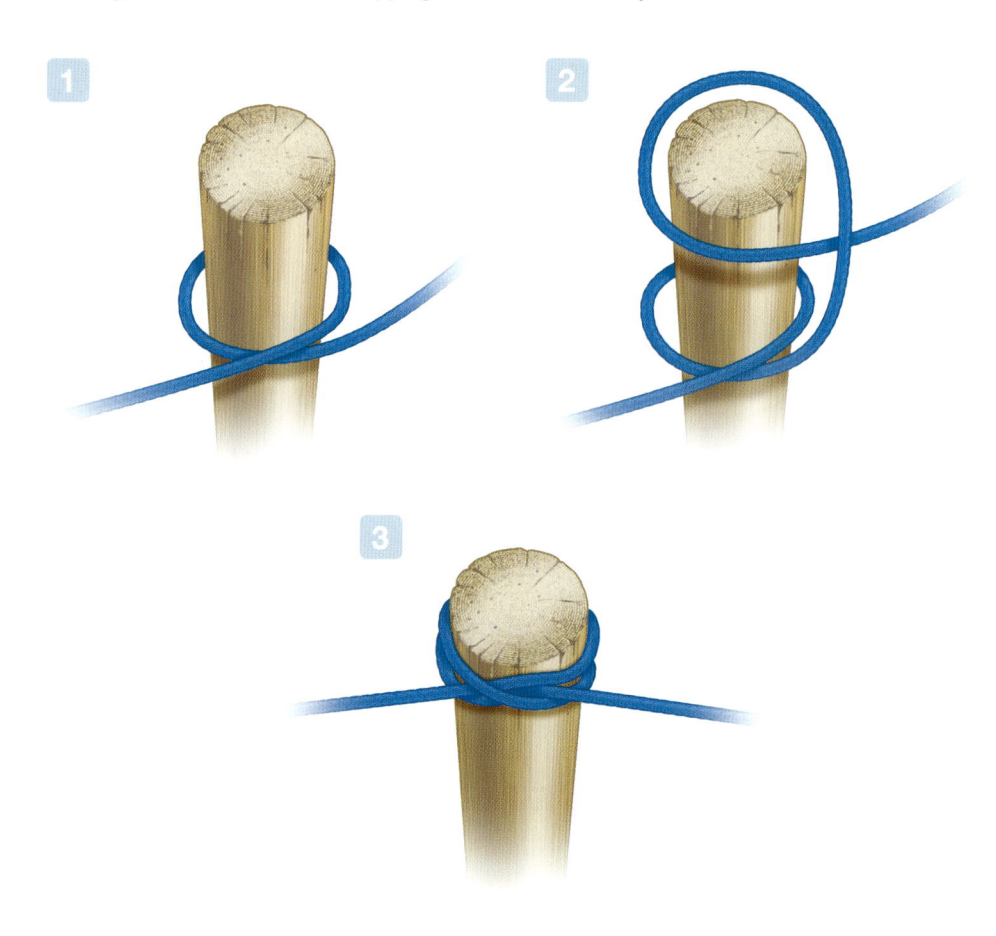

HITCHES

CONSTRICTOR KNOT

Here is a really ingenious knot with so many uses that it is like a third hand; yet surprisingly very under rated, under taught and under used. The Constrictor Knot is really a 'Binding Knot' and when tied in small lines and twine has a firm and reliable grip; so much so that it can be very difficult to untie. Among the many legitimate uses for this knot, perhaps its most useful role is as a temporary whipping or stop; when splicing, securing the neck of a bag or a bundle, or even clamping two objects being glued.

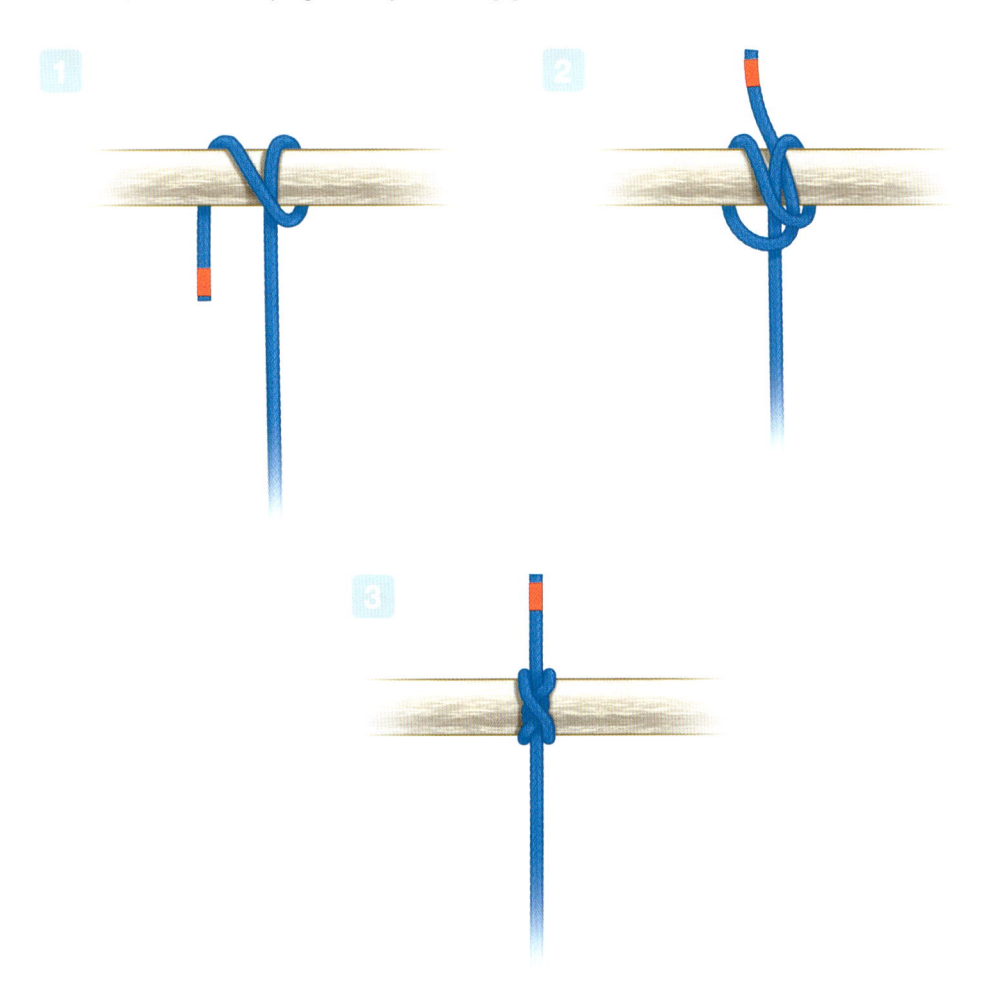

There is more than one way of tying the Constrictor Knot, which will be explained later in the book – but for ease of learning, here is a method which is easy to remember. First make a loose Clove Hitch, then take the working end over the standing part of the first turn and then under it, to emerge between the two turns. You should now have now formed a Half Knot, which, when the standing part and working end are pulled up really tight, will be locked under the crossing turn. The ends can be cut quite close to the knot without fear of it coming undone.

MAGNUS HITCH

Progressing from the Clove Hitch, the Magnus Hitch is formed with just one extra turn; this gives it the ability to take, not only a perpendicular load, but also a sideways load, suitable to attach a line to a sheet when transferring the load from one winch to another, or removing a riding turn. Other variations of this knot, such as the Taut Line Hitch and Tree Surgeon's Knot are explained in later chapters.

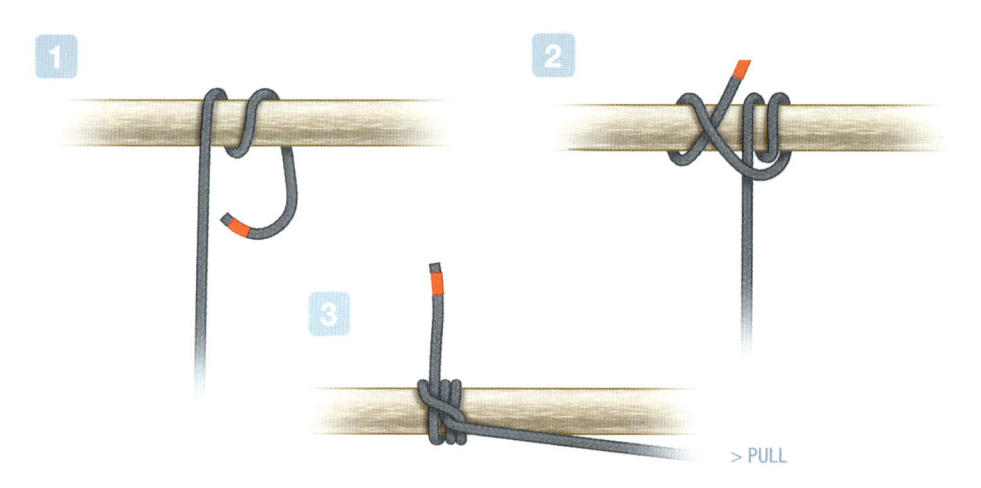

> PULL

First determine the direction of pull, or load. Form a round turn around the sheet, rail or rope, making the turns beside the standing part on the same side as the direction of pull. Cross the working end over the round turn and tie off with a Half Hitch.

ROLLING HITCH

Much the same as the Magnus Hitch, but this knot will grip a little better on wet ropes and smoother surfaces.

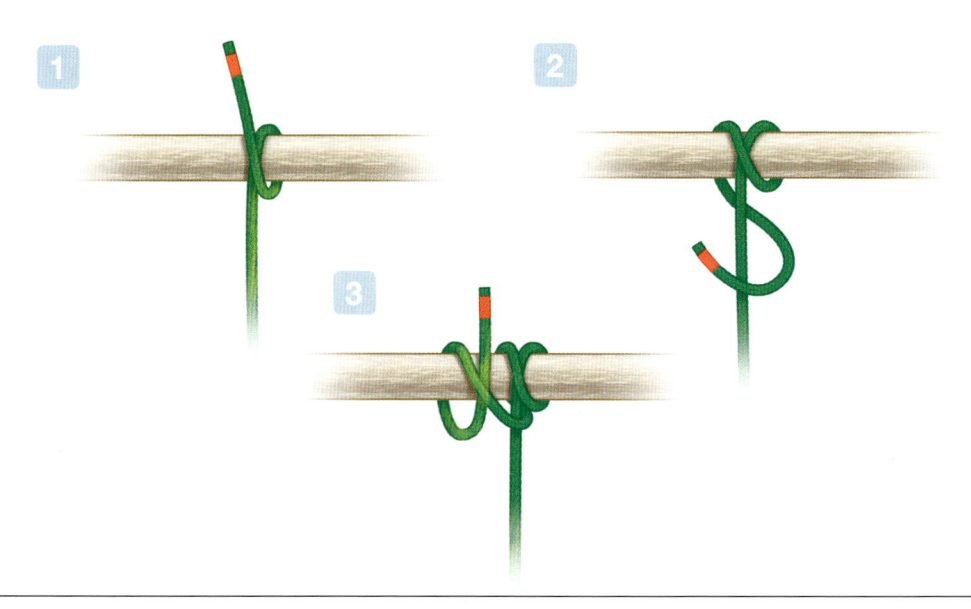

HITCHES | 53

Make a crossing turn around the spar or rope, take the working end over and back on the same side of the standing part as the first turn – cross this one over the standing part to complete two turns. Tie off with a Half Hitch, then pull the knot up 'snug'.

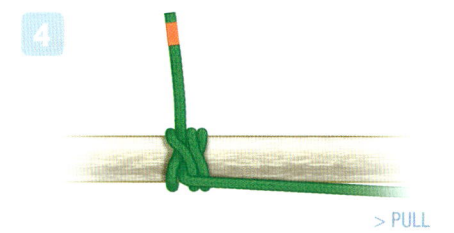

> PULL

ROUND TURNS

Before learning the Round Turn and Two Half Hitches, it is worth first considering how the friction factor of the Round Turns work, not only in the tying of this knot, but for use on a winch drum, bollard or cleat. This is the basis on which a human being can hold, veer, surge and control quite large loads, single handed.

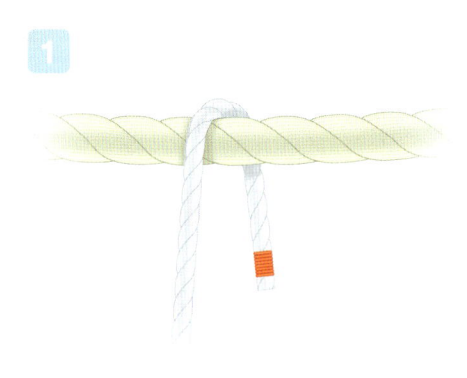

Find a secure and stout stanchion, bollard or rail then with your line, take a single turn (1) on it. If you now load one end, you will need to apply equal and opposite effort to hold that load. If you take one more turn (to complete a Round Turn), it is now possible to hold the load with much less effort. One more turn and you will find that little or no effort is required. By reducing the effort holding the turns, the friction is released and the load will slip, but under control, so by securing the working end instead of holding it the turns will have the weight and the tie off holds the turns in place. Hence the need to put Half Hitches around the standing part of the Round Turn and Two Half Hitches – one will hold the turns but is best backed up with another Half Hitch for security.

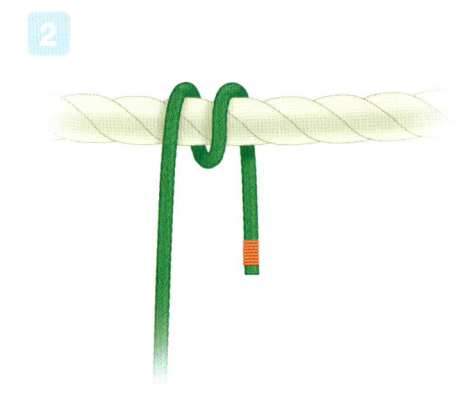

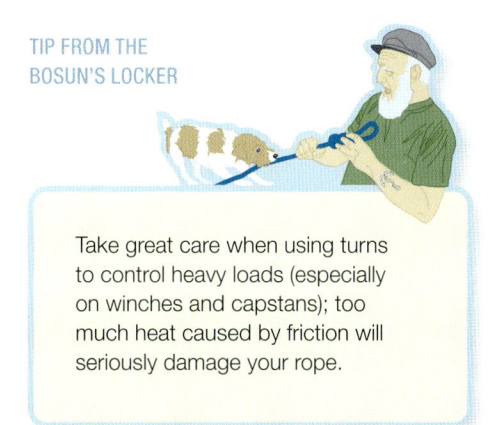

TIP FROM THE BOSUN'S LOCKER

Take great care when using turns to control heavy loads (especially on winches and capstans); too much heat caused by friction will seriously damage your rope.

Progressive Knot Tying

ROUND TURN & TWO HALF HITCHES

Probably the most used 'general purpose' knot in boating, the Round Turn and Two Half Hitches is one of the safest, secure and reliable knots you will ever use on the water.

Make a Round Turn around the rail, post, ring or bollard. Bring the working end in front of the standing part then around the back and tuck under itself to form a Half Hitch around the standing part, now complete a second Half Hitch in the same direction. Dress the knot so that the two Half Hitches are up close to the Round Turn. If the knot is going to form a semi-permanent bend, it is also advisable to whip or seize the working end to the standing part.

ANCHOR BEND OR FISHERMAN'S BEND

As the name implies, this knot is ideal for securing a rope to an anchor ring, or a fishing hook to a line; as well as many other uses. It works on the same principle as the Round Turn and Two Half Hitches, but the working end is locked between the Round Turn and the ring, before being tied off with a Half Hitch. This makes it even more secure (the greater the load the tighter it grips the working end) and is much easier to untie than the Round Turn and Two Half Hitches when wet.

Make a loose Round Turn around the ring or rail. Bring the working end in front of the standing part then pass it between the turns and the ring. Tie off the working end with a Half Hitch around the standing part. Dress the knot so that the turns hold the working end and the Half Hitch is close up to the ring.

Loops

BOWLINE (Common)

Another much used general purpose knot, the Common Bowline (there are many others) forms a temporary fixed loop in the end of a rope which can be used, among other things, to secure sheets to sails, make a loop in a temporary mooring line or as a general safety line, if a proper harness is not available. There are no less than four different methods of tying this knot, but for ease of learning I have chosen the method shown in the following diagrams; other methods, which you may eventually prefer, are explained later in the book.

Take the standing part in the left hand and pull enough line through to form the required size fixed working loop and a couple of feet or so to make the knot. Make a small overhand loop (to the left – like you would write a figure 6) with the standing part, in the left hand.

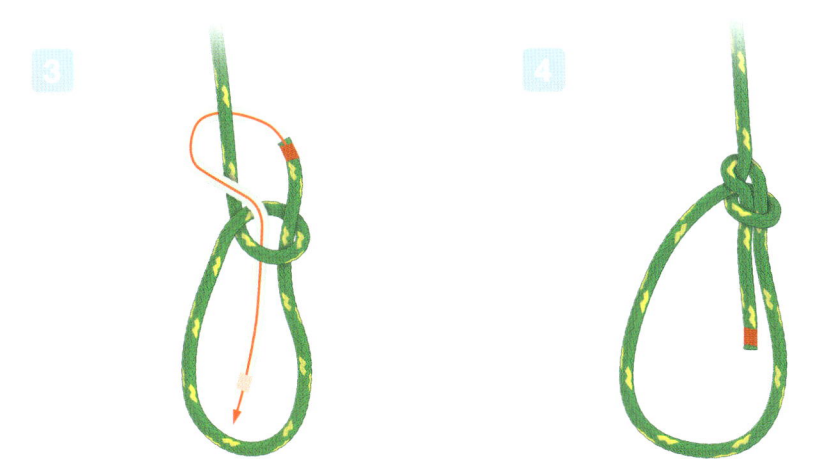

Take the working end and pass it from back to front through that loop, then around the back of the standing part from right to left before passing in back down through the loop – from whence it came. If, while learning, you want to remember this using the old adage "The rabbit comes out of its hole, goes round the tree and back down the hole" that's fine, because at least you will always tie it correctly, which is the important thing. When complete make sure the working end is inside the working loop (to prevent it snagging and capsizing the knot) and that it is at least long enough to put a Half Hitch around the adjacent working loop leg for added security.

ANGLER'S LOOP (Perfection Loop)

The Angler's Loop or as it is sometimes known the Perfection Loop, is one of those knots favoured by fishermen because it can be tied in slippery wet line with cold fingers – but is equally at home in almost any size or type of rope. Looking around quaysides at mooring and berthing lines and the knots people use (yes, some are quite amazing!) if it isn't a Common Bowline, then the chances are it is another of the Bowline (fixed loop) knots - the Angler's Loop.

Having learned this knot the conventional way, and as a reward for ploughing your way through this chapter, here too, is the 'Flying Bowline' – the 'party piece' way of tying the same knot.

1

Tie a Slipped Overhand Knot, with a fairly long working end.

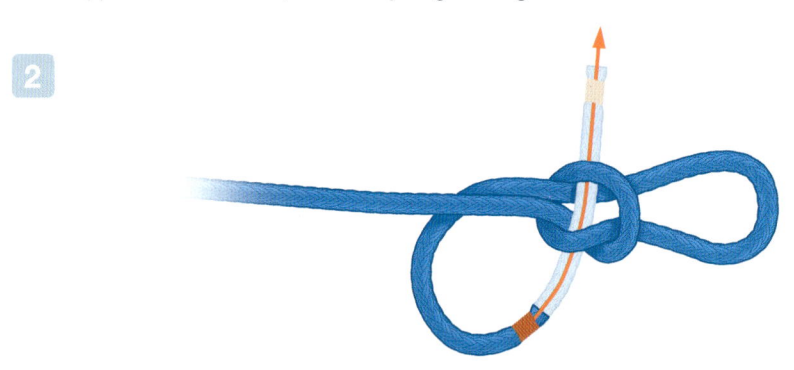

2

Pass the working end behind the standing part then through the Overhand Knot as shown above.

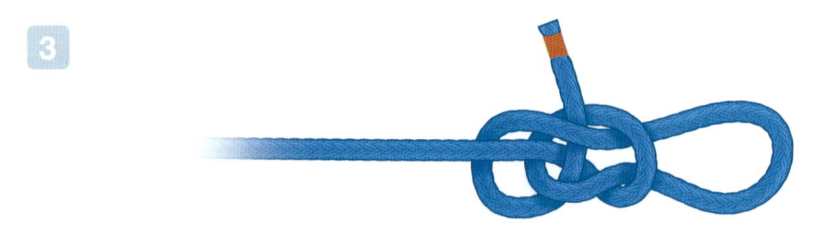

3

Pull on the standing part and the eye to pull the knot up snug.

4

FLYING BOWLINE

Now that you have mastered the basic knots – here is a bonus, which with practice will impress your friends no end. It is actually a variation of the Angler's Loop, but being as it is a fixed loop the term 'bowline' can be used.

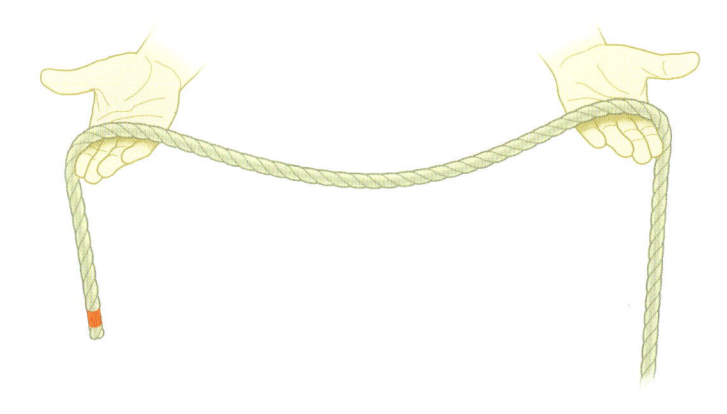

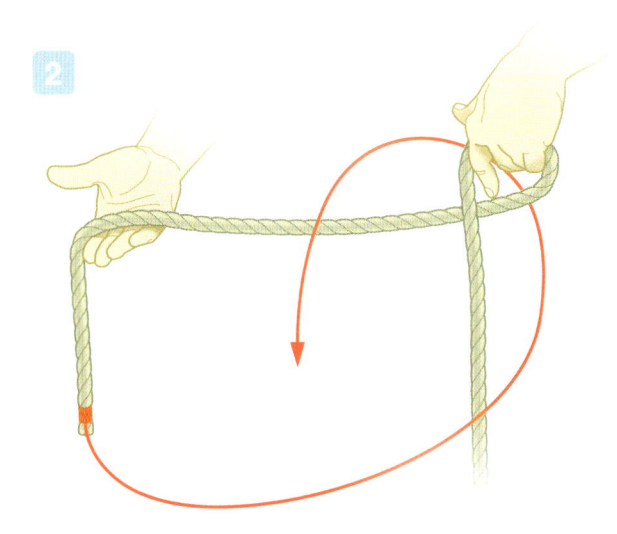

1

2

Take your line in the left hand and pull about a metre or so through with the right hand placed about 30cm from the working end. Now turn both palms upwards so that the rope lays across the top of them, hands shoulder width apart and well away from the body. Grasp the rope with the left hand and turn it inwards (twist to the right) to form a crossing loop.

58 LOOPS

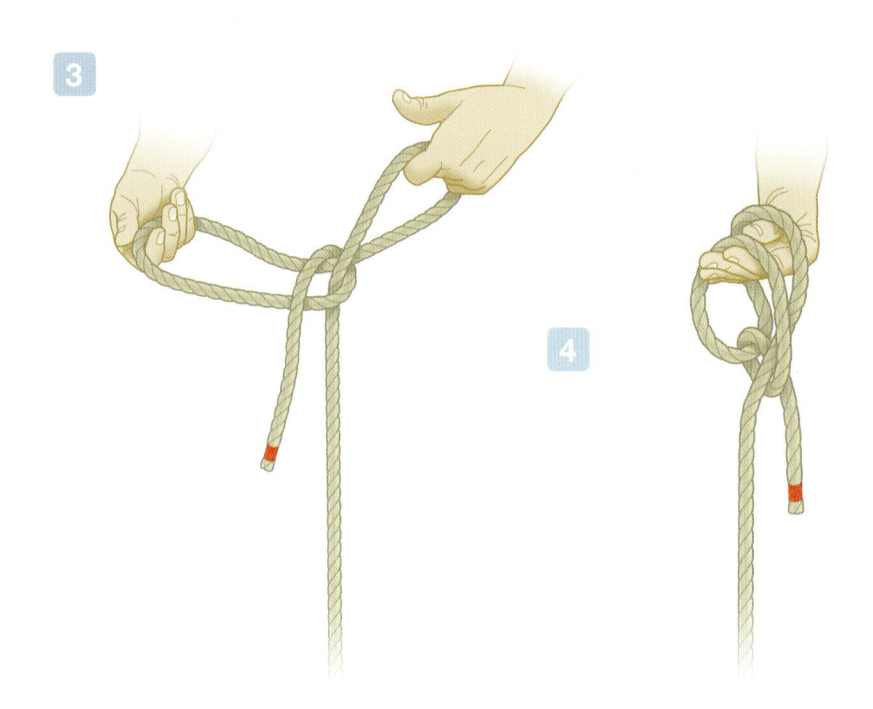

Keeping the hands well away from the body, now 'flick' the working end between the rope and your body and over the top, out to the front. You should now have a loop in the left hand and another in the right. Pass the right hand loop through the left loop, grasp it with the left hand and at the same time let the left hand loop slide off.

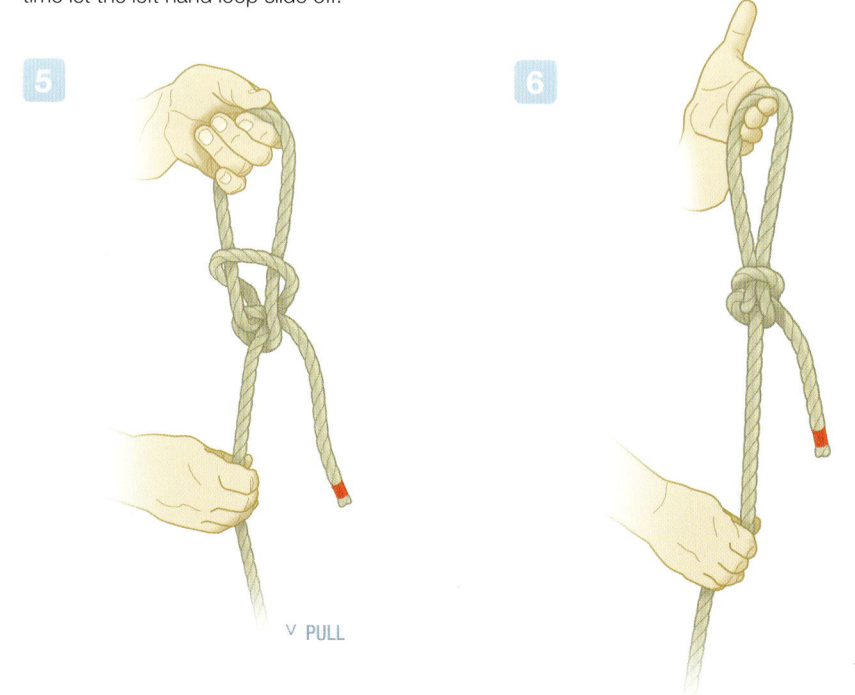

∨ PULL

Now pull down on the standing part – "Voila" – one Angler's Loop, or 'Flying Bowline'. Lots of practice and you will get very fast and impress many a friend with this one.

Progressive Knot Tying

CHAPTER 5:

ROPE END & STOPPER KNOTS

OVERHAND & FIGURE OF EIGHT KNOTS

HEAVING LINE KNOT

MONKEY'S FIST

MATTHEW WALKER KNOT

MANROPE KNOT

COMMON WHIPPING

SAILMAKER'S WHIPPING

PALM & NEEDLE WHIPPING

Introduction:
Rope End & Stopper Knots

In this chapter you will find knots which are used as 'stopper' knots (to prevent the end from passing through an aperture), the 'lump' knots which weight the end of a line or decorate the end of hand ropes and three of the more common types of permanent whipping to prevent the end of a rope from fraying.

Overhand & Figure of Eight Knots

The Overhand Knot in its various forms and the Figure of Eight Knot have been covered in Chapter 4 but are illustrated here as a reminder and for completeness of the chapter.

OVERHAND KNOT (p39)

DOUBLE OVERHAND KNOT (p40)

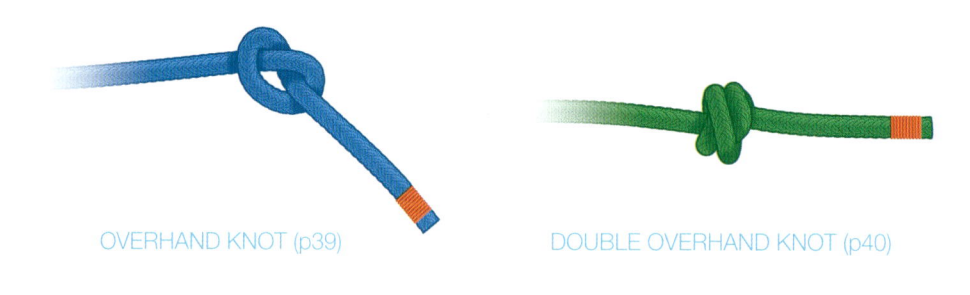

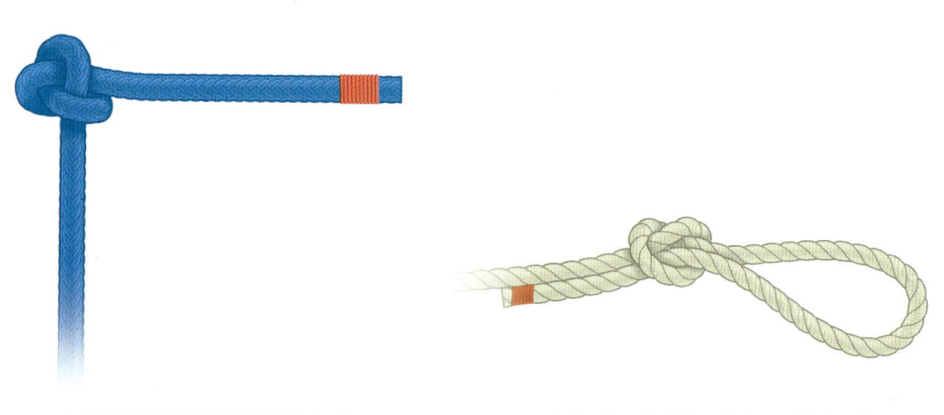

FIGURE OF EIGHT KNOT (p42)

SLIPPED OVERHAND KNOT (p39)

Heaving Line Knot

Heaving, or throwing lines need their ends weighted and the Heaving Line Knot is perhaps the quickest of the line weighting knots to tie.

1

Make an underhand crossing loop at about 1 metre from the end.

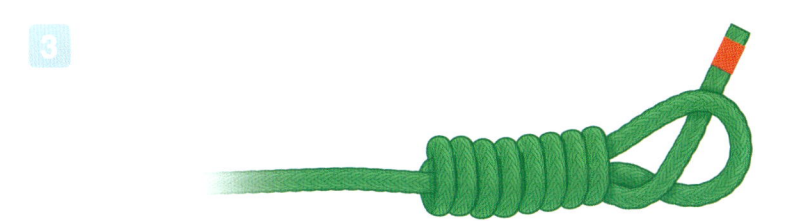

2

Wrap the working end around the loop about 6 to 8 times.

3

Tighten the turns, pass the working end through the loop, then pull the loop to tighten in the first turn snug up to the standing part.

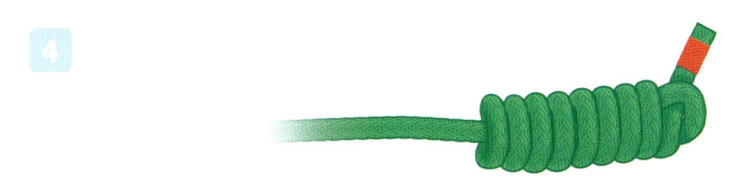

4

Pull on the standing part to trap the working end in the loop.

Monkey's Fist

Perhaps the most traditional of the heaving line knots – this knot has a certain fascination and is probably the knot most people really want to learn; maybe it is because of its symmetry, rather like Turk's Head Knots their under/over/under/over weave is pleasing to the human eye. As a decorative knot it can be used to cover spherical objects – like a cork ball on a key ring - in which case the size of line and the number of turns will need to be estimated before you start.

Start by winding the line around your hand about 12 times – don't worry this is one knot where you will not use or cut off any line that is not necessary. The knot is tied in the hand as is referred to below, but has been omitted from the diagrams for clarity.

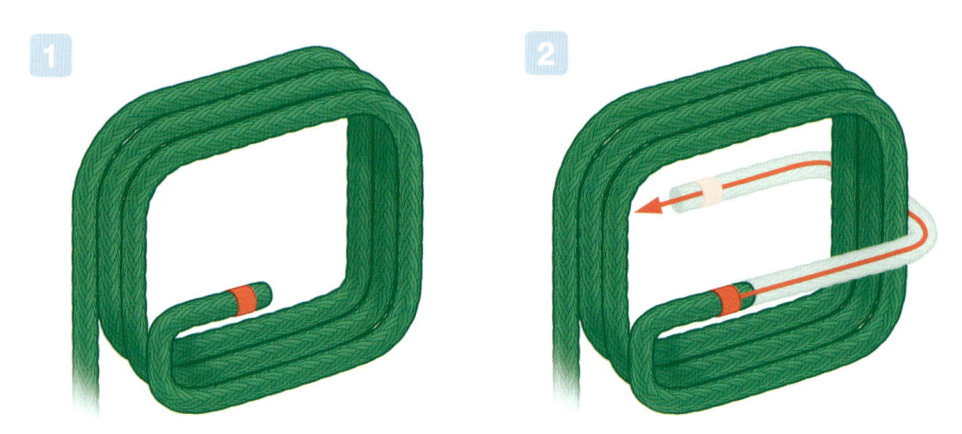

Hold the line at the point you measured, in your hand then, using the working end, wind it round clockwise three times (1). Now pass the working end between your two middle fingers from front to back, remove your hand and hold the first three turns (just below the working end) between your thumb and forefinger while you wind the working end around the first three turns in an anti-clockwise direction.

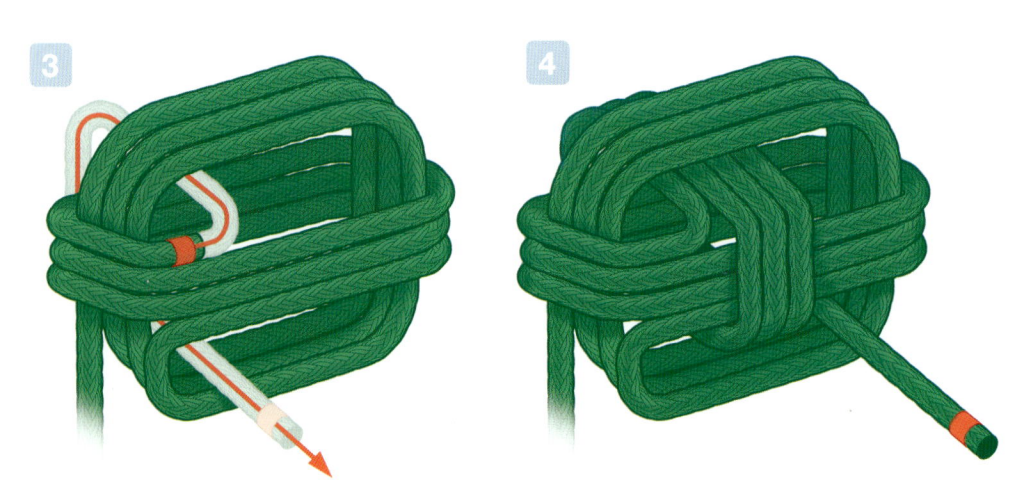

Now make three turns as shown in (3) around the second three and inside the first three.

MONKEY'S FIST 63

5

Tie a stopper knot in the end and tuck it inside the knot – this will give it something to form around. The secret to tightening the knot up is to do it gradually from the end to the standing part of the line – it may take 3 or even 4 times around. You may have to use a fid to tighten the last round.

6

TIP FROM THE BOSUN'S LOCKER

NEVER put anything hard or heavy inside a heaving line Monkey's Fist – it might hurt someone!

Rope End & Stopper Knots

Matthew Walker Knot

Mostly seen today as a decorative knot, but it is an 'end stopper knot' which is used on deadeye lanyards. It can be formed in any number of cords more than 2; however any combination over about 6 will need a core and careful pulling up. Shown here is a Three Strand Matthew Walker for use as a stopper knot, but the principle is the same for any number of leads.

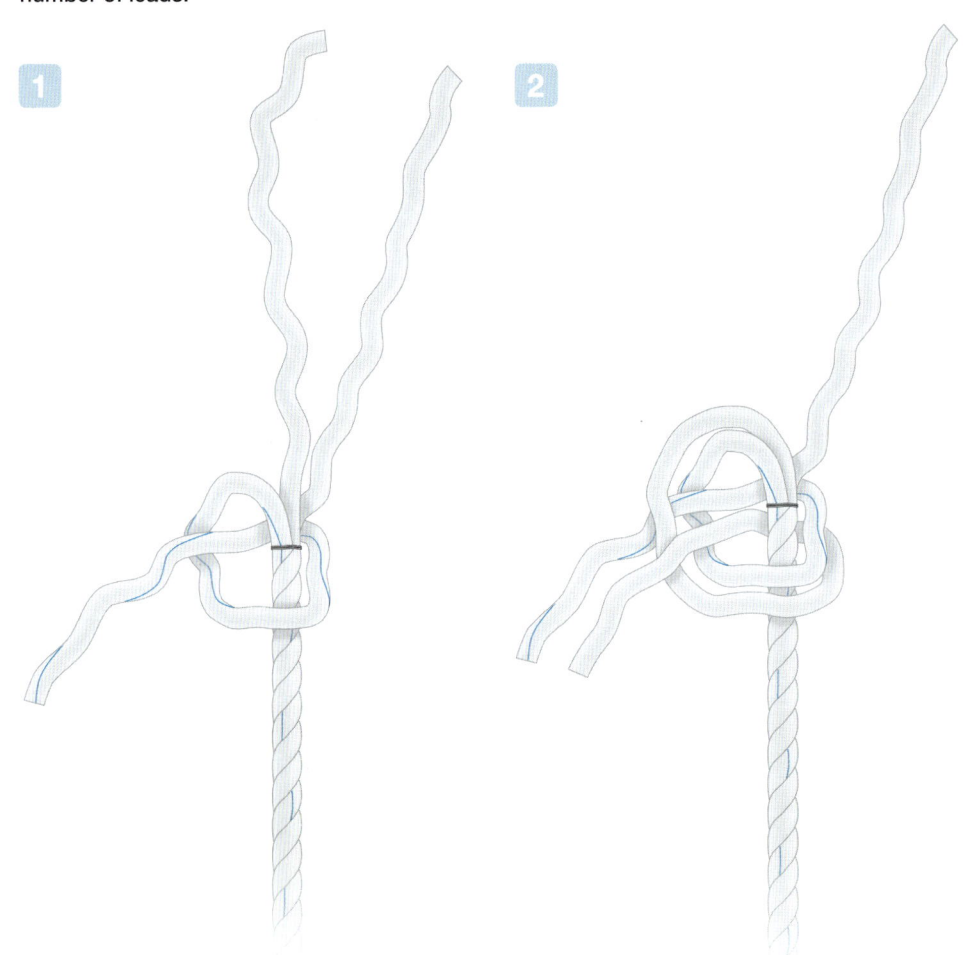

Put on a temporary stop at the point where you want the knot to form. Carefully unlay the three strands down to the stop. Bring the left hand strand in a bight in front of the standing part of the rope and tuck it through itself (1). Repeat with the second strand, but pass the end outside (to lay below) the first bight and up through both bights (2).

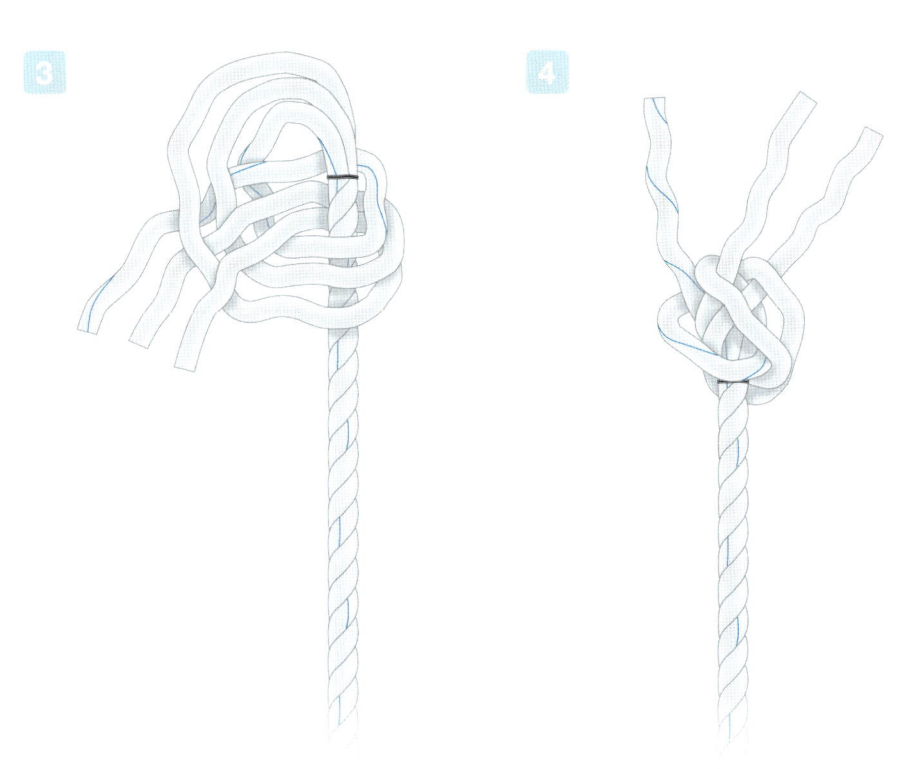

Pass the third strand round in a bight outside the first two and up through all three bights (3). Hold the three strand ends and bring them up in line with the rope, at the same time giving them a slight twist and pull to the left.

Now pull each strand in turn gently until the knot begins to form in a spiral – support the knot in one hand and pull up with the other. Once the knot is fully pulled up the stop can be removed and the strands laid up again, whipped and cut off if necessary.

Manrope Knot

The Manrope Knot is a large decorative knot which can be used at the end of a hand rope beside a ladder, on the ends of a Chest Becket pin, at the end of a rope rail on a gangway or even at home in the garden on the deck ropes or fence ropes. It may look complicated at first but it is nothing more than the clever combination of a Wall Knot with a Crown Knot on top of it. All you have to remember is – first a Wall and then a Crown, double the lead by following round.

First measure back along the rope 20 times the diameter – put on a temporary stop. Unlay the strands back to the stop and tape the ends.

Tie a very loose Wall Knot (remember "The strands of a wall go up and tall") as shown in diagram 1. Now Crown the three strands on top of the wall, again very loosely because you are going to have to follow the lead around at least once more if not twice, so leave room. "The leads of a Crown always go down". You will now find that the three strands from the Crown Knot lay nicely beside the bights of the Wall Knot – all you have to do now is to follow them round with each strand in turn, to make either a two or three pass knot. The final stage is to tuck the ends down through the centre of the knot to emerge alongside the standing part of the rope, where they can either be cut off or spliced into the rope with a gradual taper.

Whipping

There are several different types of whipping which can be used to stop the ends of a rope from fraying; the three methods shown here are those commonly used and sufficient to cover all types of rope construction. Temporary whipping using the Constrictor Knot or tape is covered in the Splicing chapter.

Whipping twine can be obtained in various sizes, materials and colours – as a rule of thumb a whipping should be laid on using a twine of a diameter that will not cut into the rope and be about one to one and a half times the diameter of the rope in length.

Do not confuse Whipping with Serving and Seizing which are covered in the Splicing chapter later in the book.

COMMON WHIPPING

The Common Whipping is a quick and easy whipping that can be used at the end of natural fibre ropes and at the throat of an eye splice. Its drawbacks are that if one wrap breaks or is cut, the whole whipping will come off as it has no other support than its tight wrap, secondly it can slip off the end of man-made fibre ropes that are slippery. The turns here are shown open for illustration purposes.

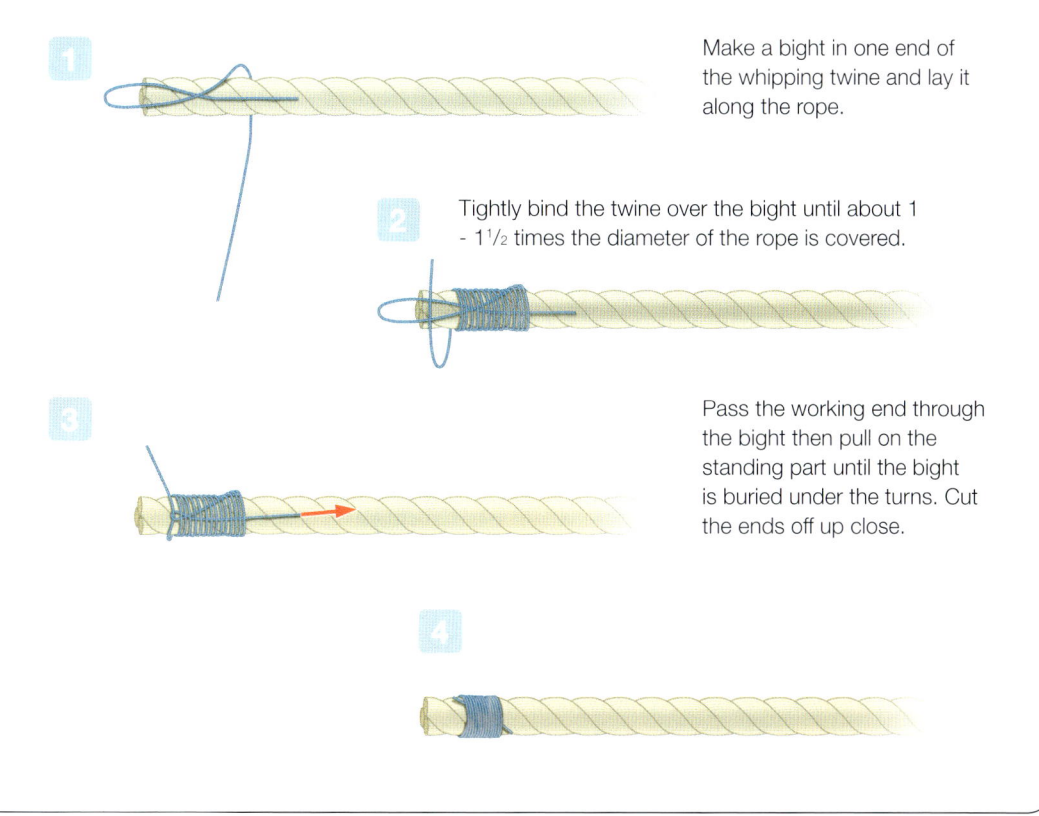

1 Make a bight in one end of the whipping twine and lay it along the rope.

2 Tightly bind the twine over the bight until about 1 - 1½ times the diameter of the rope is covered.

3 Pass the working end through the bight then pull on the standing part until the bight is buried under the turns. Cut the ends off up close.

4

SAILMAKER'S WHIPPING

There is no better or more seamanlike whipping for three strand rope than the traditional Sailmaker's Whipping. It is suitable for both natural and man-made fibre ropes and done well, it is not only practical but makes a decorative end to a rope.

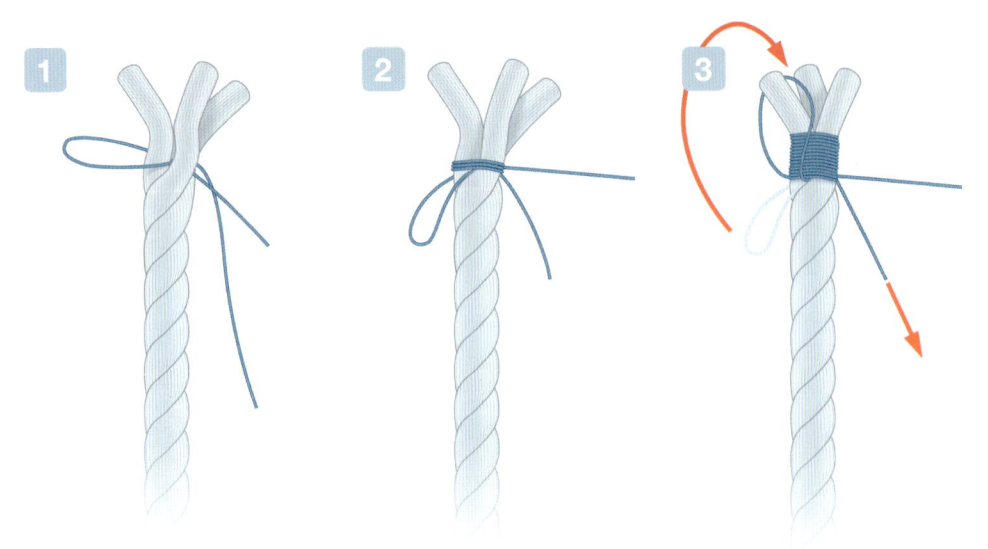

Make a long bight in the end of your whipping twine, unlay about two turns of the rope and lay the bight of the twine over one of the strands as shown in diagram 1. Commence winding on the whipping, above the bight and about 3 rope diameters from the end. Working towards the end lay on nice neat tight turns around the rope – for about one to one and a half times the diameter of the rope. Now take the bight in the whipping twine and place it over the strand which it straddled, then pull the end of the twine to tighten in down into the centre of the rope.

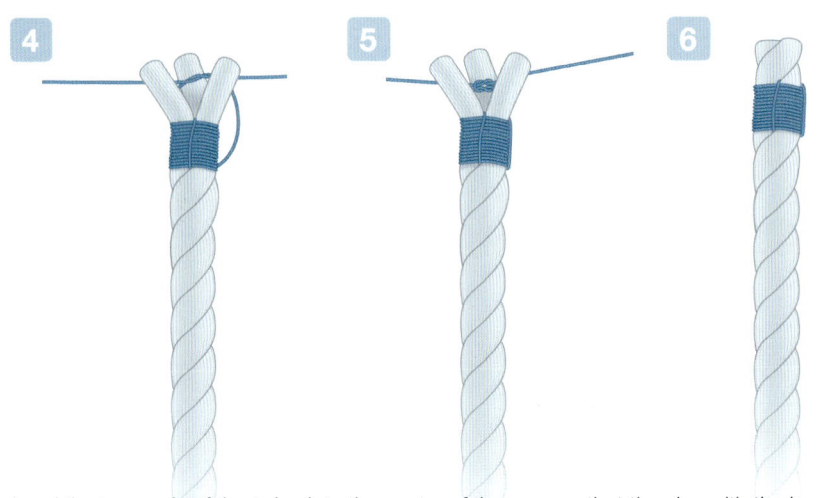

Lead the two ends of the twine into the centre of the rope so that they lay with the lay of the rope (one strand of twine in each lay) and tighten down with a Half Knot, followed by another to form a Reef Knot in the centre. Lay the emerging strands back up and cut them off short.

PALM & NEEDLE WHIPPING

A Palm and Needle Whipping is the only really secure whipping to use on braided ropes as others like the Common Whipping tend to slide off the slippery man-made fibres. All braided rope ends should be whipped; it is not seamanlike to rely on the heat seal to stop the ends from fraying out.

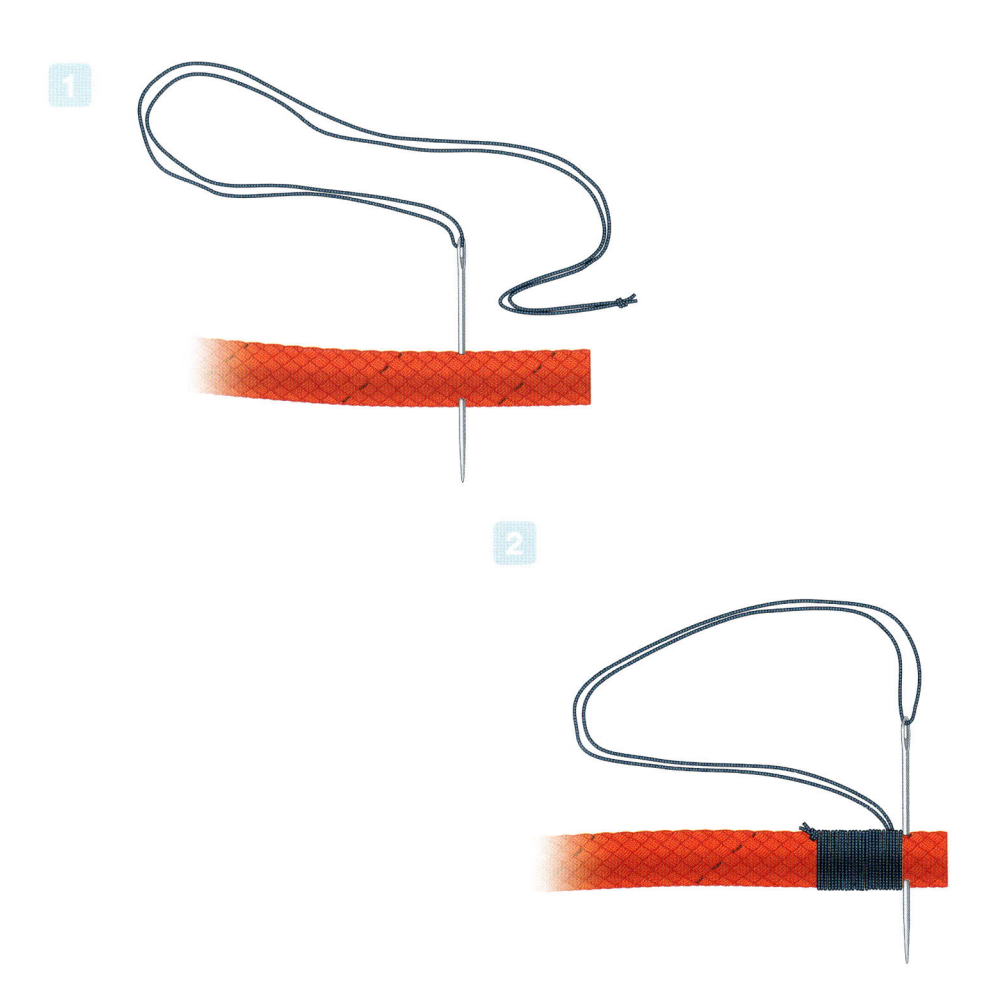

Take about a fathom of whipping twine, thread it on to a sail needle, middle it and put a Thumb Knot in the ends. Pass the needle through the centre of the rope and core, about 2 diameters from the end - pull up to the stopper knot. Wind the whipping twine on tight and neat towards the end covering about one and a half times the diameter of the rope. At the end of the whipping, pass the needle through the cover and core once more.

PALM & NEEDLE WHIPPING

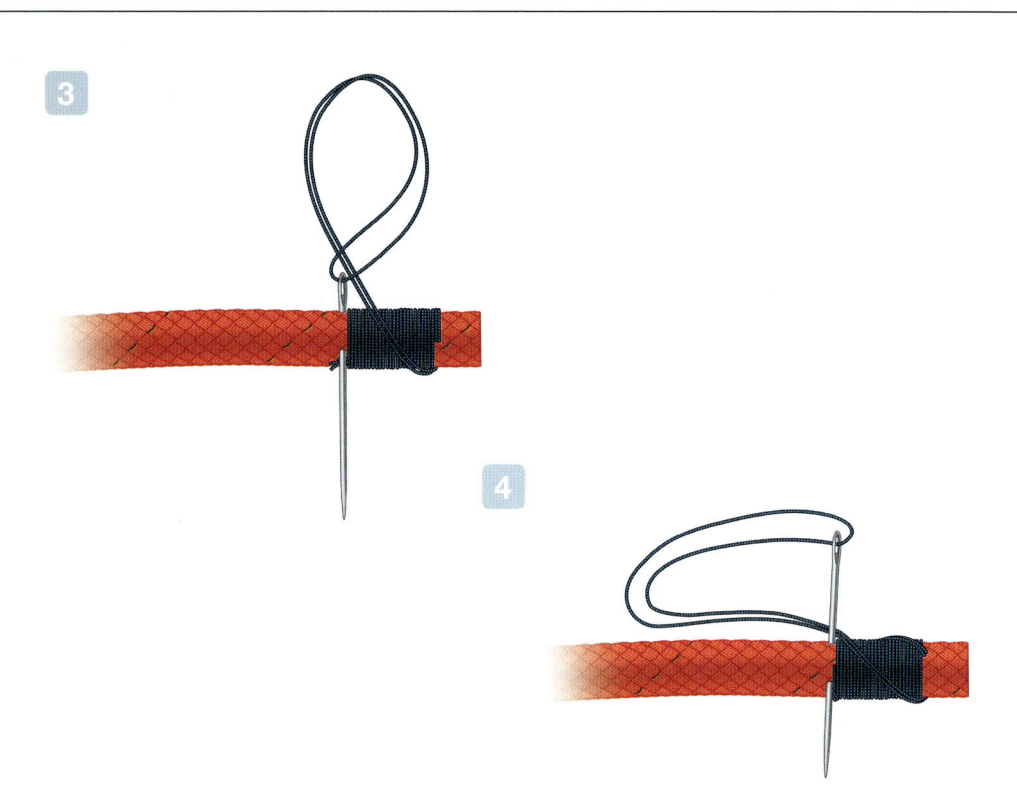

3

4

Now pass the twine over the whipping and pass the needle through about a third of the rope as shown in diagram 3. Then back towards the end (forming a mock Sailmaker's Whipping pattern), pass through a third again before ending where the stopper knot rests on the cover of the rope.

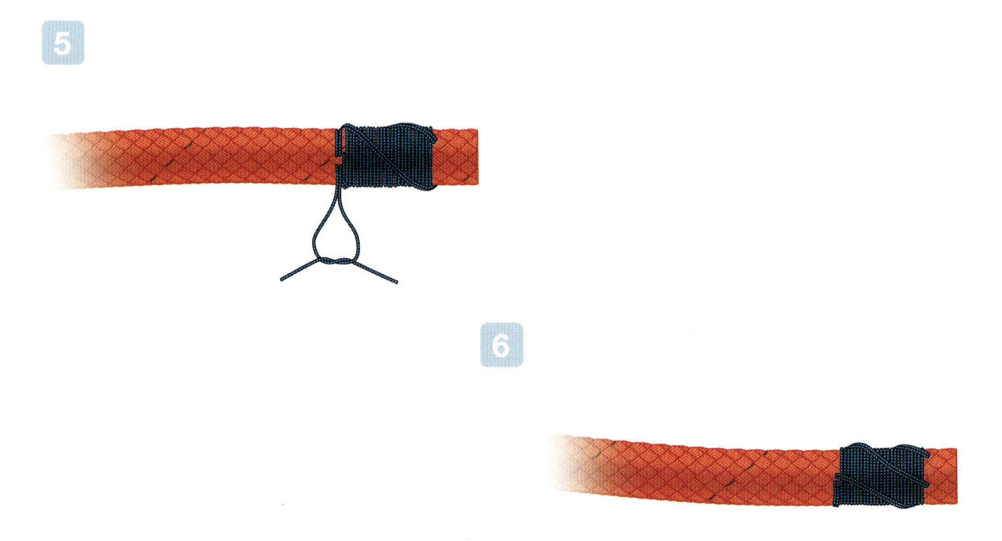

5

6

Cut the whipping twine so that you leave one end threaded – pass this through the cover once more and secure with a Half Knot. Re-thread the needle and bury the ends in the rope.

CHAPTER 6:

BENDS

SHEET BEND - VARIANTS

SHEET BEND - DOUBLE

SHEET BEND - ONE WAY

HEAVING LINE BEND

RACKING BEND

SEIZING BEND

ALPINE BUTTERFLY BEND

ASHLEY'S BEND

RIGGER'S BEND

FISHERMAN'S KNOT

FISHERMAN'S EIGHT KNOT

HARNESS BEND

BLOOD KNOT BEND

CARRICK BEND

BOWLINE BEND

Introduction: Bends

Bends are those knots which join two ends of rope, tape or bungee cord as a temporary expedient; be those two ends of different ropes or two ends of the same rope. Where a more permanent join is required, a Splice should be employed.

When considering the 'Safety' aspect of bends, remember that bends tied with ropes of different thicknesses are not as reliable as those tied in ropes of similar or equal thickness – unless that is, they are designed specifically for that purpose; like the Heaving Line and Racking Bends. Some readers may be wondering why the Reef Knot is not in this chapter; the reason being that it is a Binding Knot and can be unreliable if used as a bend, for the reasons pointed out in the Progressive Knotting chapter.

Sheet Bend - Variants

Although the Sheet Bend in its basic form has been covered in the Progressive Knotting chapter, it is also included here, together with some variations which are traditionally used afloat, on rings, thimbles, eyes, hooks or bights of rope. These have a variety of different names, although they are all tied in the manner of a Sheet Bend.

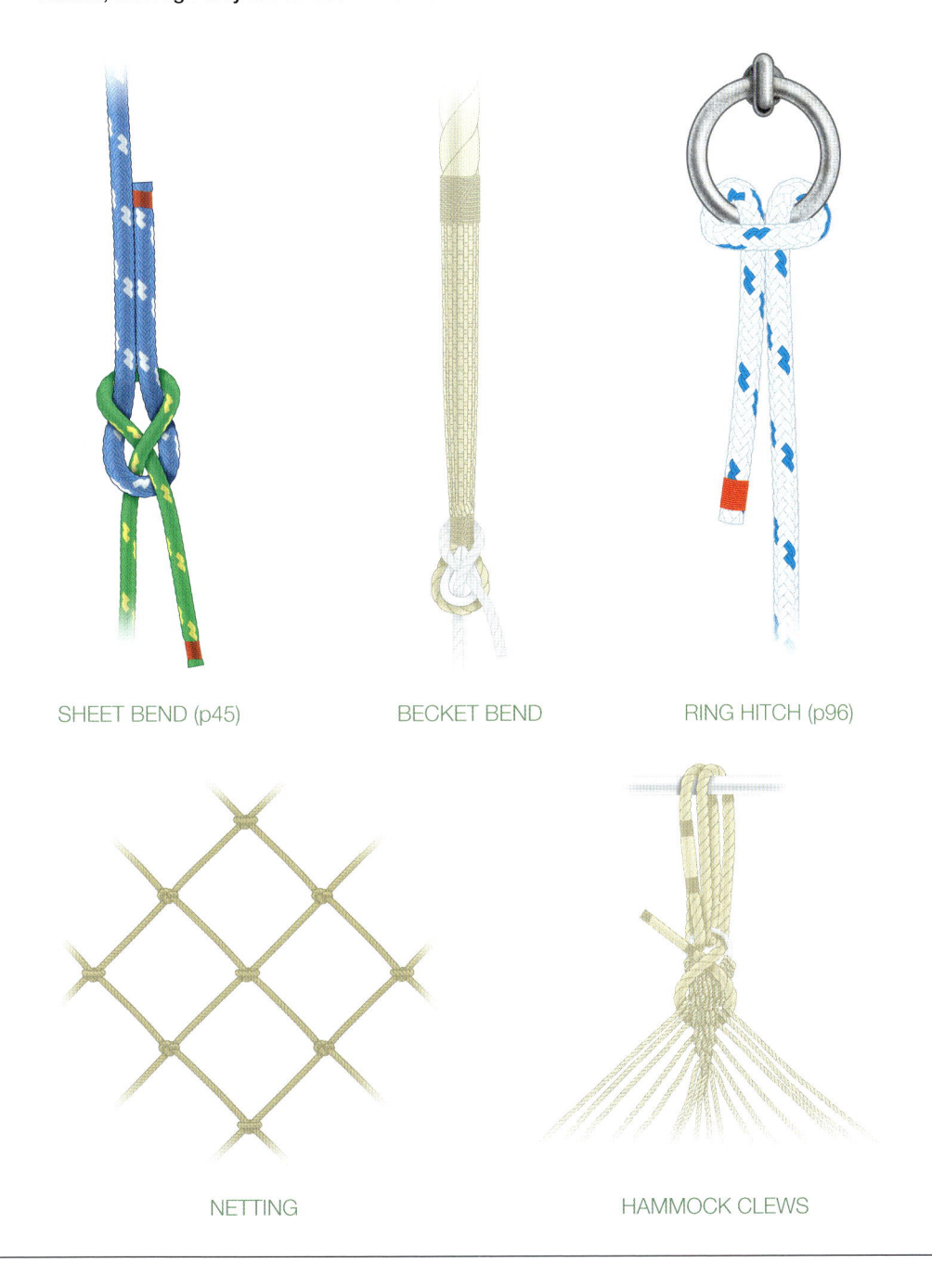

SHEET BEND (p45)

BECKET BEND

RING HITCH (p96)

NETTING

HAMMOCK CLEWS

Sheet Bend - Double

The Double Sheet Bend is more secure than the Sheet Bend and is recommended if the two ropes are of different thickness.

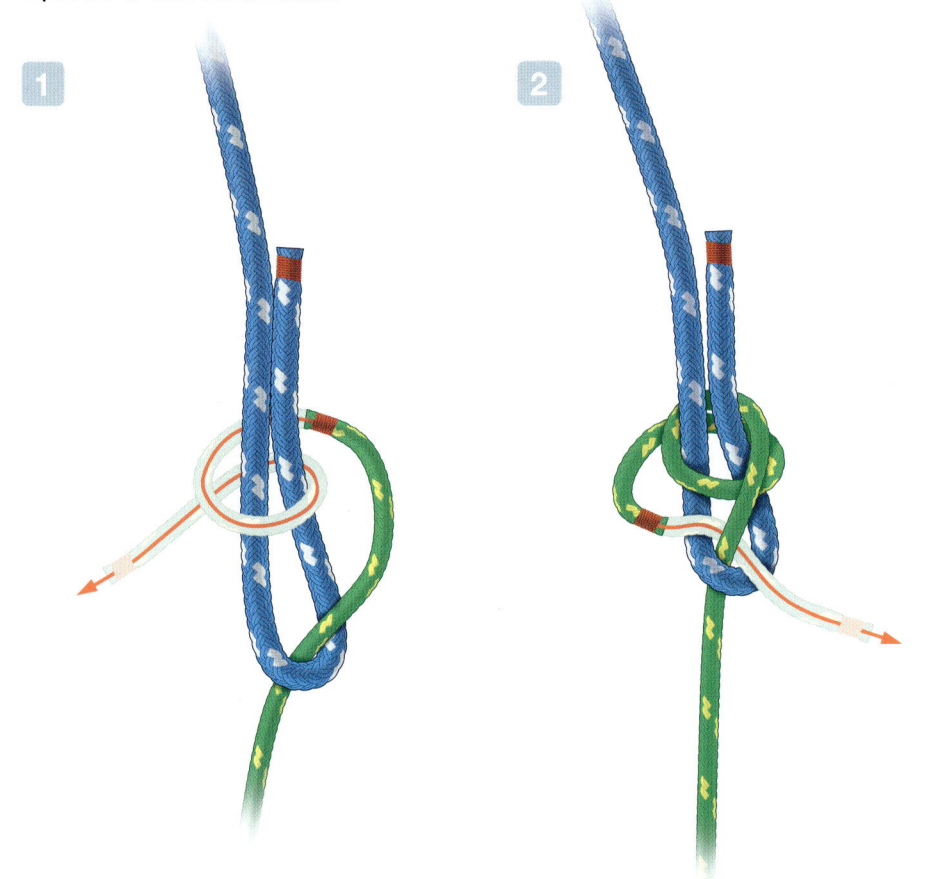

1

2

Form a closed loop in the end of the thicker rope. Pass the other line up through the loop and round the bight in the direction shown (behind the short end first).

Tuck the working end under its own standing part, across the top of the bight of the thicker rope. Hold the loop in place then pull on the standing part of the thinner rope.

3

Sheet Bend - One Way

By tucking the working end of a heaving line or messenger back alongside the standing part of the rope to be hauled, the knot can be safely pulled over a deck edge, through a bull ring or fairlead, a mooring ring or round a pile, without the ends snagging.

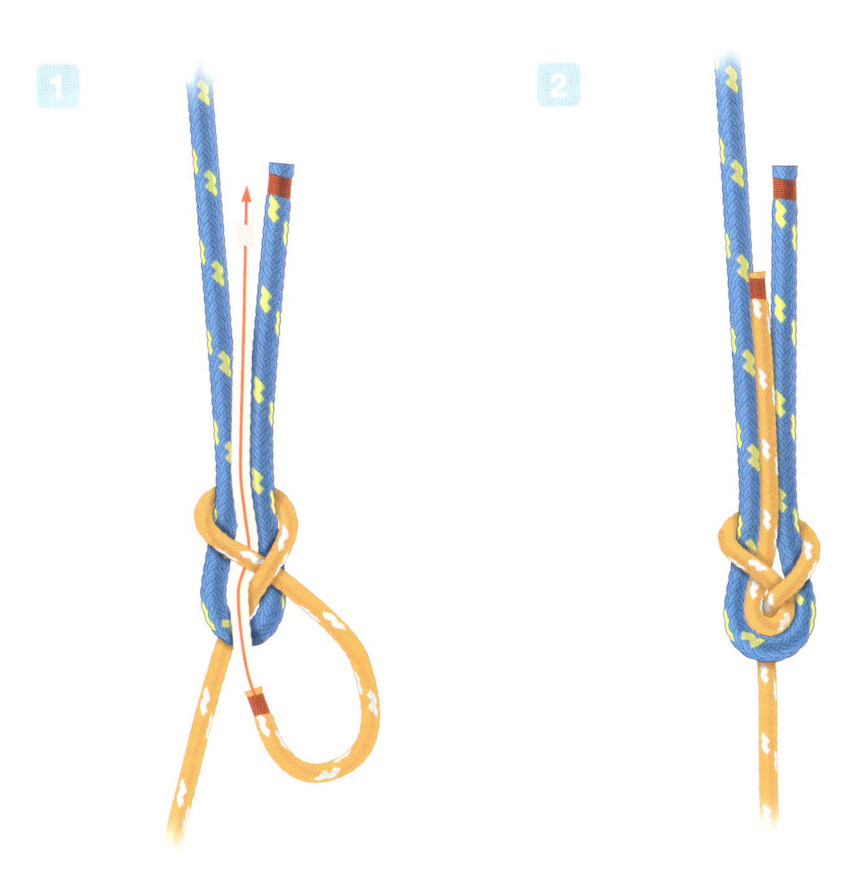

1

2

Tie a Single Sheet Bend (p45) then tuck the working end of the hauling rope under itself and up alongside the standing part of the rope being hauled.

TIP FROM THE BOSUN'S LOCKER

If you need to join lines of considerably differing diameters – consider using a Racking Bend (p77) or Seizing Bend (p78).

Heaving Line Bend

This knot is used to attach a heaving/throwing line to the eye or bight in a heavier rope, such as a berthing hawser, to haul it to a securing point. It is, as its name implies, for attaching a heaving line as a temporary expedient – it is not a very secure knot unless it is under load; but having been under a load it is easy to untie, by pulling the standing part and the working end of the thicker rope apart.

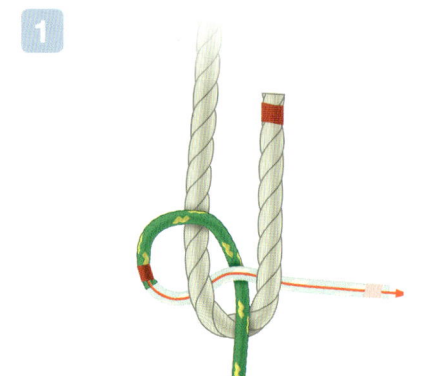

1

2

Form a bight in the hawser/mooring rope. Lay the heaving line over the top of the bight then pass it back under the bight, over itself, under the bight, then back over the bight.

Tuck the working end under the standing part of the line (diagram 2), leaving a long end, then haul the knot up with the standing part of the heaving line.

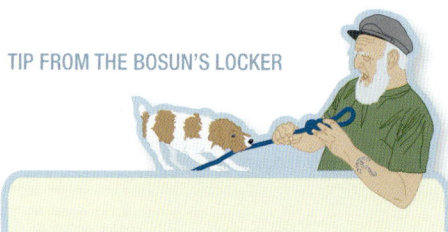

3

TIP FROM THE BOSUN'S LOCKER

A soft (leather or canvas) bag containing sand is the safest weight for the end of a heaving/throwing line. The traditional Monkey's Fist or Heaving Line Knot can also be used but under NO circumstances should they be 'loaded' with solid objects.

Racking Bend

If the end of a large hawser, that has to be hauled by a messenger or heaving line, is heavy and stiff, the Racking Bend is used; firstly because it will pull the bight in the larger rope together and secondly it will prevent it from pulling straight and spilling the knot. If there is any doubt about whether it is going to hold, the working end of the messenger should be stopped to the standing part of the hawser.

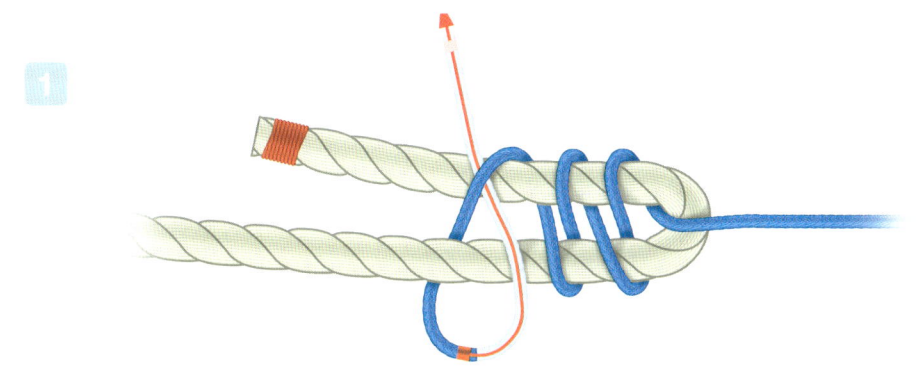

1

Form as tight a bight as possible in the large hawser – you may even have to stop the working end to the standing part in very springy ropes. Take the end of the heaving/messenger line and form a figure of eight weave, as shown. Pull each turn up as tight as you can before starting the next. Three or more turns will be required, depending on the ropes being used.

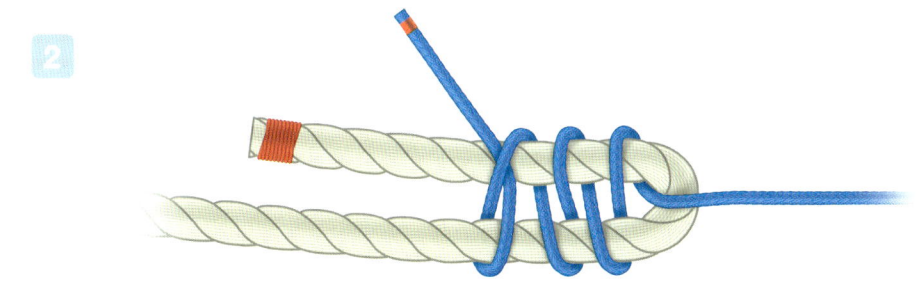

2

Tuck the working end under the last turn, as shown, then work back towards the standing part and tighten the turns as much as possible, before taking the weight on the heaving line.

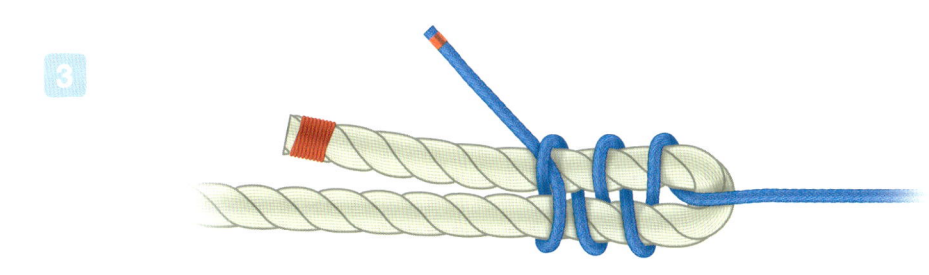

3

Seizing Bend

For joining two ropes of different thickness, where the joined ropes are going to be rove through an aperture and perhaps be subjected to alternating load or no load, the Seizing Bend is the most secure bend to use.

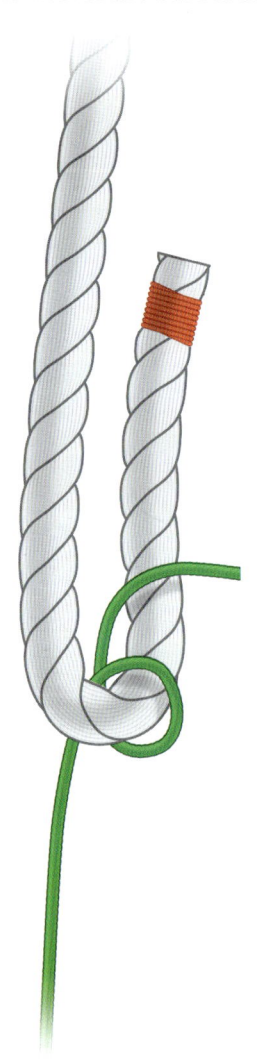

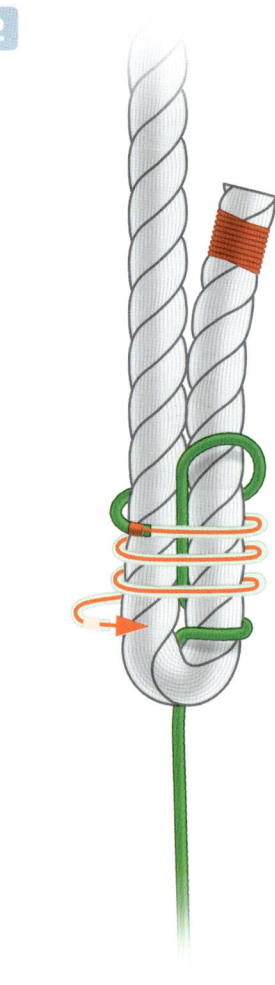

1 Form a bight in the thicker rope, pass the heaving line through the bight and make a turn, as shown.

2 Make at least four wraps around the bight above the round turn. (Take care not to trap the standing part of the heaving line.)

SEIZING BEND | 79

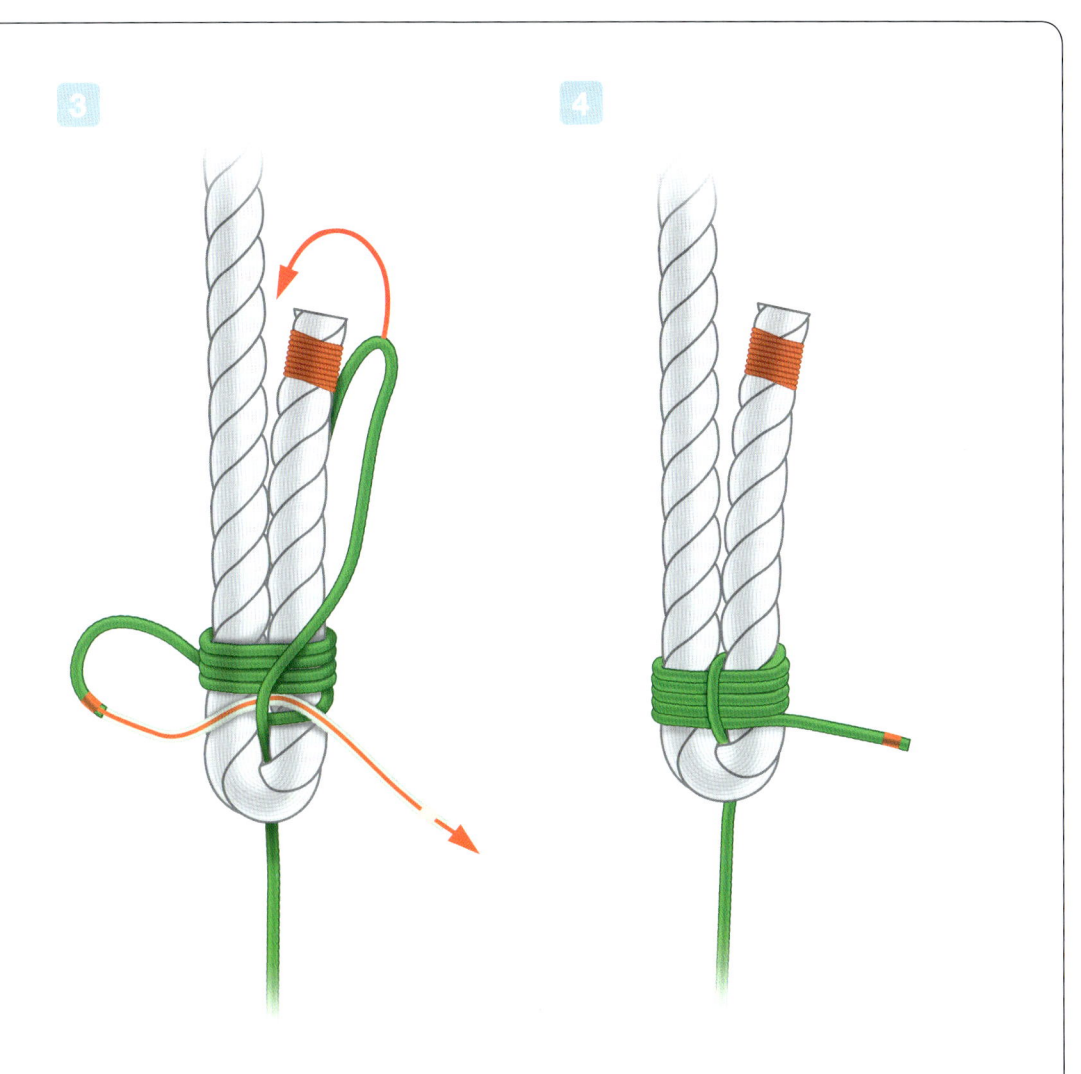

Pull the standing part of the heaving line, to make a loop large enough to pass over the working end of the hawser. Pass the loop between the standing part and the working end, tuck the working end of the heaving line under it and pull on the standing part of the heaving line to tighten the knot.

Bends

Alpine Butterfly Bend

This adaptation of the Alpine Butterfly Loop provides an easily tied, secure and safe bend with which to join two warps or lines of equal thickness.

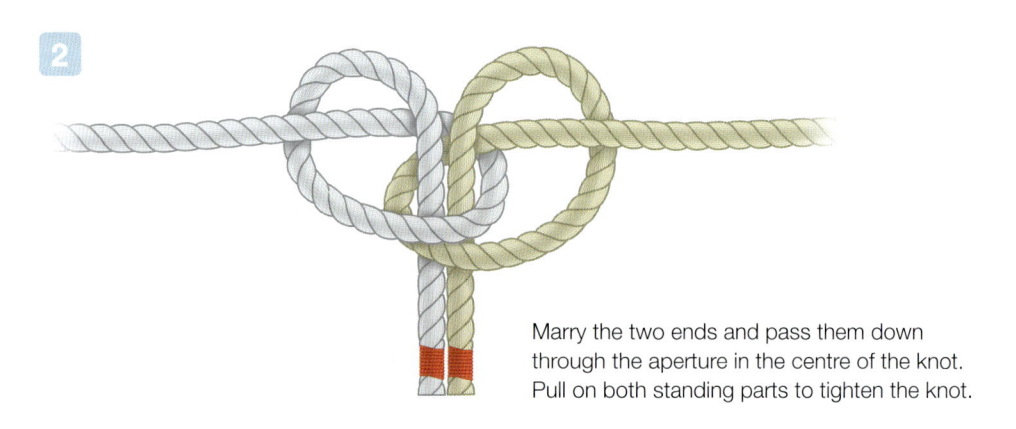

1

Make an underhand crossing loop with the left hand rope. Pass the working end of the right hand rope up through the loop in the first rope and form another crossing loop, as shown above.

2

Marry the two ends and pass them down through the aperture in the centre of the knot. Pull on both standing parts to tighten the knot.

3

Ashley's Bend

This knot appears in the Ashley Book of Knots with no name, just the number 1452 and the simple statement that it is probably original. No wonder the Knot Tyers of the world have now opted to call 1452 'Ashley's Bend' for it is really one of the most versatile bends ever to be published. Rope, cord and even bungee can be united using this knot and it will take a load on combinations of any one, two, three or all four of its parts. Perhaps a little clumsy to tie, but well worth the effort.

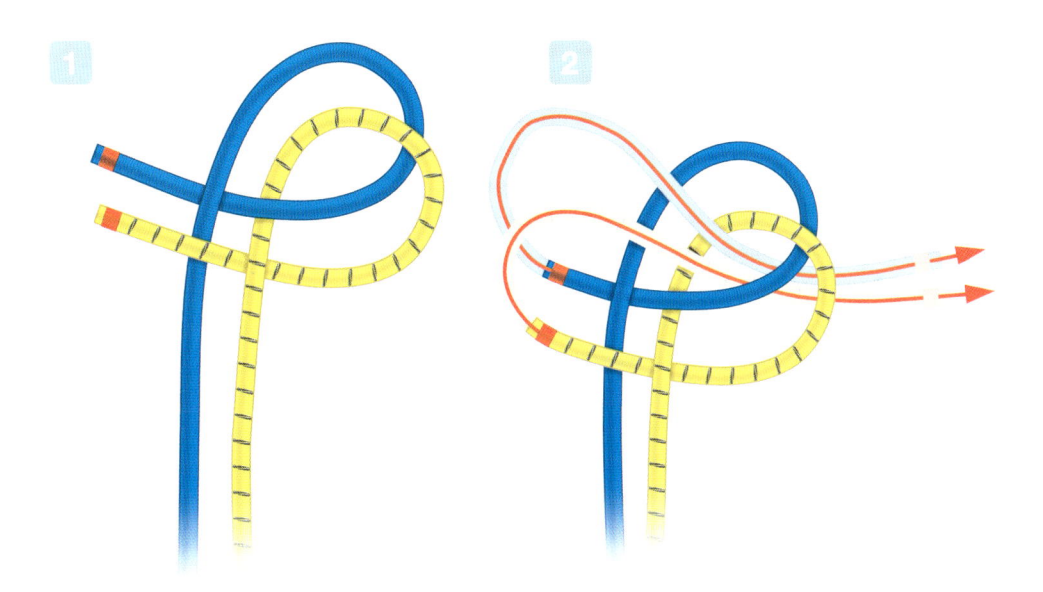

Make an underhand crossing loop in one cord (yellow). Pass the working end of the second cord (blue) behind the first, then up through the first loop before forming another underhand crossing loop.

Marry the two working ends and pass them down through both the loops. Hold the working ends and pull up on the standing parts to tighten the knot.

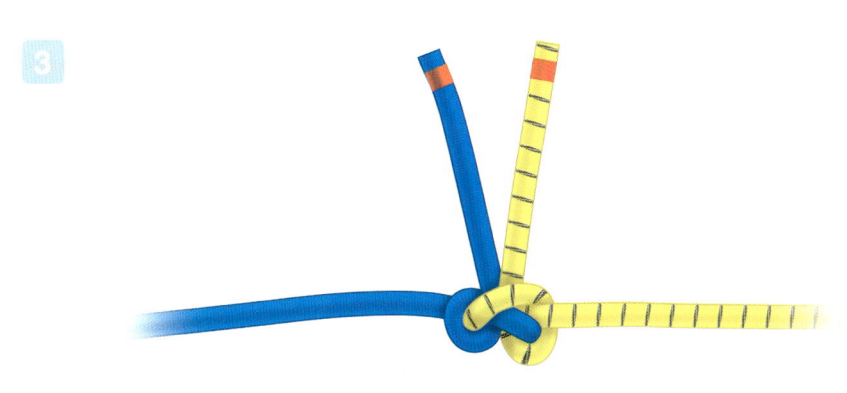

Rigger's Bend *(Hunter's Bend)*

Like Ashley's Bend, the Rigger's Bend, or Hunter's Bend (named by Dr Hunter), is also a knot tied with interwoven Overhand Knots. In this knot however, the two working ends emerge from opposite sides of the knot – making it suitable as a centre bend for a four way lashing etc.

1

Lay both ropes end for end, with a large overlap.

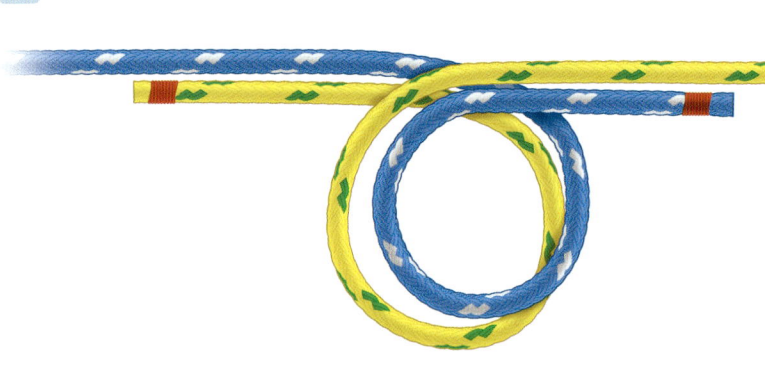

2

Take the working end and adjacent standing part in each hand and twist a crossing loop in both ropes together, as above.

3

Tuck the left hand working end through the centre from front to back and the right hand working end through from back to front.

RIGGER'S BEND | 83

4

Dress the knot by pulling up the two working ends first, then tighten using both standing parts.

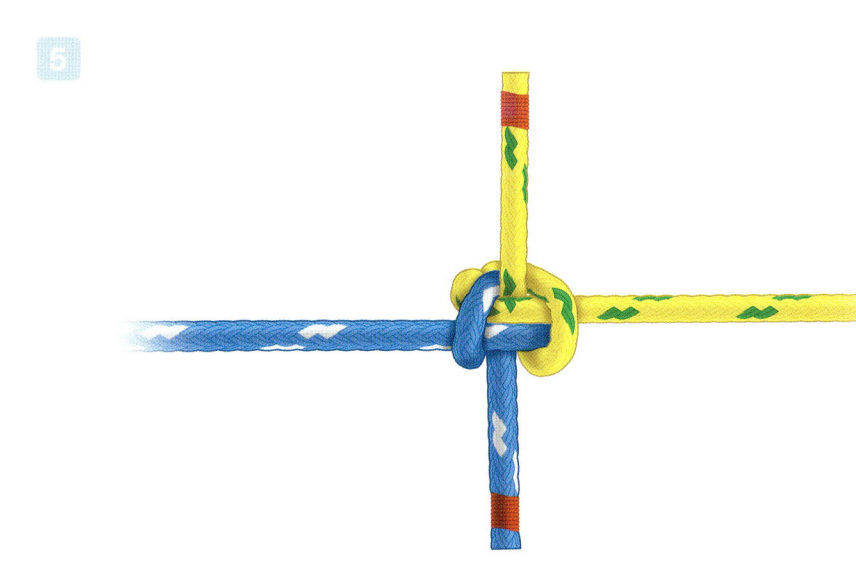

5

Bends

TIP FROM THE BOSUN'S LOCKER

When using 'bends' to join shock (bungee) cord – always leave very long ends and ensure the knot is pulled up tight before loading.

TEST BEFORE USING.

Fisherman's Knot

A 'knot' among bends – the reason is that there is also a Fisherman's Bend (or Anchor Bend) and as this particular method of joining two ropes' ends employs the Overhand or Double Overhand Knot, the names have stuck. The single Overhand Knot variant of the knot is one of the most efficient ways of tying two lines together. However, for joining 'slippery' lines, the Double (or even Triple) Overhand Knot is not only more secure but it does not reduce the strength in the rope quite so much as the Single Overhand. A useful knot for joining ropes that are used for climbing, or working aloft.

1

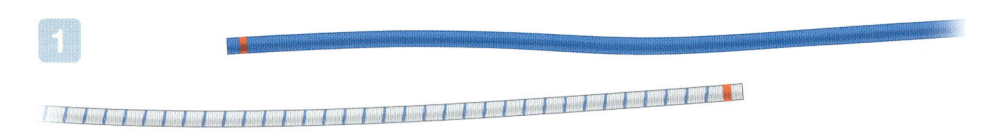

Lay the two pieces of line to be joined, end for end – leaving enough line to tie the overhand knot in the working end.

2

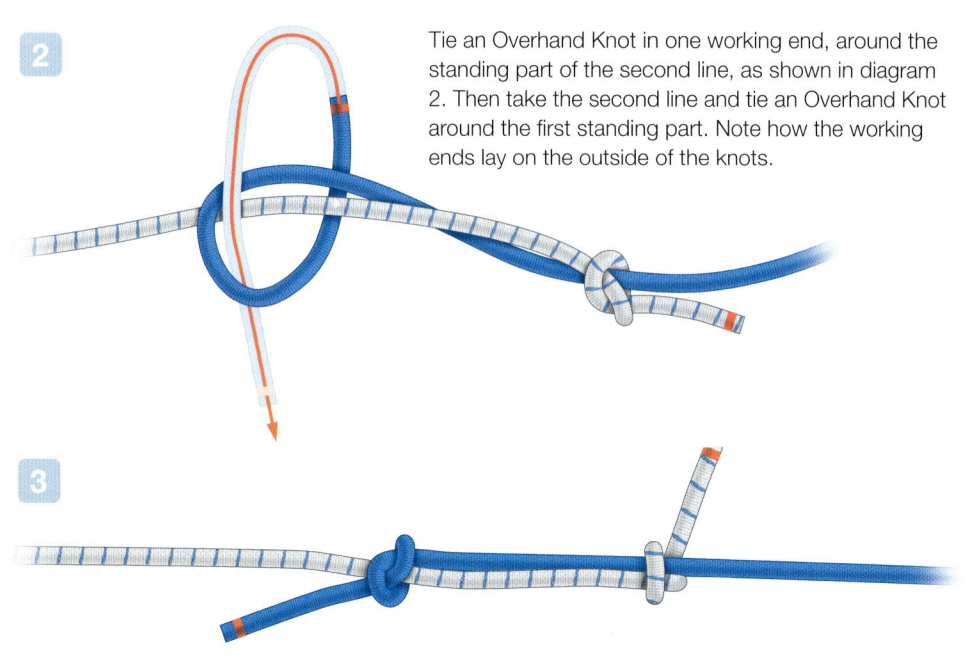

Tie an Overhand Knot in one working end, around the standing part of the second line, as shown in diagram 2. Then take the second line and tie an Overhand Knot around the first standing part. Note how the working ends lay on the outside of the knots.

3

Pull both Overhand Knots up tight, then pull on both working ends and draw the knots together. For a more permanent join the two working ends can now be taped or stopped to the standing parts.

4

Fisherman's Eight Knot

Used and tied in much the same way as the Fisherman's Knot, the Fisherman's Eight Knot is tied with a Figure of Eight Knot instead of an Overhand Knot.

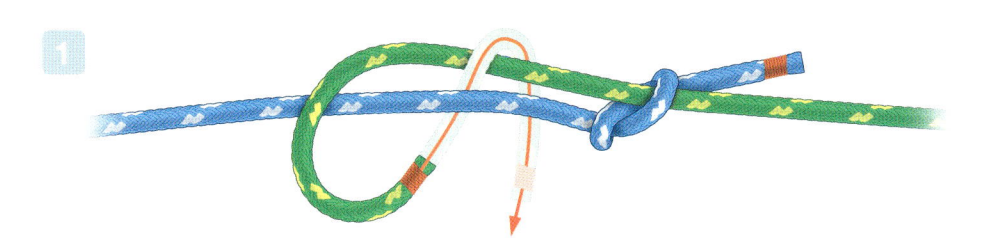

Lay the two lines end for end allowing enough working end to tie the Figure of Eight Knots. With the working end of one line tie a Figure of Eight Knot around the standing part of the second line – ensuring that the working end lays parallel with the standing part of the second line.

Tie the second Figure of Eight around the first standing part, also ensuring that the working end lays parallel to the standing part.

Tighten both Figure of Eight Knots then draw them together by pulling on both standing parts. The two knots should lay snug together as shown in the diagram below.

Harness Bend

Broken sail tape, strapping or leather tack can be quickly and safely re-joined using this combination of two opposing Half Hitches. But care must be taken to dress the tapes flat or the knot will spill.

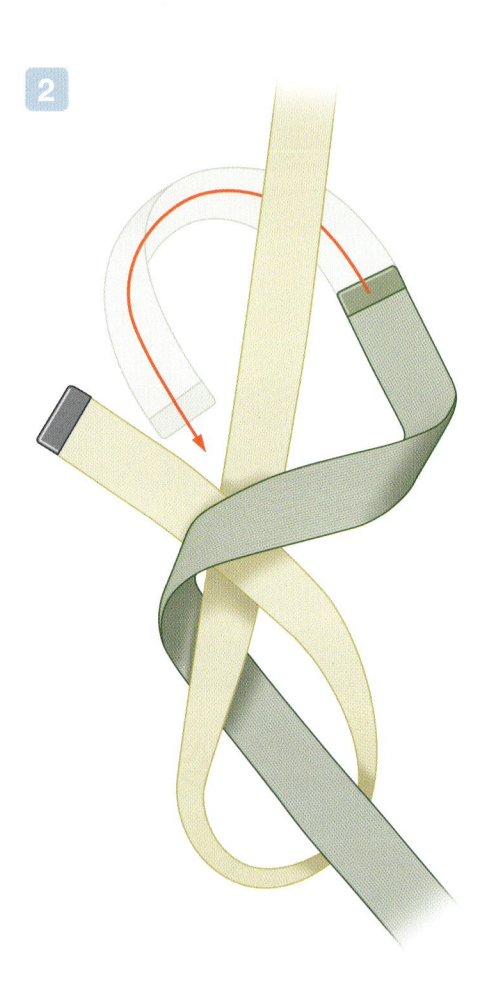

1

Make an overhand crossing loop. Then pass the second strap through it from front to back.

2

Pass the second strap around the standing part of the first, then lay it on top of the first working end.

CHAPTER 7:

HITCHES

HALF HITCHES

COW HITCHES

CLOVE HITCH

PRUSIK HITCH

BLAKE'S HITCH

HIGH POST HITCH

PILE HITCH

ICICLE HITCH

ANCHOR BEND

TIMBER HITCH & KILLICK HITCH

SCAFFOLD HITCH

BUNTLINE HITCH

GUYLINE HITCH

HALYARD KNOT

Introduction: Hitches

The knots in this chapter are collectively known as 'Hitches', although you will actually come across some which are known as a Bend or Knot; nevertheless they are all used to make fast a rope to another object, even another rope.

Some of the knots in this chapter were covered in the Progressive Knotting chapter, but are repeated here briefly to make this chapter complete.

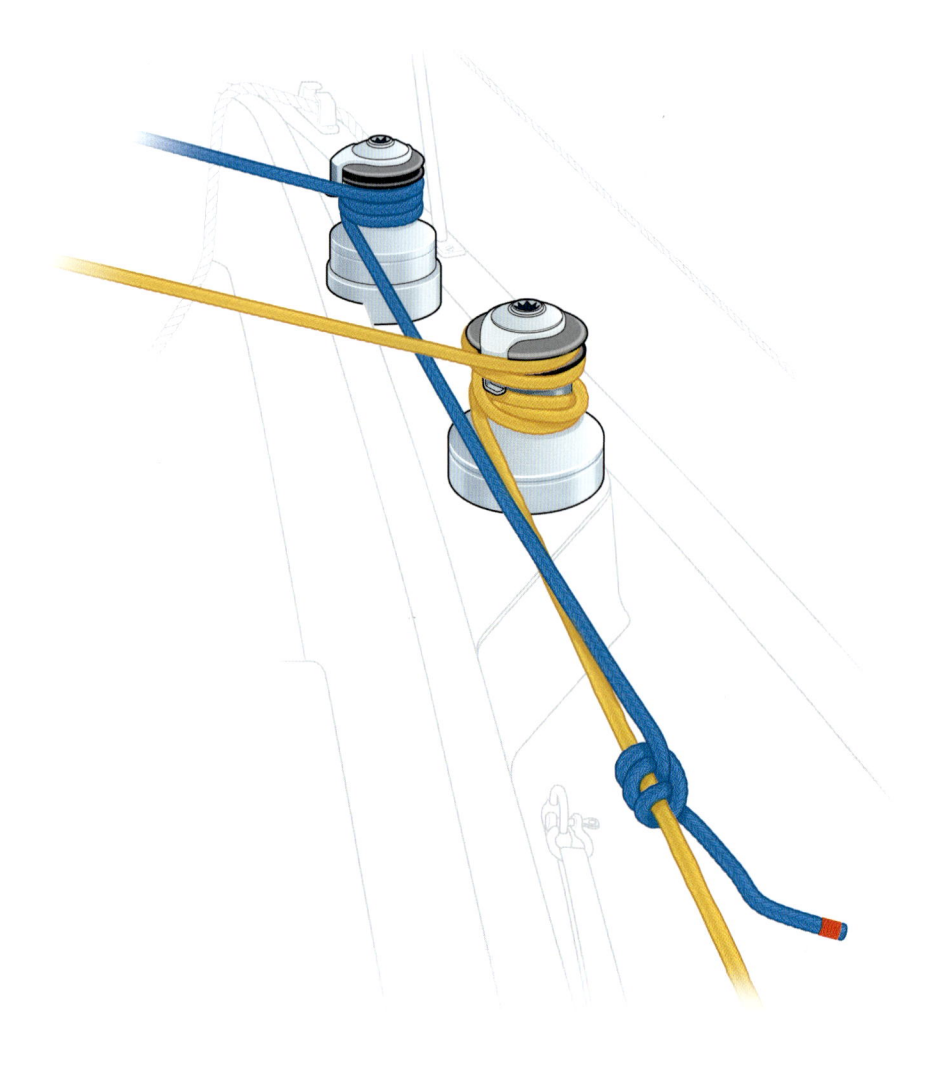

HARNESS BEND 87

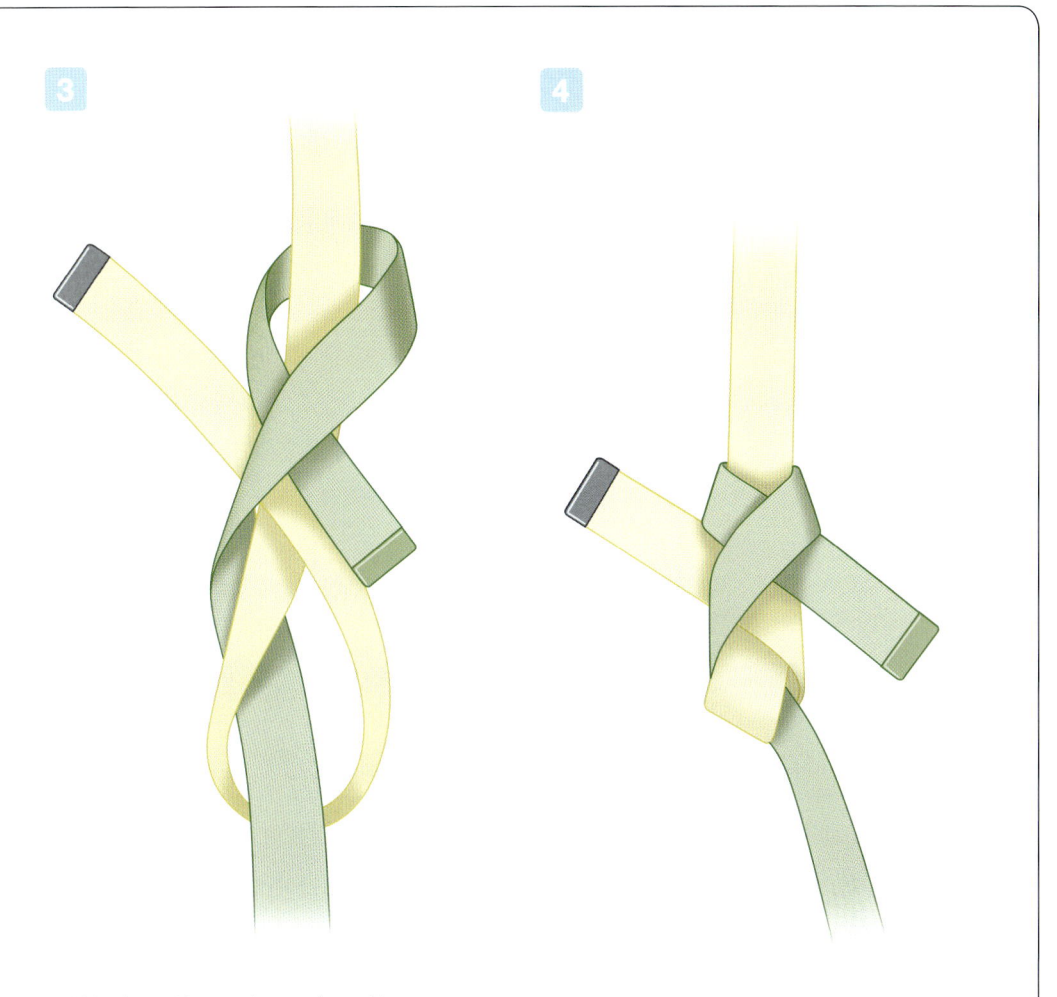

3

4

Hold both working ends together with one hand, and pull the knot up with the standing parts, ensuring that the tape lays flat and neat throughout the knot.

Bends

Blood Knot Bend

Monofilament and slippery thin lines are difficult to tie together securely, but this knot from the Angler's repertoire is perhaps the most efficient.

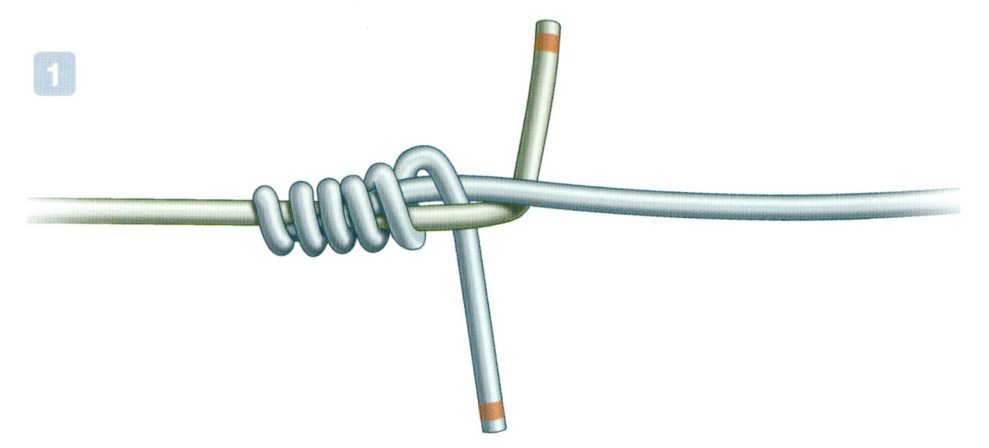

1

Lay both lines end for end, allowing a generous length for the turns. Wind on at least 4 turns back over the standing part and the second line, finishing by tucking the working end between the two lines.

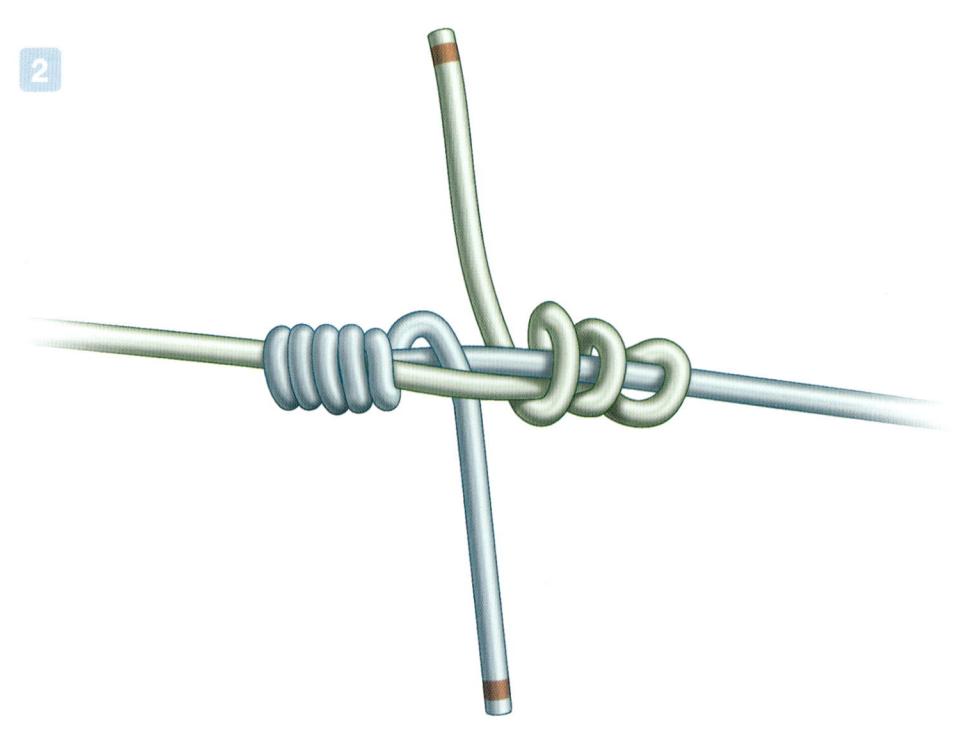

2

Take the second working end and wind the same number of turns back toward the centre of the knot, finishing by tucking the working end in between the two lines, in the opposite direction to the first, as shown in diagram 3.

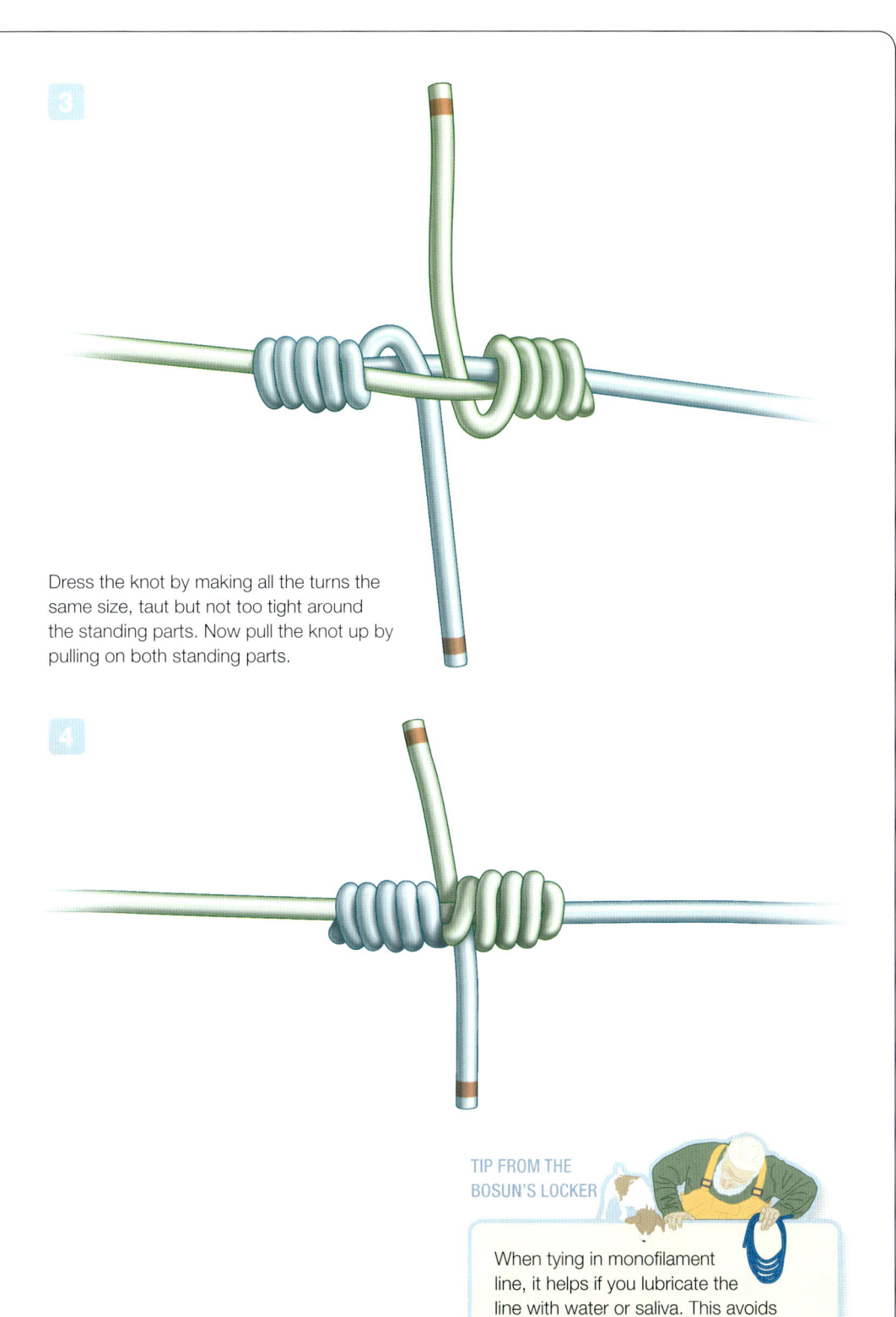

BLOOD KNOT BEND | 89

3

Dress the knot by making all the turns the same size, taut but not too tight around the standing parts. Now pull the knot up by pulling on both standing parts.

4

TIP FROM THE BOSUN'S LOCKER

When tying in monofilament line, it helps if you lubricate the line with water or saliva. This avoids causing friction burns to the line.

Bends

Carrick Bend

There are two variations of the Carrick Bend, one which is used to bend two heavy hawsers together, especially if the join has to pass around a capstan or windlass, where the ends emerge on different sides of the knot. The other is the decorative version, sometimes called a 'Check Knot' or 'Josephine Knot' where the two working ends emerge on the same side of the knot.

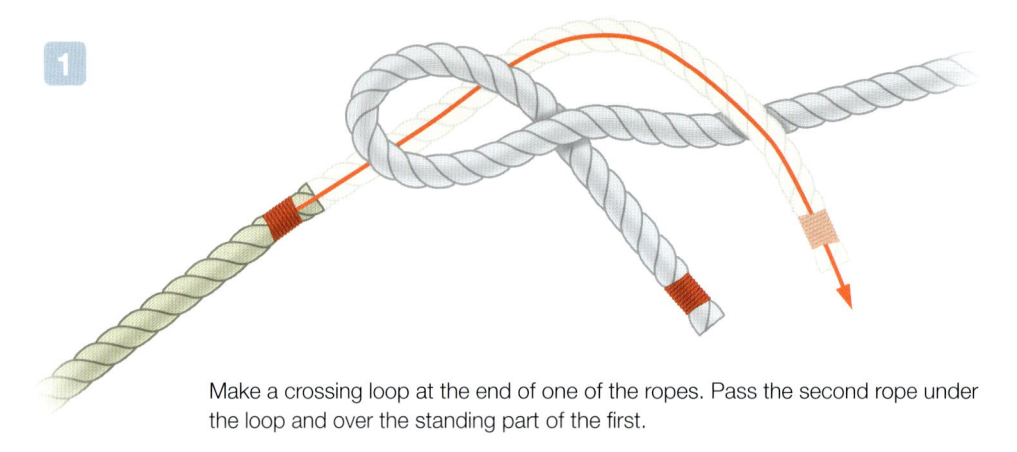

1

Make a crossing loop at the end of one of the ropes. Pass the second rope under the loop and over the standing part of the first.

2

Continue an under-over-under-over sequence through the knot, as shown above.

3

Then, either dress the knot so that it looks like the one above (seizing the working ends to the standing parts if necessary), which is the normal method, or, in small diameter ropes, by pulling on the standing parts to tighten the knot, which will result in a knot like the one in diagram 4.

CARRICK BEND | 91

4

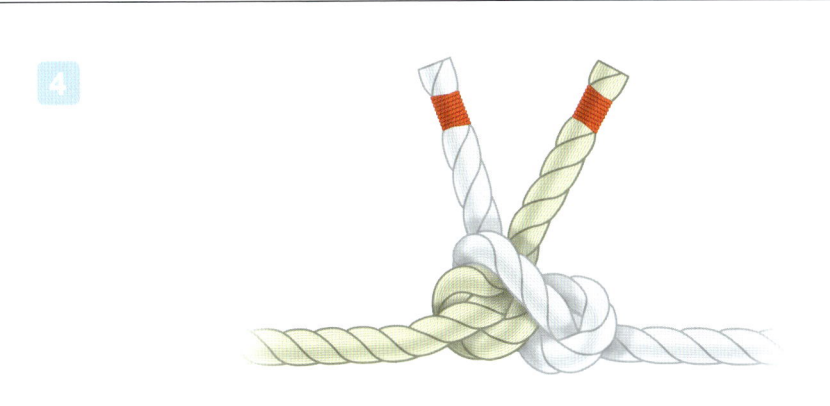

Check Knot

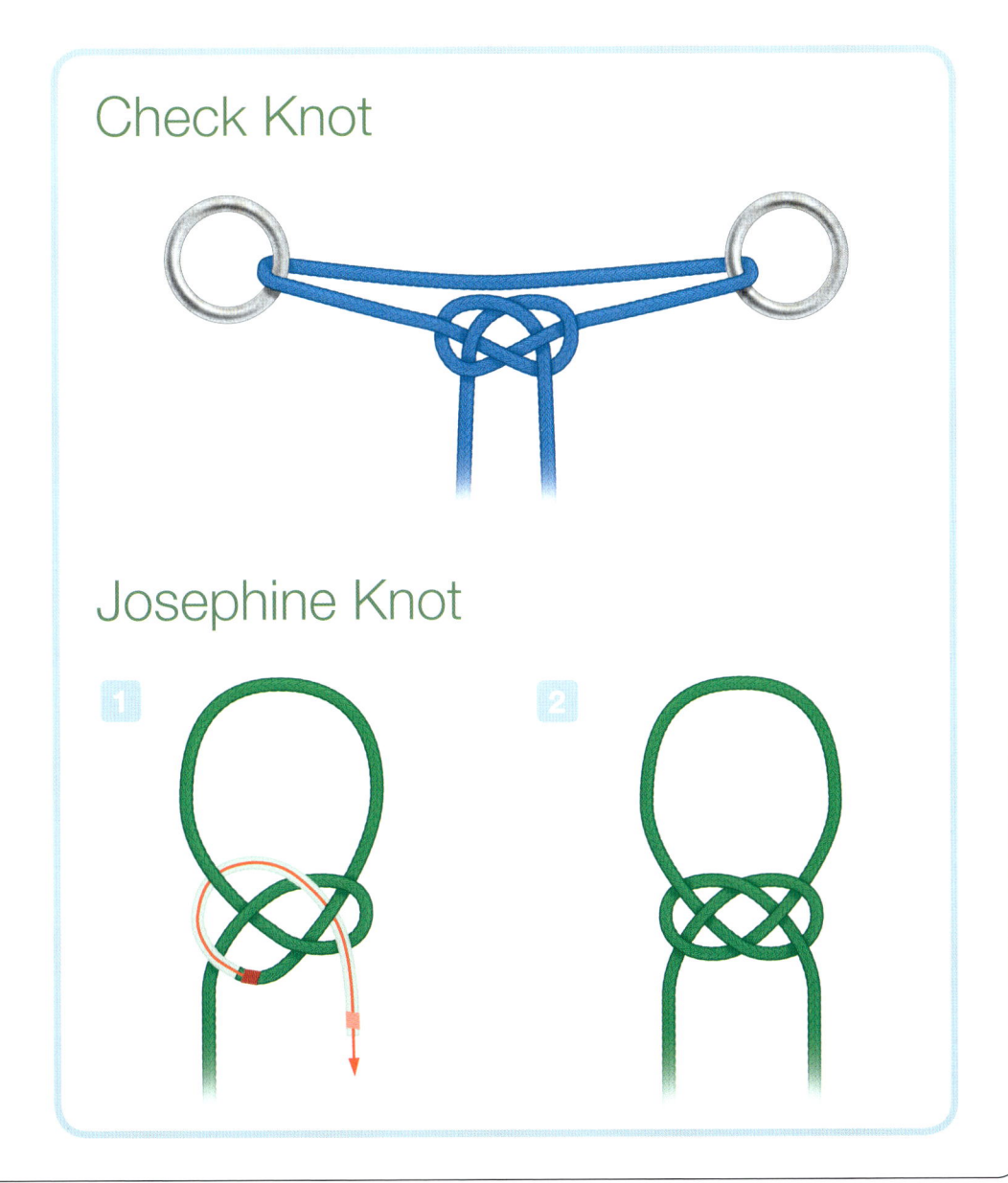

Josephine Knot

1

2

Bends

Bowline Bend

The Bowline Bend is another useful bend for heavy berthing hawsers, particularly if one is larger than the other. The method shown here employs two Bowlines which have been 'through-footed' to form a Reef Knot in the loops where they join; this is to distribute the load at the join so as not to have a sharp bend or single friction point.

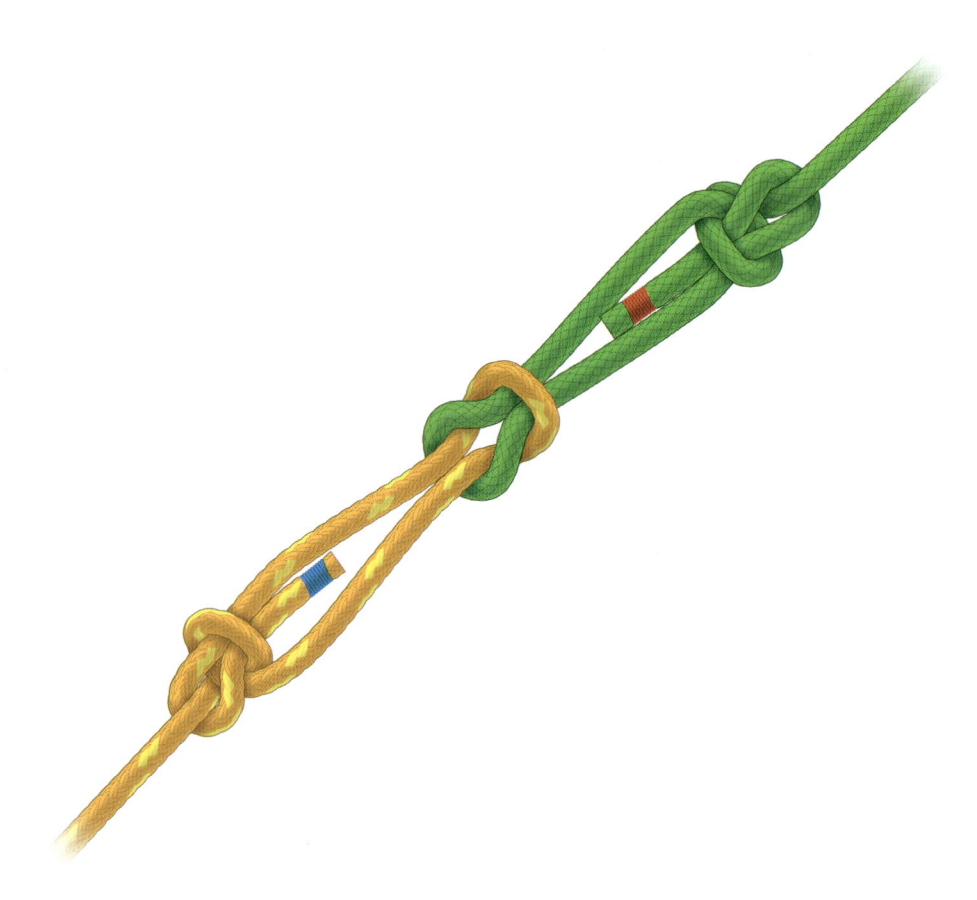

Tie a Bowline in one rope, then pass the working end of the second rope through the eye of the first to form a Reef Knot – tie a Bowline in the second rope then dress the Reef Knot to make sure the load is equal on both sides of each of the Bowline eyes.

HALF HITCHES | 95

Half Hitch, Round Turn & Two Half Hitches & Slipped Half Hitch

A Slipped Half Hitch is formed by tucking the bight and pulling down on the standing part which will grip a rail, spar or rope quite nicely, making it a handy hitch for tying off a lanyard which may need releasing quickly.

HALF HITCH (p48)   SLIPPED HALF HITCH (p20)   ROUND TURN & TWO HALF HITCHES (p54)

Hitches

TIP FROM THE BOSUN'S LOCKER

To prevent the Slipped Half Hitch from spilling accidentally, tuck the working end through the bight.

Cow Hitches

The Cow Hitch is two Half Hitches in which the standing part and working end both emerge on the same side of the knot. The Cow Hitch has a standing part and a short working end (1) – the disadvantage of this is that the knot can rotate round the object it is tied to and the end work its way through the knot and release. To prevent this happening, Harry Asher devised the Pedigree Cow Hitch (2), which has its working end tucked between the object and the standing and working parts. The Ring Hitch (3) is self explanatory and the Lark's Head (4) is a Cow Hitch but where both parts are used – mostly in Macrame projects, making Baggy Wrinkle, securing small strops and label ties.

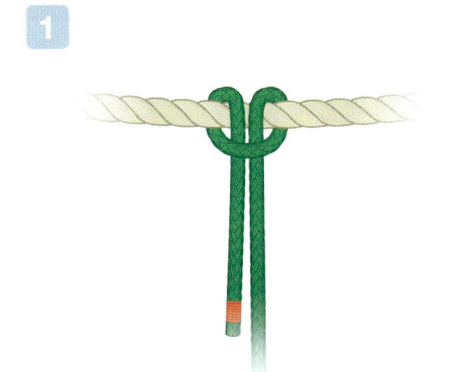

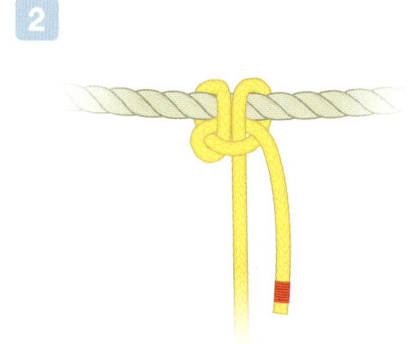

COW HITCH
Make a turn around the rope or spar, bring the working end in front of the standing part then round the rope and through itself.

PEDIGREE COW HITCH
Tie as for a Cow Hitch but before tightening pass the working end between the rope and the turns.

RING HITCH
Pass the working end down through the ring, then in front of the standing part, up through the ring and down through itself.

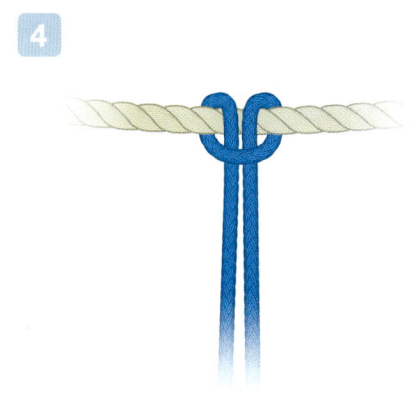

LARK'S HEAD
The Lark's Head can be tied by holding the bight behind the rope then pass the two ends through the loop.

Clove Hitch

The most common knot used to secure a line to a rail, post or ring that has a load at right-angles to it, is the Clove Hitch. It can be tied either with the working end or in the bight if the end of the rail or post is exposed. This is another knot that can be completed with a bight instead of the working end passing through, to make it easily slipped. Useful for handling fender lanyards on a guardrail for example.

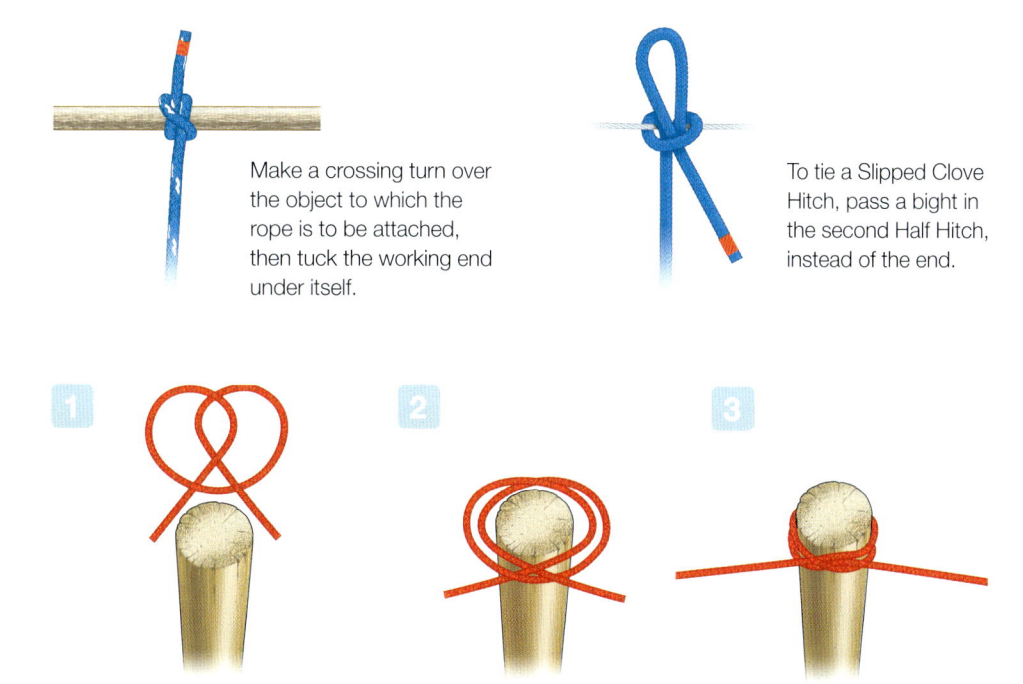

Make a crossing turn over the object to which the rope is to be attached, then tuck the working end under itself.

To tie a Slipped Clove Hitch, pass a bight in the second Half Hitch, instead of the end.

There are two quick methods of tying a Clove Hitch in the bight of a rope when the end of the post or upright is available. The first, shown here, is to make two underhand loops in the same direction – place the right hand loop directly behind the left hand loop then place over the end of the object before pulling on both ends to draw the knot tight.

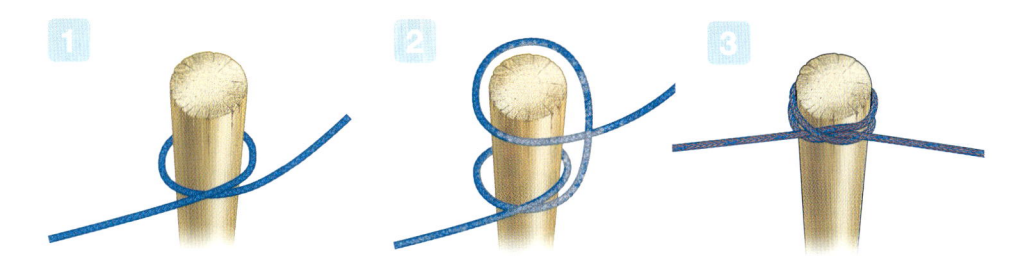

The second method, favoured more by the seaman when tying off is to throw two half hitches over the post or bollard etc, by forming a Half Hitch and simultaneously placing it over the top of the object, then forming a second Half Hitch (in the same direction) on top of the first.

Prusik Hitch

Although the Prusik Hitch is a climbing knot, it has many useful adaptations for sailing, heaving on lines and attaching strops on halyards or stays of larger boats. It can also be used in lieu of the Magnus Hitch to take the weight off a sheet to remove a riding turn. The main advantage of this knot over the Rolling Hitch variants, is that it will take a pull in either direction and will hold when loaded but is easy to move when the load is taken off.

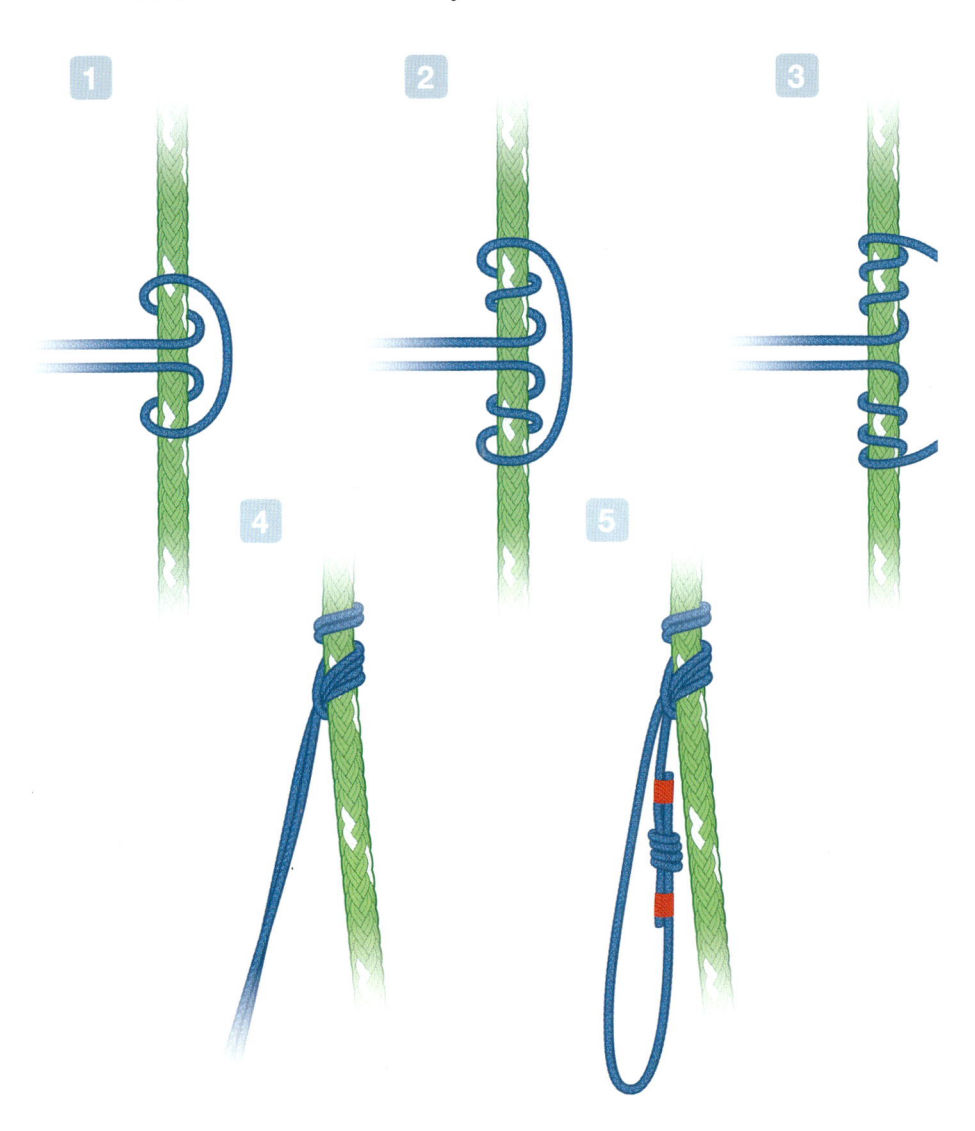

The Prusik is best made up using a strop (using a line which is between half and three quarters the diameter of the rope to which it is to be attached), as shown in diagram 5, but provided a long working end is allowed, it can also be tied using the bight of a rope. Place a fairly large bight in front of the rope, pass the other end of the strop around the rope and through the bight, repeating at least 3 times as shown in diagrams 2 and 3. Work the knot up snug around the rope.

Blake's Hitch

Another useful single line hitch with a sideways pull is the Blake's Hitch, from the world of the Tree Surgeon. This knot is particularly good if you are dealing with a wet or slippery rope that has to be hauled by another line.

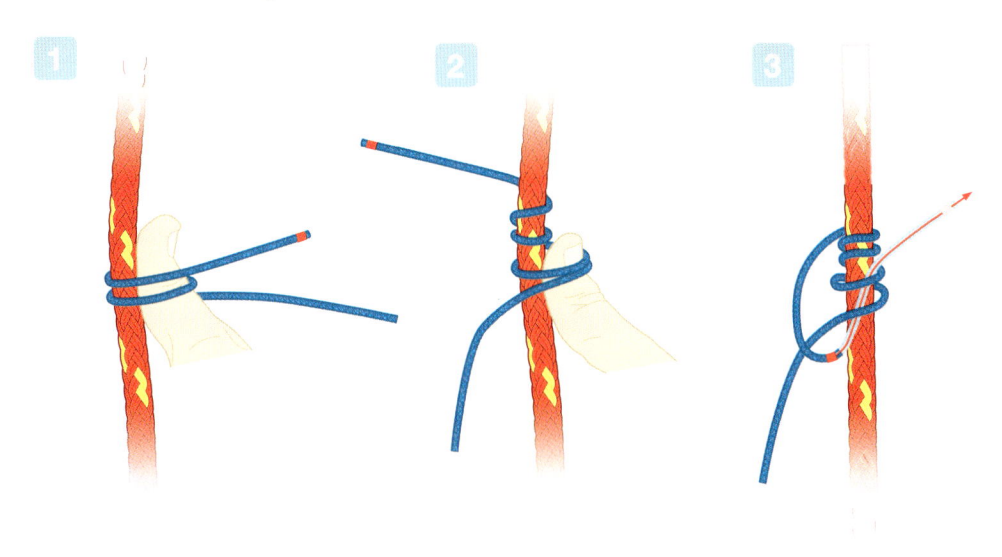

Take a round turn around your thumb and the static line, followed by another round turn above the thumb. Pass the working end OVER the standing part and tuck it from bottom to top of the first round turn in place of your thumb.

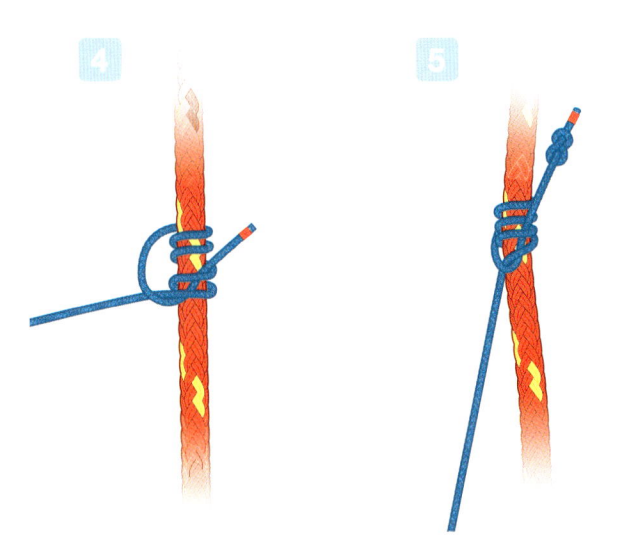

Pull the knot up snug, leaving a LONG working end. Complete the knot by putting a Figure of Eight Knot in the working end – this is VITAL, otherwise if the line rotates around the static line the working end can work its way through the knot and it will spill.

High Post Hitch

Should you have to recover a line when the object around which it is to be tied may become inaccessible, the High Post Hitch can be released by pulling the working end. In the illustrations below, the working end is shown short but it can be longer or attached to another line back into the boat.

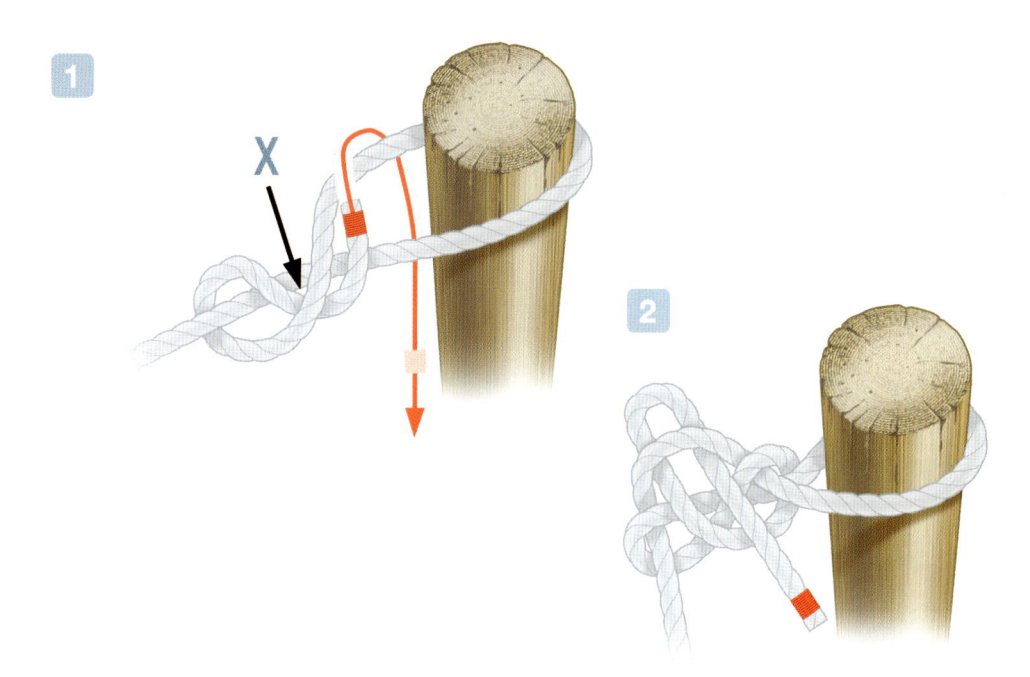

1

X

2

Take a turn around the post, bollard or fixing, then take a turn around the standing part and back over the working part – at this stage the configuration does not form a knot, so you will have to hold the turn and standing part (marked 'X') while you complete the knot. Make a bight in the working end and tuck it between the standing part and the working part at 'X' – pull the knot up tight with the standing part.

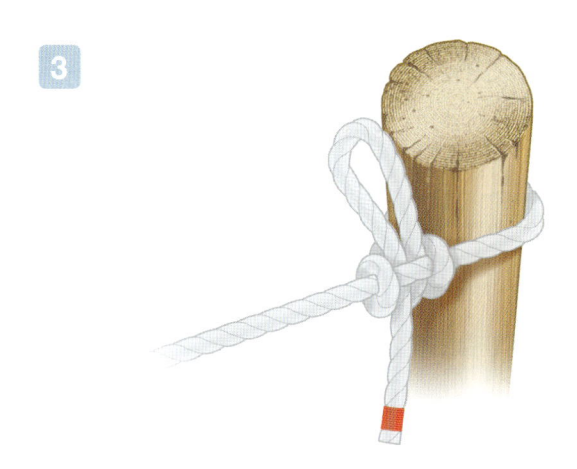

3

Pile Hitch

As its name implies, this knot can be used to moor to a pile, bollard if the top is accessible (don't forget the tide range) or to attach a line to a post. This knot is both simple and effective and will not jam, so it is easily untied when not under load.

Pass the bight around the object, under the standing parts – open the bight and pass it over the top of the object. Pull up snug with the standing parts.

TIP FROM THE BOSUN'S LOCKER

Think of others before employing this hitch – only use it if you are certain that you will be the sole user of the bollard.

Icicle Hitch

Developed from the Pile Hitch by John Smith, this ingenious Icicle Hitch will take a sideways pull on just about anything from rope to rail, rough or smooth, straight or tapered.

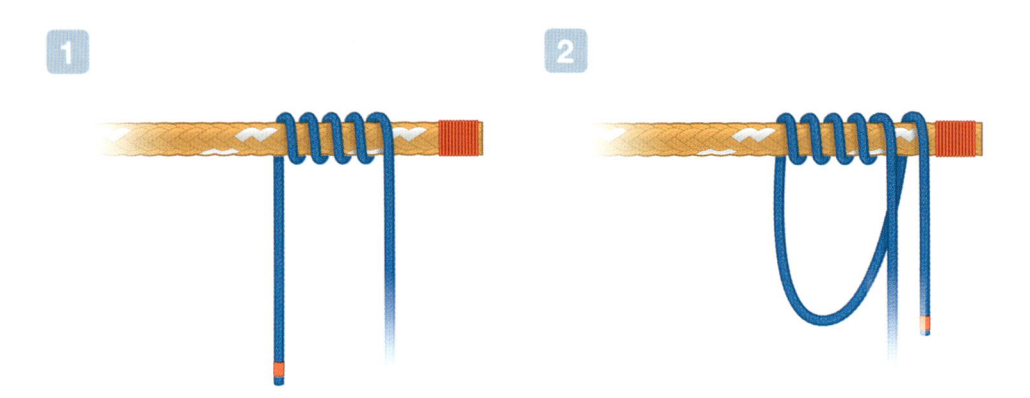

1

2

Make at least four turns with the working end, away from the direction of pull. Form a bight in the working end and lay it over the object and parallel with the standing part.

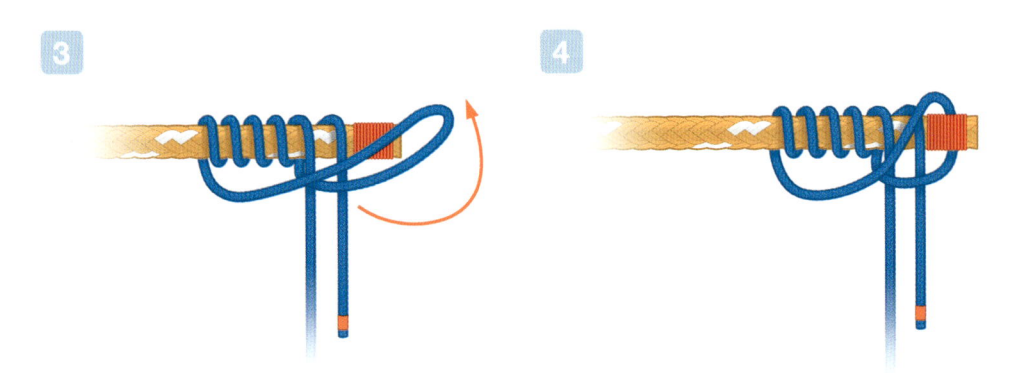

3

4

Bring the bight in front of the standing part and pass it over the end of the object. Pull the working end to tighten the knot. Make sure all the turns are tight around the object then pull on the standing part to pull the knot into its working position.

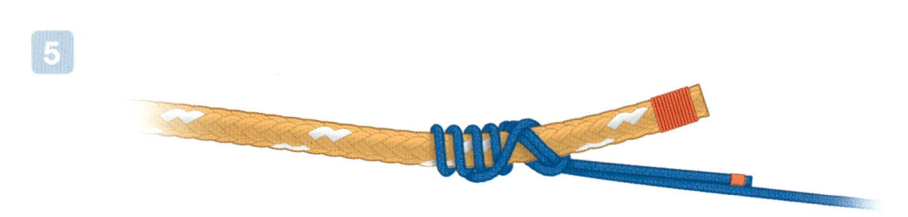

5

Anchor Bend

The bend among hitches – the Anchor Bend is a variation on the Round Turn and Two Half Hitches, only in that the working end is passed between the round turn and the object before being secured with a Half Hitch. As its name implies, this knot is useful for securing a line to an anchor – either as a cable or as a trip line. It is also used when a slightly more secure knot is required than a Round Turn and Two Half Hitches.

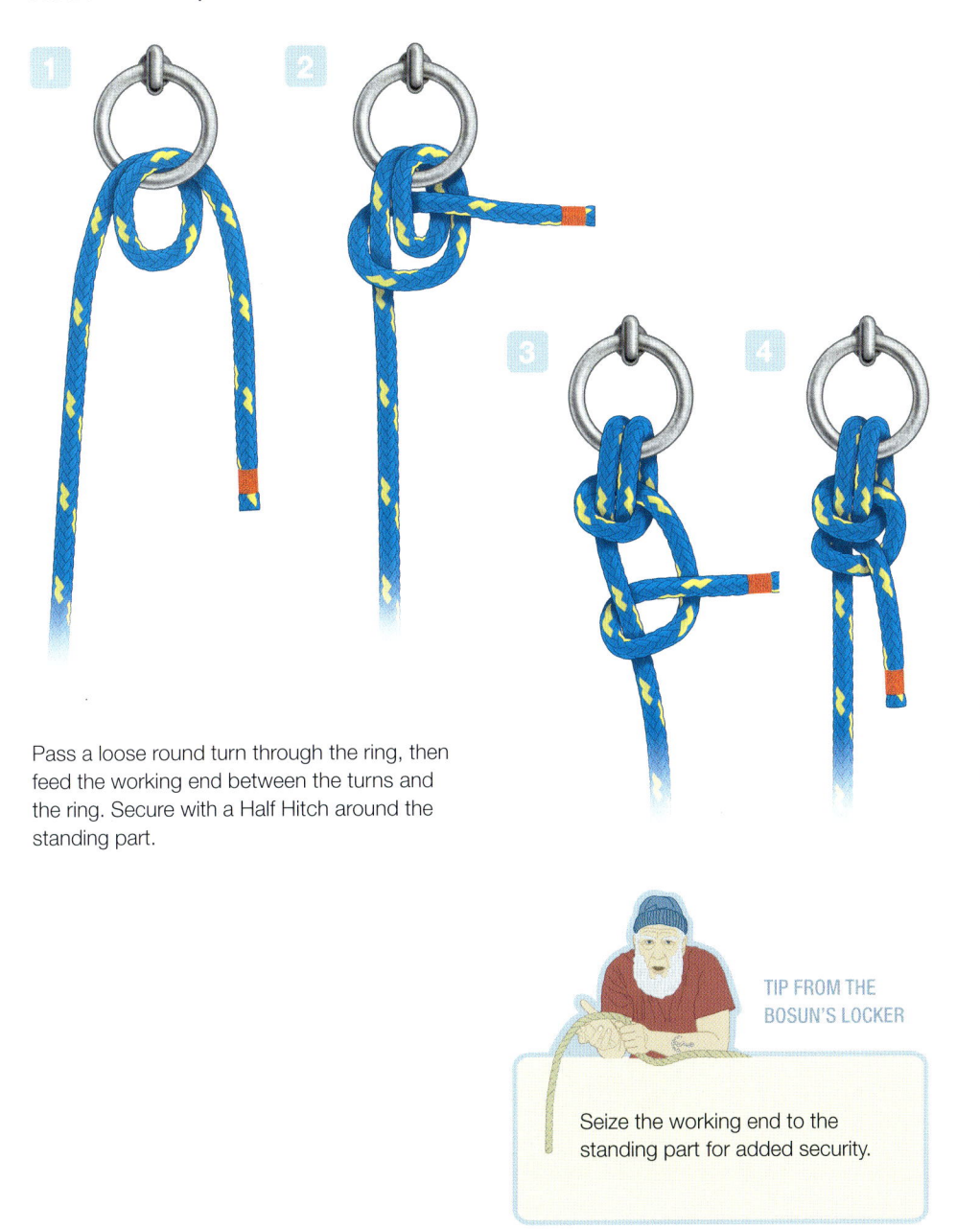

Pass a loose round turn through the ring, then feed the working end between the turns and the ring. Secure with a Half Hitch around the standing part.

TIP FROM THE BOSUN'S LOCKER

Seize the working end to the standing part for added security.

Timber Hitch & Killick Hitch

The Timber Hitch is used to hold the end of a line around a cylindrical object when there is no eye splice in the end of the line. It is commonly used to start lashings, or to support the end of a rope which is going to be Half Hitched or Marling Hitched. When tied around a cylinder together with a Marling Hitch, it is called a Killick Hitch – a killick being an anchor, this knot could be used around a boulder to provide an emergency second anchor, such as a kedge.

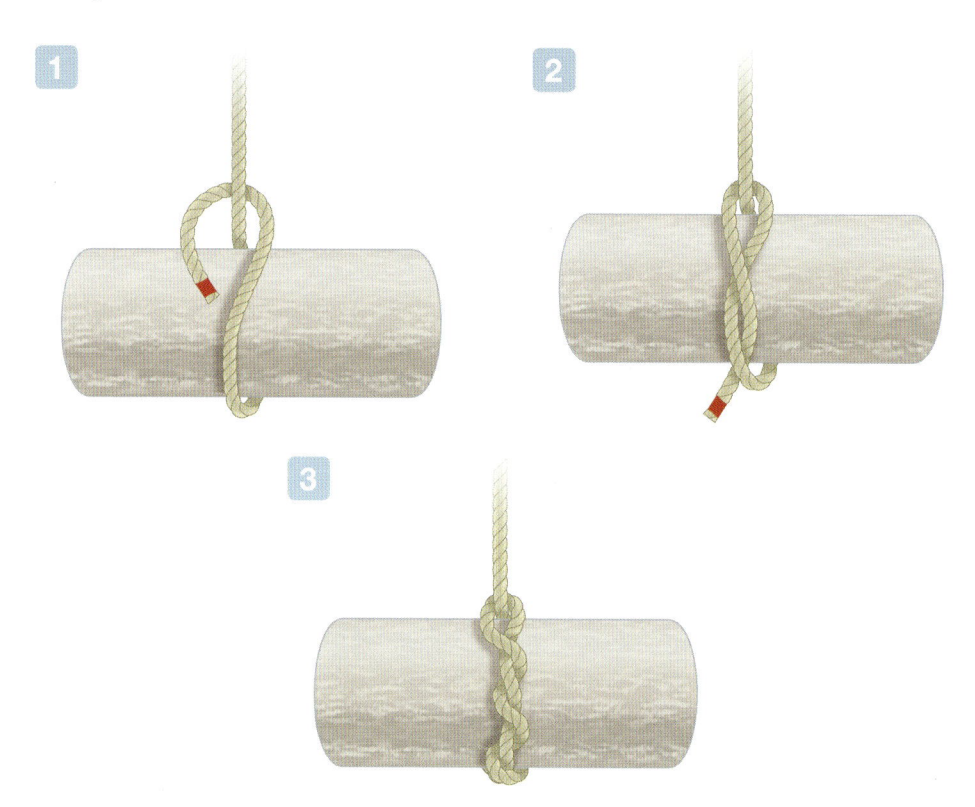

Pass the line around the spar, cylinder or similar object then pass the working end around the standing part and wind it around itself at least 3 times; more if the circumference of the object will accept it. Pull on the standing part, to tighten the grip around the object. When using 3 or 4 strand laid rope always wind the working end round 'with' the lay of the rope.

KILLICK HITCH

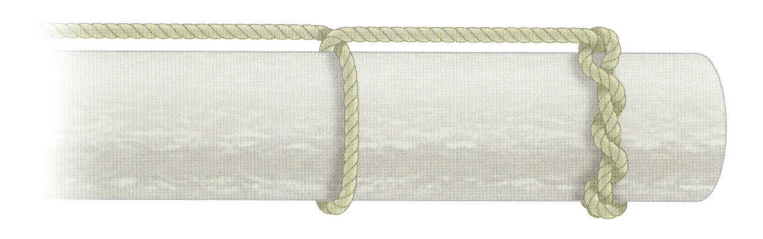

Scaffold Hitch

This is another name which is applied to more than one knot, depending on which book you read. However, think of it as a knot supporting one end of a short scaffold plank (maybe as a Bosun's chair). It can also be very useful for tying together bundles of poles, rods, oars etc. To support a plank the working end is attached to the standing part with a Bowline; used as a bundle the two ends are tied together using a Reef Knot.

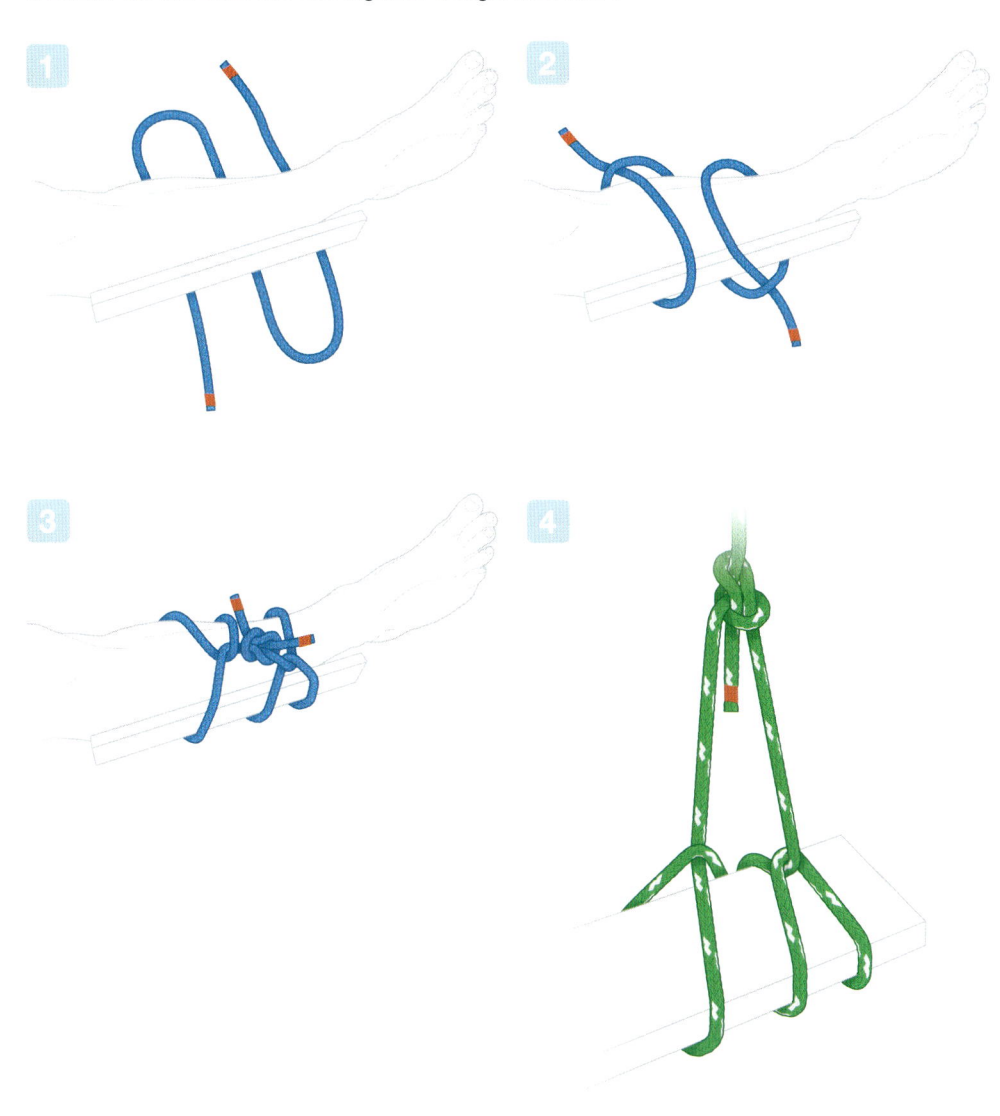

There is more than one way of tying this knot, but this method is considered the easiest to remember. Lay the line under the object in the form of a letter 'Z' as shown. Take each end and pass it through the bight opposite. Pull both ends tight and secure, either with a Bowline or Reef Knot, as described above.

Buntline Hitch

Traditionally used to attach the 'buntline' to the foot of a square sail, this knot has found many other uses over the years, including tying a necktie. The structure is simply a Clove Hitch made inside the noose around the standing part of a rope – similar to Two Half Hitches, but more secure because it jams. Ideal for securing lines to hooks, swivel eyes, snap shackles and cylindrical objects, it still has many uses today.

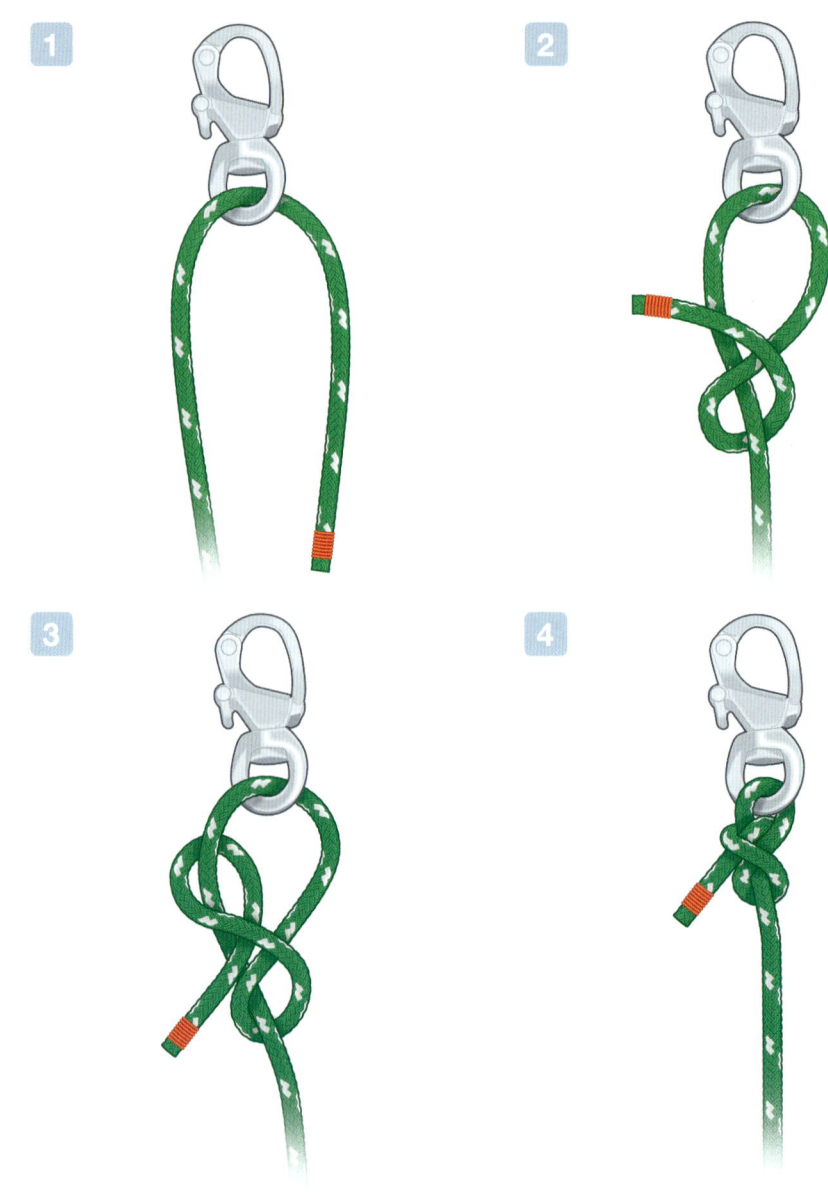

Pass the working end through the eye, cringle, ring or around an object, take a turn around the standing part, then form a Half Hitch, inside the turn, to form what is effectively an 'Inside Clove Hitch'.

Guyline Hitch

This quick and very simple hitch to hold a guy line taut was published in 'Knotting Matters', the magazine of the International Guild of Knot Tyers, by a Scouter who first saw it used in Malta. Although intended for use in tent guys, instead of a wooden slider, it could prove useful for tightening lines both above and below decks.

1

Form two Overhand Knots in the standing part of the line, then pass the working end around a suitable fixing point.

2

Bring the working end first through the upper Overhand Knot, then down through the lower one, leaving a fairly long end.

3

To tighten, pull on the working end.
Note: The knot holds much better if the working end is passed through the Overhand Knot in the opposite direction to the lower exit line.

Halyard Knot

The Halyard Knot is a stable, strong and secure knot with which to attach a snap shackle to a halyard. It also has advantages over other knots, one of which is that the working end can be cut quite short or tapered and taped to the standing part to get the knot 'close up' to a sheave if necessary.

1

Pass the working end through the shackle ring twice, forming a round turn. Bring the working end alongside the standing part and make 3 loose turns around the standing part as in diagram 1.

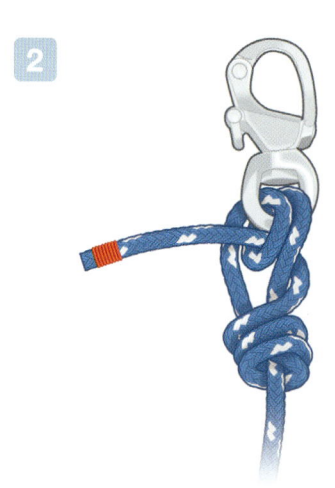

2

Now pass the working end through the round turn between the halyard and the shackle ring.

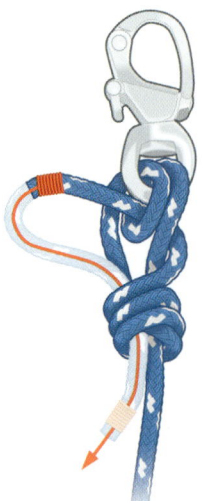

3

Tuck the working end down through the turns alongside the standing part. Pull the knot up tight by adjusting the turns and pulling on the standing part to snug the knot to the shackle.

4

Trim the end and if necessary tape it to the standing part of the halyard.

CHAPTER 8:

LOOPS & NOOSES

OVERHAND LOOP

DOUBLE OVERHAND LOOP

ARTILLERYMAN'S KNOT

ALPINE BUTTERFLY LOOP

BOWLINE - COMMON

BOWLINE - CLIMBER'S METHOD

BOWLINE - TUCKED

BOWLINE - ON A BIGHT

BOWLINE - WATER

BOWLINE - RUNNING

FIGURE OF EIGHT LOOP

PACKER'S KNOT

BOTTLE KNOT

DOUBLE FISHERMAN'S LOOP

JURY MAST KNOT

Introduction: Loops and Nooses

In this chapter, you will find a selection of loops and nooses which can be used afloat in halyards, sheets, mooring lines, flag hoists and many other roles. For the purposes of identification, a 'loop knot' is considered to be a fixed eye formed by a knot in a rope or tape and a 'noose' is an adjustable or sliding eye. You may have already met the 'Bowline' either in the Progressive Knotting chapter, or elsewhere but here you will find a few more variations (there are over 80 known 'Bowlines') which boat users will find useful in different circumstances. These, together with a selection of general purpose knots for use both above and below decks (even one to suspend a bottle in the water to keep it cool) complete the chapter.

Bowline - On A Bight

As the name implies, this knot can be tied using a bight of rope; in addition to which it provides two loops which can be adjusted to different sizes.

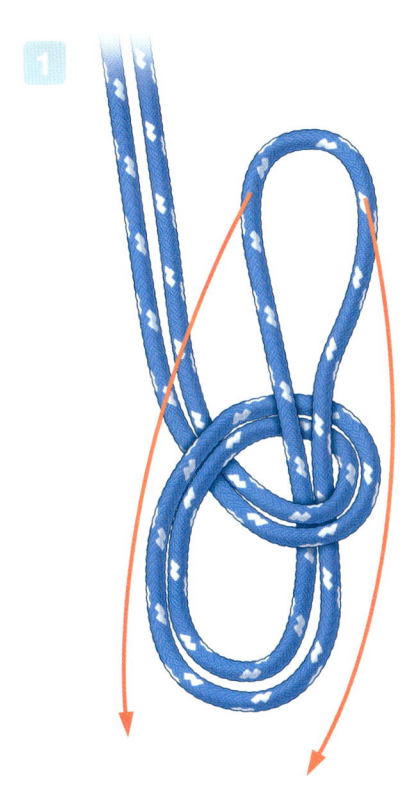

Double the rope, to form a long bight. Double the bight back along the rope to the size of eyes required - at this point form an overhand crossing loop. Pass the bight up through the loop, open it up and fold it down over the front of the knot.

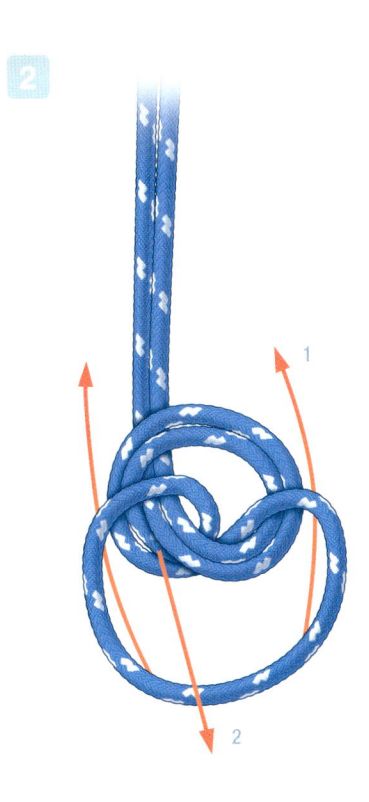

Now pass the bight behind everything and up to the standing part above the knot. Pull down on the eyes, adjusting them as necessary, until the bight is snug against the standing part.

Bowline - Water

Because this knot was devised for natural fibre ropes that were subjected to submersion in water (resulting in shrinkage and difficult to untie) it is not seen so much today. That said, it is still worth knowing because natural fibre is still used in traditional boats and even some of the man-made fibres can be difficult to untie, even when dry. The principle of this knot, is that the majority of the weight is taken on the lower crossing loop, leaving the upper one easy to move and untie.

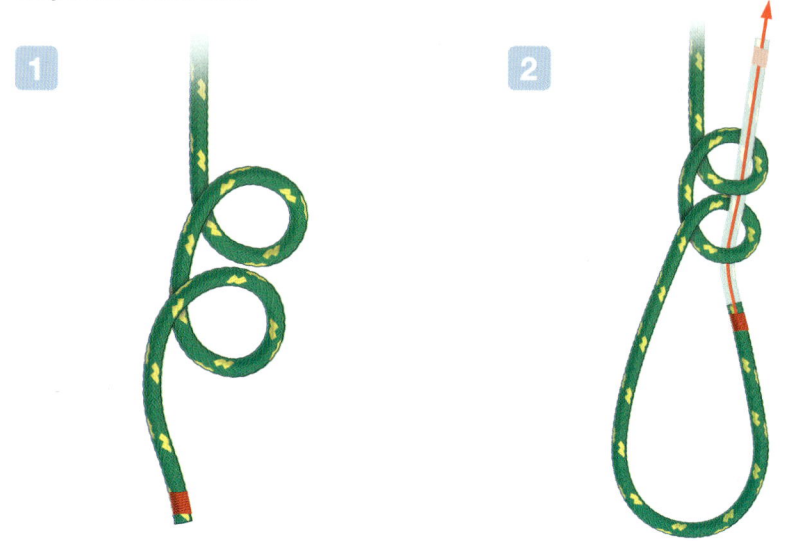

Start, just as you would for a Common Bowline, by doubling the rope back to estimate the size of the eye – but instead of forming one crossover loop, make two, keeping the lower one behind the upper. Pass the working end up through both loops as shown.

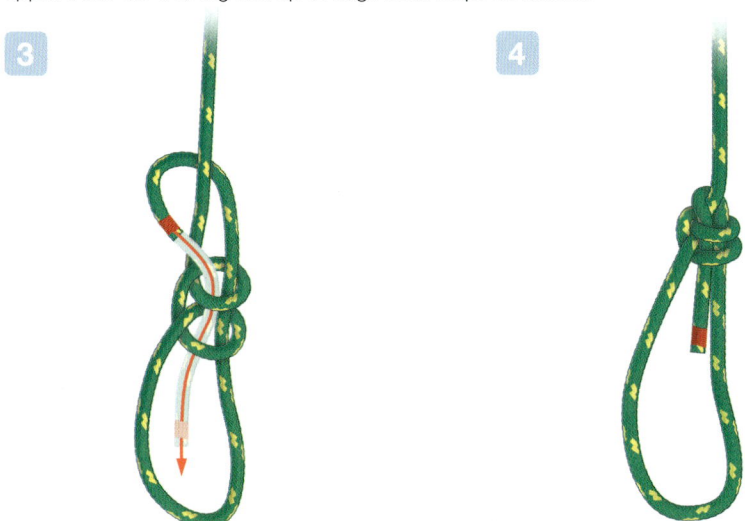

Pass the working end around the standing part then back down through the two loops. Pull up by holding the eye and pulling on the standing part, adjusting the size of the eye and the knot as you go.

Bowline - Running

The Running Bowline provides a quick and easy 'noose' with a free running loop; very useful for recovering inanimate objects from the water or to lasso a mooring buoy or bollard. If the rope being used is flexible enough, one way of tying this knot is to form a Bowline with a small eye and pull a bight of the standing part through the eye, otherwise it can be tied as shown below.

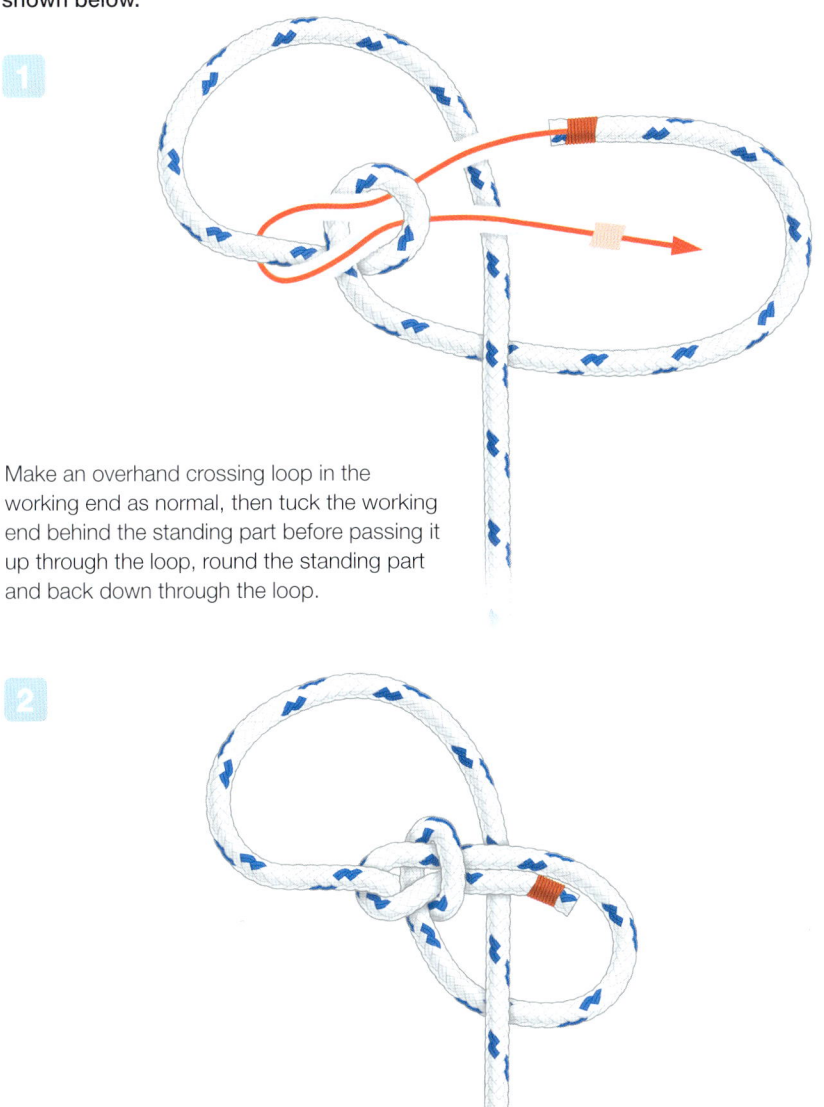

1

Make an overhand crossing loop in the working end as normal, then tuck the working end behind the standing part before passing it up through the loop, round the standing part and back down through the loop.

2

Figure of Eight Loop

Another fixed loop with its origins in climbing. It has the advantage of being able to be tied in the bight or at the end of a rope. Safe, secure and easy to tie but it should be dressed properly (remember to have standing part as the outside loop) before use otherwise it may be difficult to untie after being loaded.

1

Make a large bight at the end of the rope. With this bight form a Figure of Eight Knot.

2

Pull on the loop in one direction and the standing part and working end in the other to pull the knot up tight; taking care to dress the knot so that the outer collar around the loop is from the standing part of the rope - this makes it easier to untie after it has been under strain.

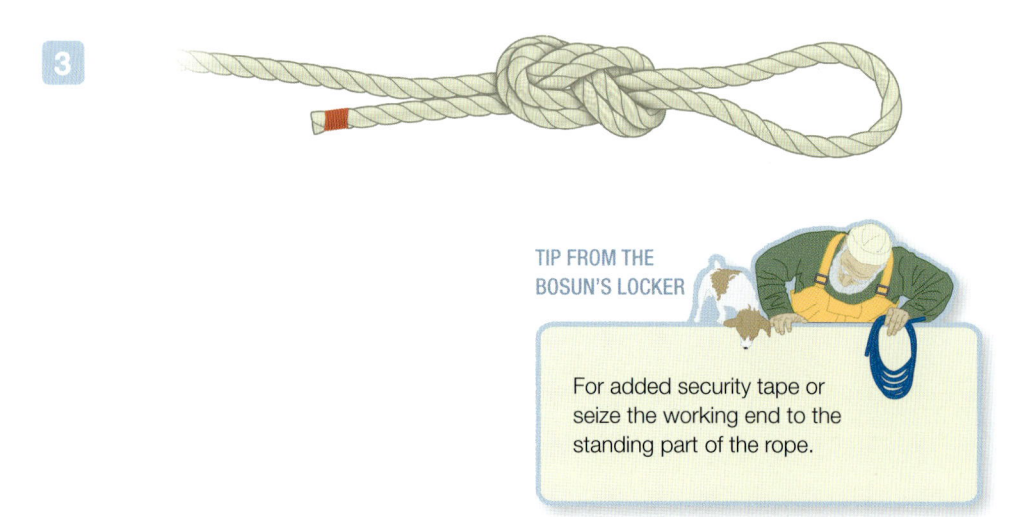

3

TIP FROM THE BOSUN'S LOCKER

For added security tape or seize the working end to the standing part of the rope.

Packer's Knot *(Butcher's Knot)*

If you have ever had to ask someone to hold their finger on a Half Knot around a parcel or bundle, while you tie the other to form a Reef Knot - those days are now over, here is a knot you can tie single handed. The Packer's Knot, or Butcher's Knot will enable you to take a turn around a parcel or bundle using a knot which has sufficient grip to hold while you pass another turn, or secure it with a Half Hitch.

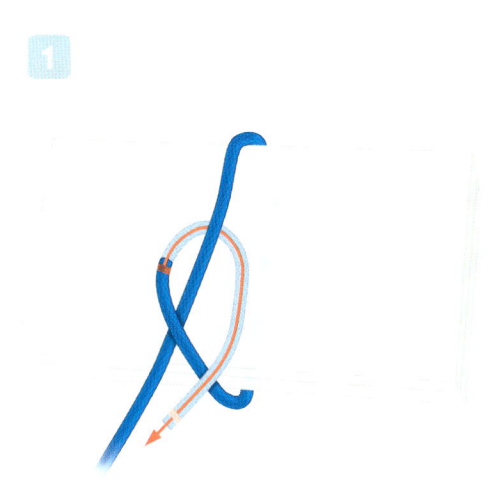

1

Pass the line around the object to be tied - leaving enough working end to form a Figure of Eight Knot with a little spare to hold and secure it.

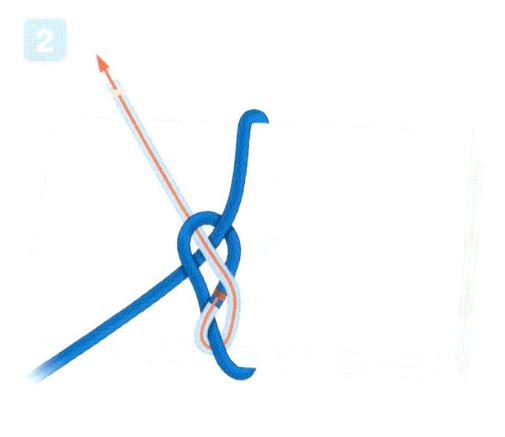

2

Form a Figure of Eight Knot in the working end as shown, ensuring that the standing part and the working end emerge from the knot on the same side.

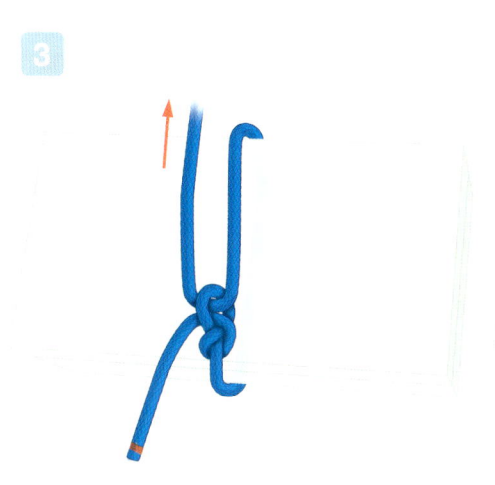

3

Pull the Figure of Eight Knot up tight before pulling on the standing part - the noose around the object should now hold, sufficient for you to make any further turns that may be necessary.

4

On completion, the standing part can be secured to the working end with a Half Hitch if required.

Loops and Nooses

Bottle Knot

This is but one version of a knot which can be used for suspending a bottle with a lip on the opening.

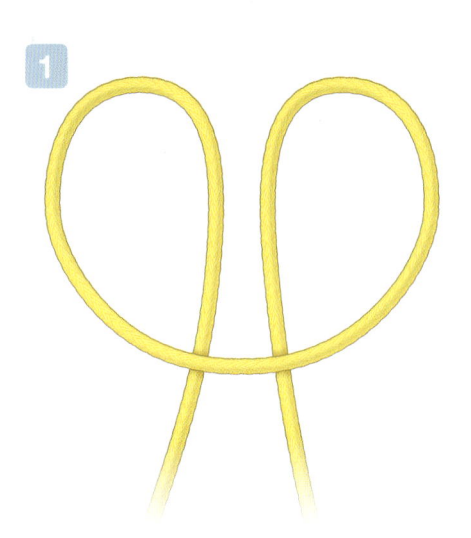

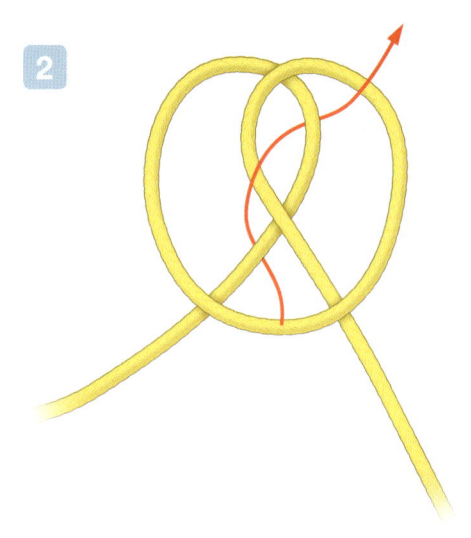

1 Middle a piece of line and lay it with the bight uppermost; then fold it down over the front of the standing parts to form two loops.

2 Cross the right loop over the left then pass the original bight under/over/under/over, through the knot, as shown above.

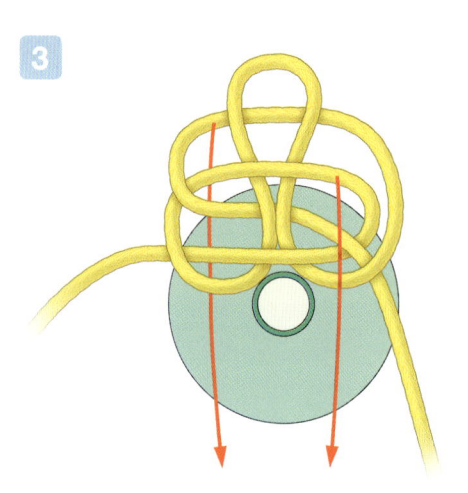

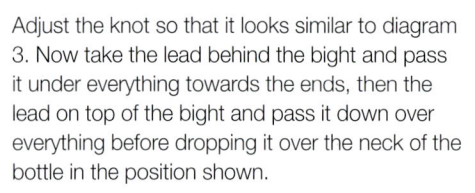

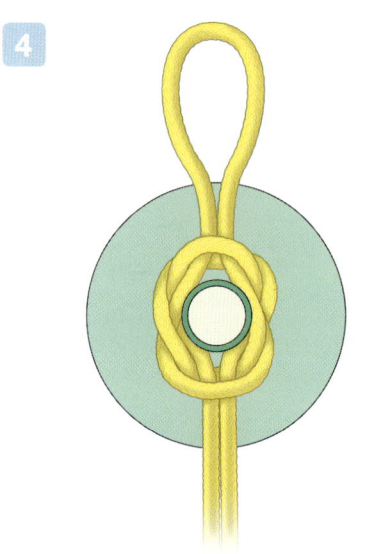

3 Adjust the knot so that it looks similar to diagram 3. Now take the lead behind the bight and pass it under everything towards the ends, then the lead on top of the bight and pass it down over everything before dropping it over the neck of the bottle in the position shown.

4 Pull the loop and two ends to tighten the knot up snug about the neck of the bottle.

Double Fisherman's Loop
(Double Overhand Noose, Poacher's Noose or Scaffold Knot)

A firm favourite of mine, having so many uses, the Double Overhand Noose is also known as a Poacher's Noose. It provides a handy sliding loop which can be varied to slide easily (like a poacher's snare), or by pulling up the Double Overhand Knot really tight, the noose will hold with sufficient grip to hold together objects being glued, or even grip a heart shaped thimble to form a hard eye in the end of a line. Because the Double Overhand has to be tied around the standing part of the line, it is tied using the 'grapevine' method; described here.

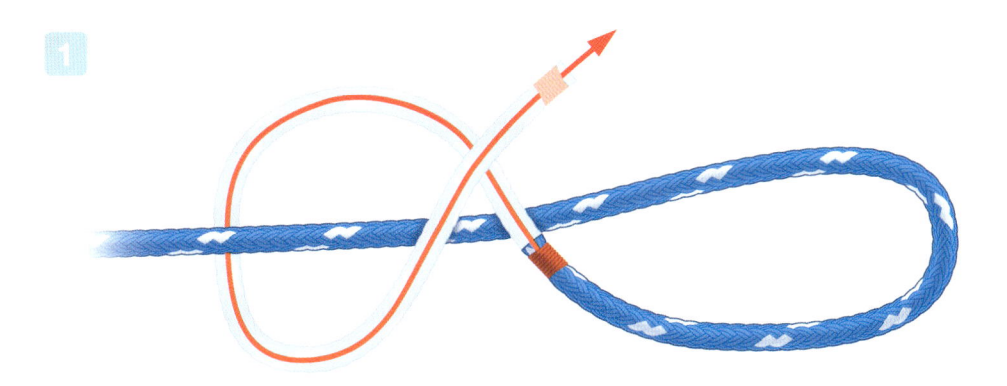

1

Form a bight in the end of the line, then pass the working end over the standing part, around behind it and back across itself. Working towards the tip of the loop, take the working end behind the loop.

2

Tuck the working end under itself, where it crosses the front of the loop, then under the first crossover to form an Overhand Knot. Hold both sides of the loop and pull the knot up with the working end to form the knot as shown below.

3

Jury Mast Knot

A simple but effective arrangement of loops to which 3 or 4 stays can be attached to a temporary or broken mast. The Jury Mast Knot can be used at any point, top, middle or bottom of a mast to hold it in position using stays, tackles or guy lines. Although the centre of the knot provides some grip when under load, it is necessary to provide a means of stopping the knot from sliding down the mast before use; this can be done with a simple whipping or lashing a short spar to the upright.

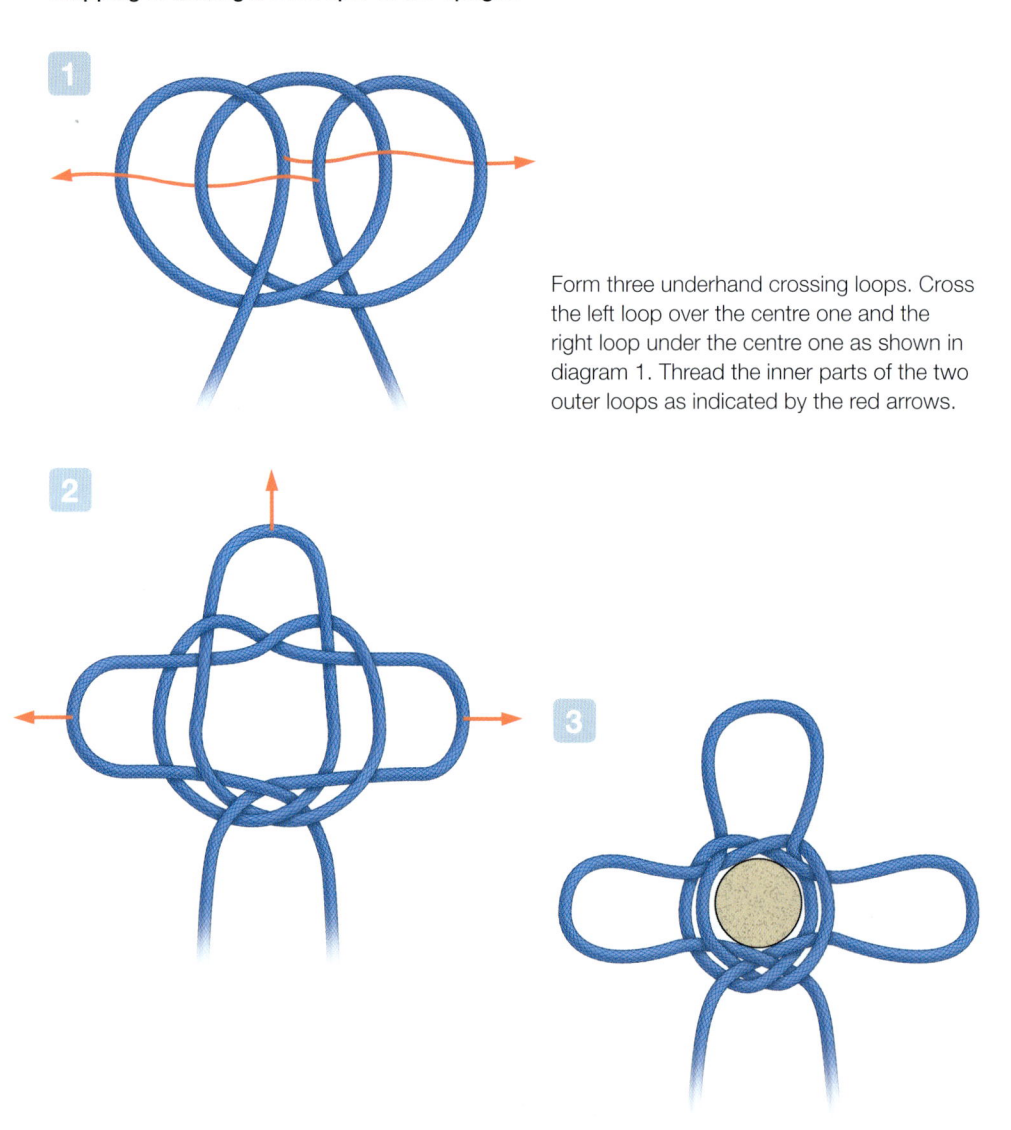

Form three underhand crossing loops. Cross the left loop over the centre one and the right loop under the centre one as shown in diagram 1. Thread the inner parts of the two outer loops as indicated by the red arrows.

Pull the three loops and the two ends, to draw the knot up into the shape above. Place the centre of the knot over the mast and pull it up tight.

Overhand Loop

The Overhand Loop is most used in the end of sewing threads, or to form a temporary loop in a line which is not going to be under too much stress - it is after all, one of the weakest loops.

1

Make a bight in the line, then using the bight as the working end, form an Overhand Knot as shown.

2

Double Overhand Loop

The Double Overhand Loop is more secure and does not weaken the line as much as a single overhand; making it very suitable for forming a fixed loop at the end of a fishing line, especially when using monofilament.

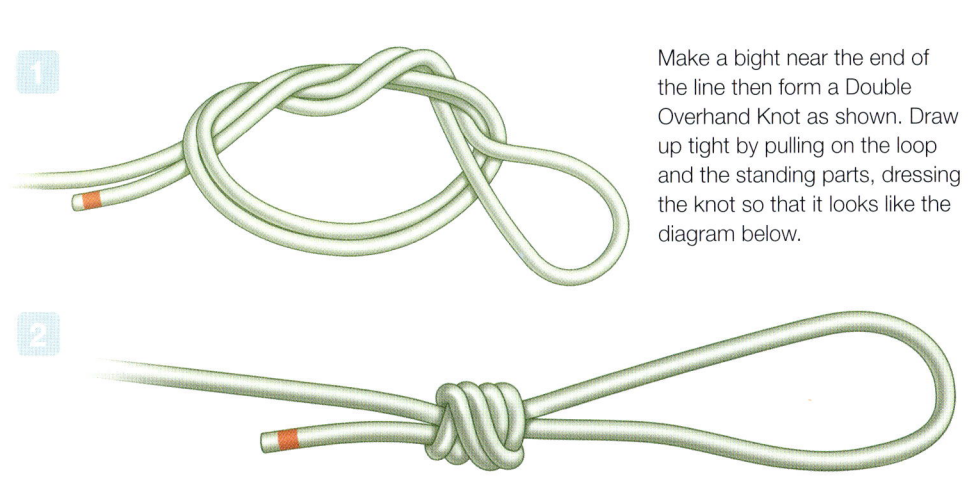

1

Make a bight near the end of the line then form a Double Overhand Knot as shown. Draw up tight by pulling on the loop and the standing parts, dressing the knot so that it looks like the diagram below.

2

Artilleryman's Knot *(Harness Hitch or Loop)*

Another knot that is usually tied in the bight of a rope, the Artilleryman's Knot forms a fixed loop, handle or shoulder loop for hauling with a rope; as it will take a pull in either direction. This knot is very useful as a stopper knot and strong-point loop when splicing braided ropes.

1

Make an underhand loop, then lay the same part over the top of that loop, as shown. Take the bight and pass it over the lead across the loop and under the loop, as shown. Draw the knot up tight by pulling on the two standing parts.

2

Alpine Butterfly Loop

The Alpine Butterfly Loop's origins are in climbing, where it is used as a 'tie in' but it can be put to many other good uses where a fixed loop is required in the bight of a rope (e.g. splicing braided ropes). The tying method shown below is a simple and efficient way of forming a fixed loop in the bight of a rope, which is safe, secure and can be untied after being under strain.

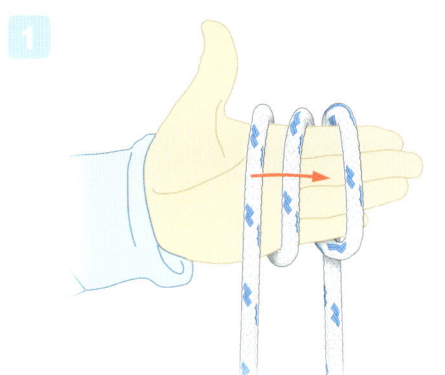

Make three turns around the hand. The centre turn can be adjusted to approximately the size of loop required. Cross the left hand lead over to the centre.

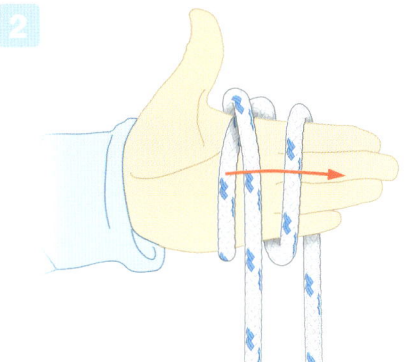

Cross the new left hand turn over the other two towards the finger tips.

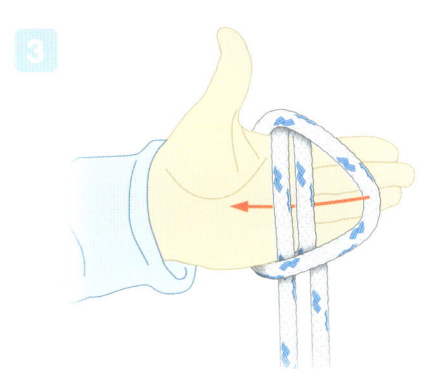

Curl the fingers over the bight to grasp it, then…

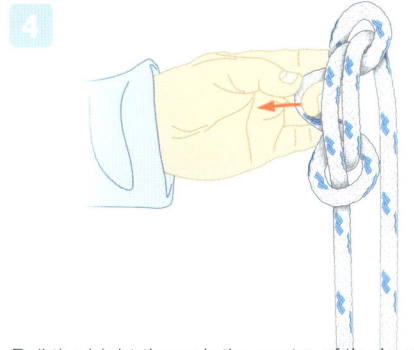

Pull the bight through the centre of the knot to form the loop. Adjust the loop to the size required, and then haul on both sides to tighten the knot.

Bowline - Common

This knot has been called the 'King' of knots, probably because it has been in everyday use afloat for centuries. It is certainly one of the most talked about. Practice makes perfect with this knot and it is so often used in critical situations like berthing lines and safety lines – practice means you will get it right in an emergency.

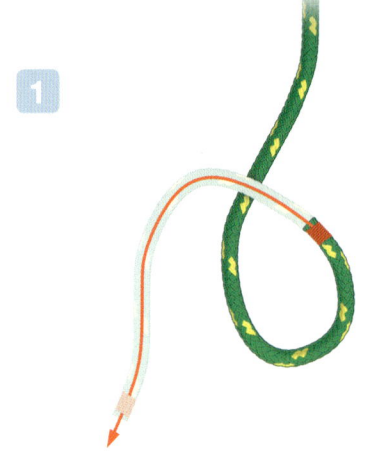

1

Double the end of the rope to roughly the size of the eye required - at this point form an overhand crossing loop (the same way that you would write a figure 6), hold this between the thumb and fingers of one hand, then…

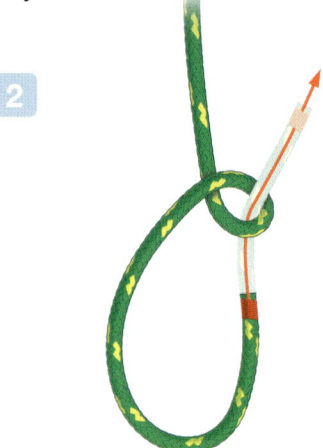

2

Pass the working end through the loop from back to front.

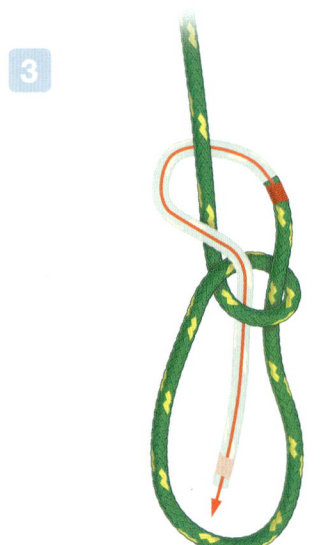

3

Now pass the working end around the standing part and back through the loop from front to rear. Pull the knot up by holding the working end and eye, pulling on the standing part.

4

Bowline - Climber's Method

The Climber's Method of tying a Bowline (which is identical to the Common Bowline when tied), can be useful to boaters, especially when mooring around a large pile or other awkward fitting. The only difference is in the method of tying, which, for those people who have learned to tie a Bowline around the waist, is an easy method of tying one the other way round.

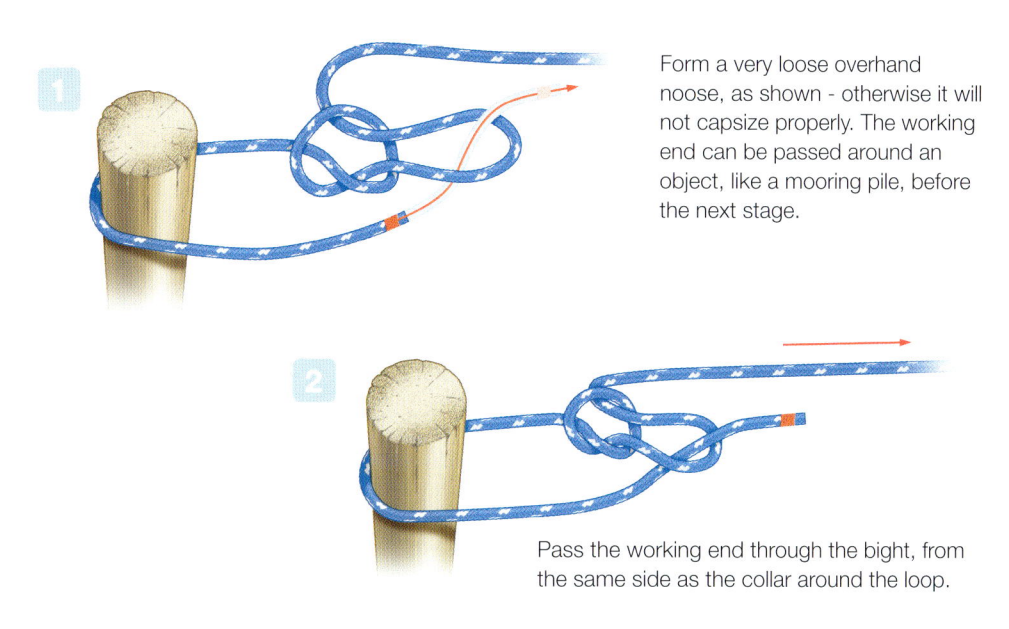

Form a very loose overhand noose, as shown - otherwise it will not capsize properly. The working end can be passed around an object, like a mooring pile, before the next stage.

Pass the working end through the bight, from the same side as the collar around the loop.

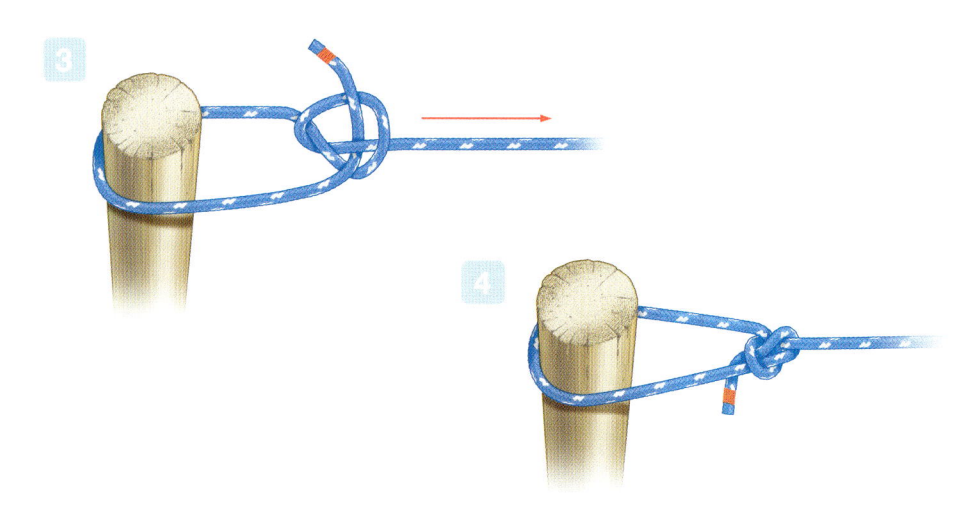

Hold the eye and pull on the standing part, pulling the bight down through the knot to capsize it into a Bowline. If the eye is around an object, hold the working end and pull on the standing part until the knot capsizes.

Loops and Nooses

Bowline - Tucked *(Yosemite Tie Off)*

Favoured by Tree Surgeons - so you may find this one more suitable when going aloft - it is a Common Bowline but the working end is tied off up through the knot and alongside the standing part; providing added security and an eye which is free from obstructions.

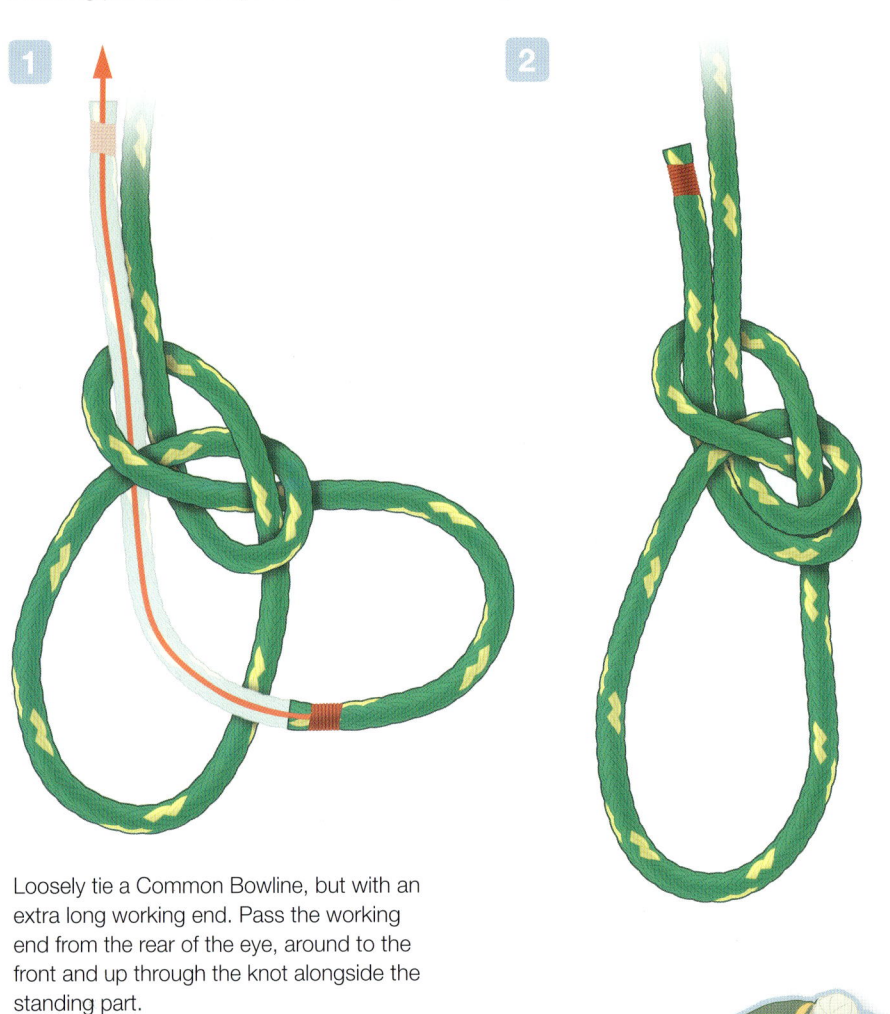

Loosely tie a Common Bowline, but with an extra long working end. Pass the working end from the rear of the eye, around to the front and up through the knot alongside the standing part.

TIP FROM THE BOSUN'S LOCKER

Tape or Half Hitch the working end to the standing part to keep it tidy and out of the way.

CHAPTER 9:

LASHINGS & BINDINGS

MOUSING HOOKS

MOUSING A SHACKLE

HALF HITCHING

MARLING HITCHING

CHAIN LASHING

TRUCKER'S HITCH

SQUARE LASHING

DIAGONAL LASHING

TRANSOM KNOT

ROPE STOPPER

CHAIN STOPPER

Introduction: Lashings and Bindings

Lashings and Bindings are the "Make it Safe and Secure" department of knotting. To 'Lash' or 'Bind' is to use rope, tape or bespoke purpose made arrangements to secure one object to another, more often than not afloat; it is to stop items of gear that cannot be stowed from moving around, maintaining a safe and damage free environment. The foot of a sail can be 'lashed' to a boom when not in use to protect it from unnecessary wear when flailing in the wind – a split oar can be temporarily repaired with a binding, and the number of jobs for these forms of knotting goes on. Two other forms of binding, Serving and Seizing, can also be found in the Splicing chapter.

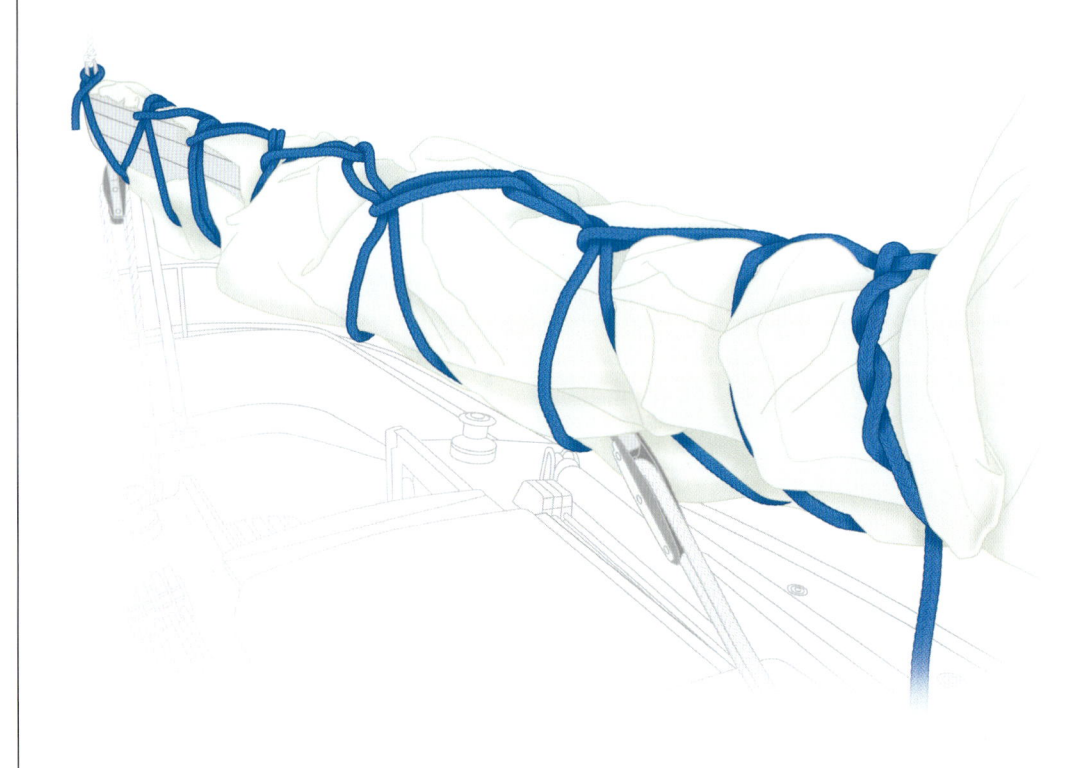

KNOTS USED FOR LASHING & BINDING

Knots Used for Lashing and Binding

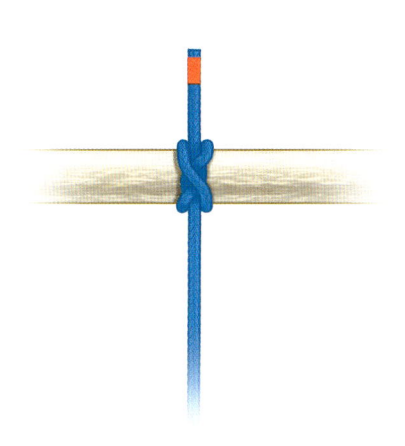

CLOVE HITCH (p97)

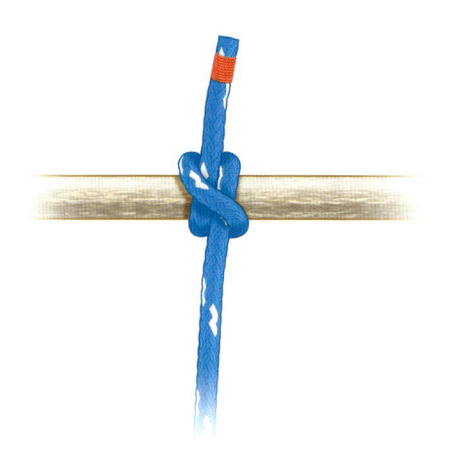

CONSTRICTOR KNOT (p51)

REEF KNOT (p46)

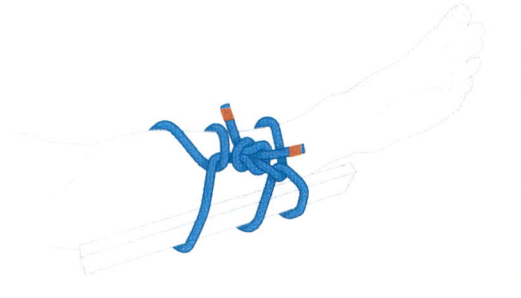

SCAFFOLD HITCH (p105)

TIMBER HITCH (p104)

Lashings and Bindings

Mousing Hooks

Tackle Open Hook
Middle a short length of small stuff and put a Lark's Head around the shank, wind the two ends around the shank and bill across the opening. Finish by making wrapping turns with one end then securing the two ends with a Reef Knot.

Scissor or Caliper Hook
Using small stuff or thin wire, make at least 6 turns around the neck of the closed hooks and secure with a Reef Knot.

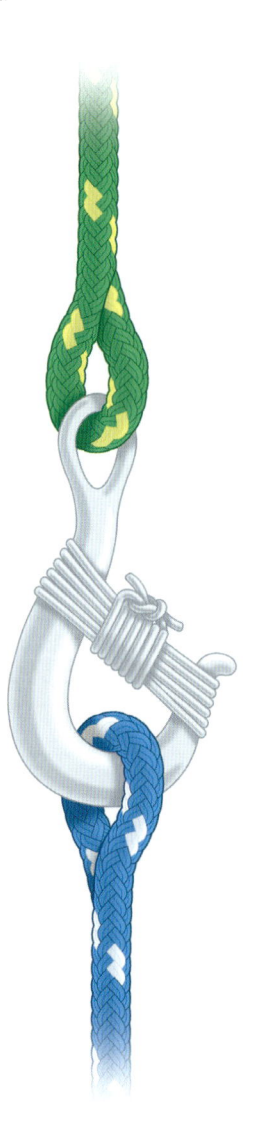

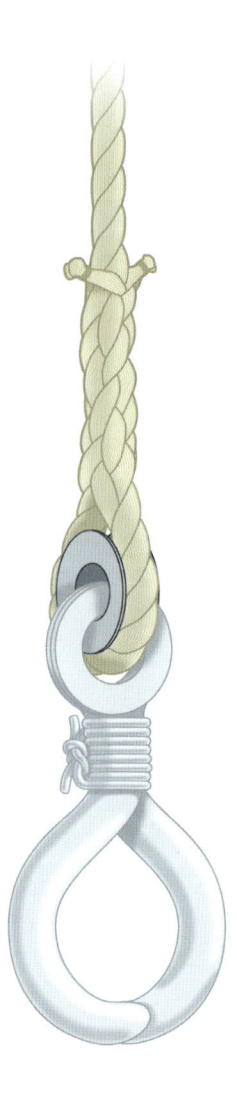

Mousing a Shackle

Shackles are used to join either a moving part to a fixture or two moving parts of rope or chain; consequently at some time or other, vibrations will be set up in the shackle, which could shake the pin loose and eventually release the pin. Prevention being better than cure – mouse all shackles when they are in use.

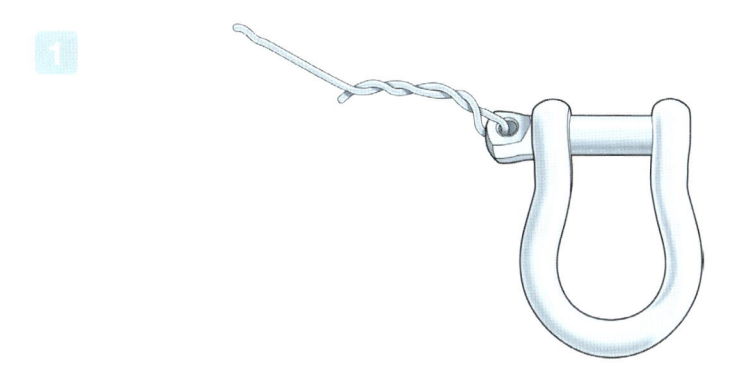

Pass the end of a piece of mild steel wire through the pin hole and twist it back around itself.

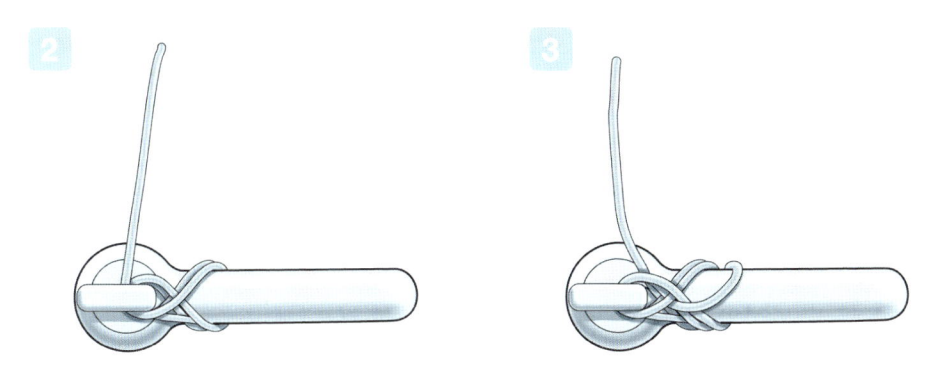

Make two or three figure eight turns around the shackle and through the pin hole – not too tight. Pass the end between the turns and the pin to make a round turn.

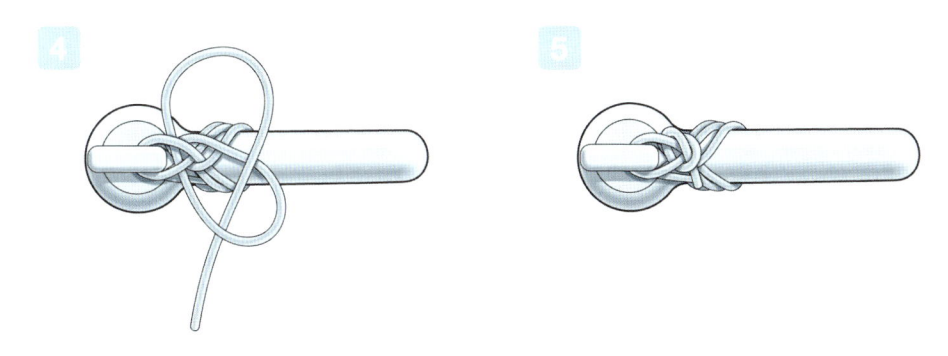

Finish off with a Half Hitch.

Half Hitching

Half Hitching is used for general lashing, either bundles or through eyelets in canvas to a boom or ridge rope etc.

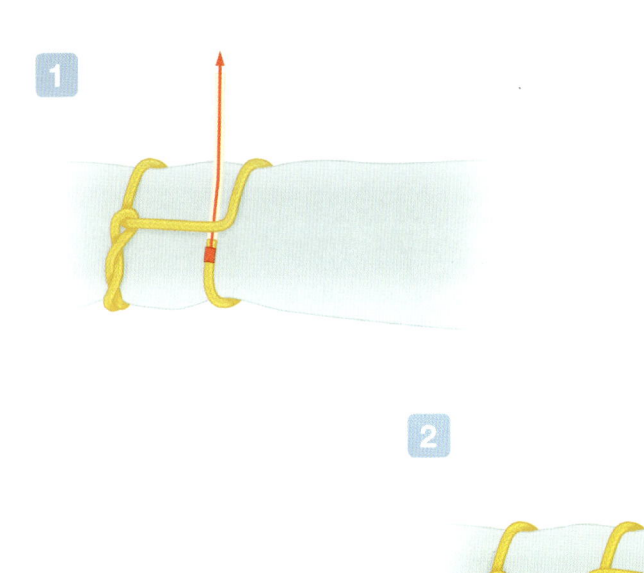

1

2

Pass the working end through an eye (Spliced or a Timber Hitch) in the end of the rope and Half Hitch at regular intervals along the bundle.

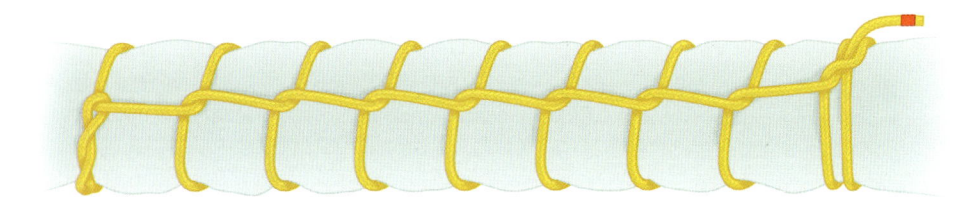

3

Finish with a Clove Hitch.

Marling Hitching

Marling Hitching is the traditional method of lashing up a hammock before stowing it in the hammock netting. Because it is effectively an Overhand Knot, it is a little more secure than Half Hitching and makes a good lashing for reefed or stowed sail on deck.

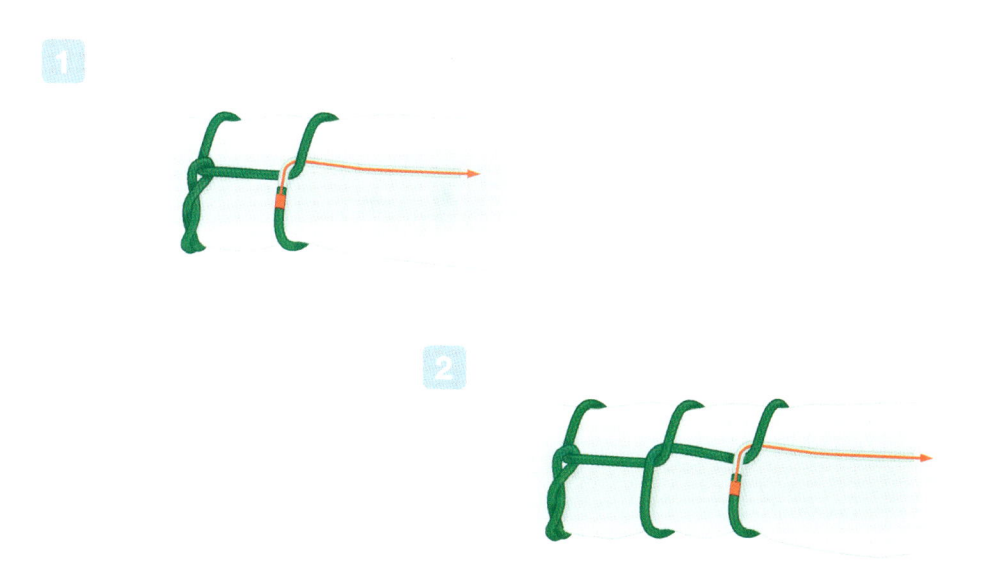

Pass the rope around the object and through an eye (Spliced or Timber Hitch) one end. Coil the rope and hold it in the right hand - pass the coil around the object, into the left hand then under the standing part and into the right hand again. Pull the coil down to the right and back parallel with the bundle to tighten the turn, then repeat with as many hitches as are necessary.

Secure the end with a Clove Hitch.

Chain Lashing

This lashing works on the same principle as the Chain Shortening or Drummers Plait and is used in situations where the lashing needs to be released quickly. Either make a Timber Hitch around the bundle or secure the line to an adjacent object if the bundle has to be released without having to untie any knots.

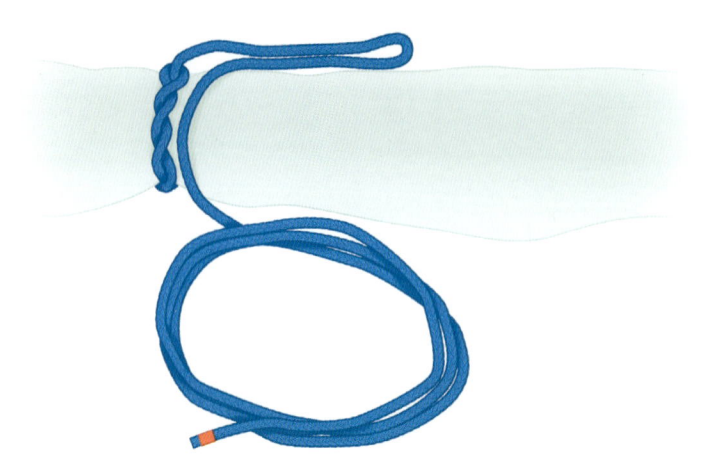

1

Secure one end of the line – coil the line so that each turn can be taken off the coil to form a bight. Make the first bight and pass it around the bundle to the right.

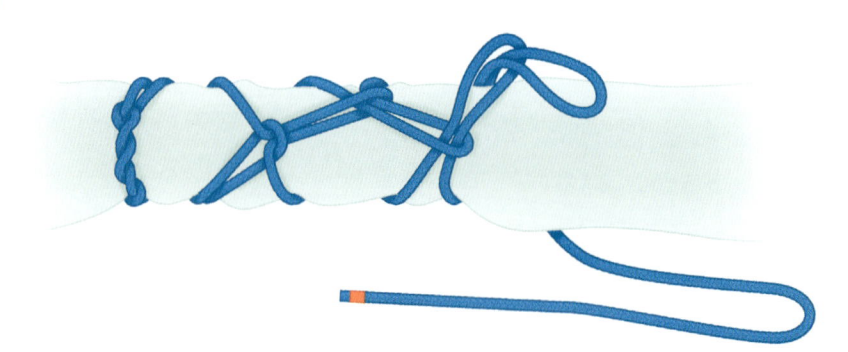

2

Make the next bight and pass it through the first then round the bundle to the left.

CHAIN LASHING

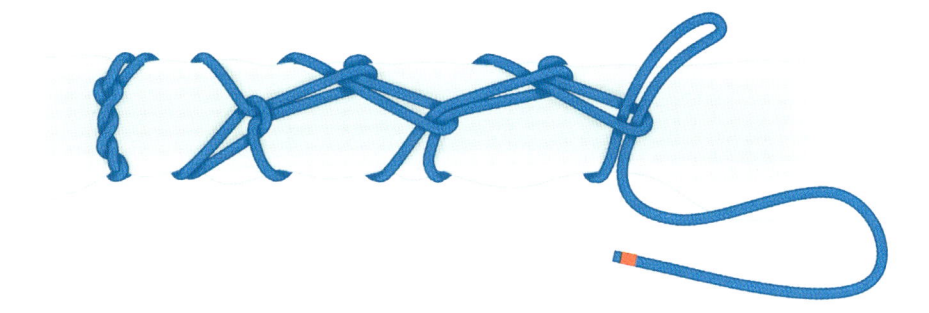

3

Continue alternate right and left passes until the lashing is complete. Form the last bight, but instead of passing a bight through it, pass the end through. In the diagram above the working end will be passed under the bundle and through the bight on the right.

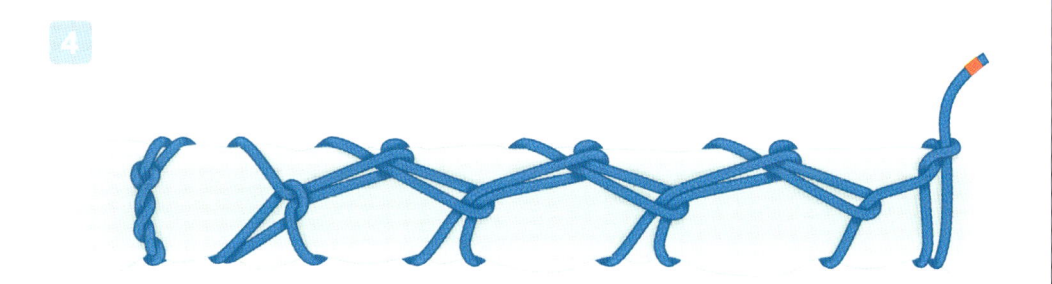

4

Secure the lashing with a Clove Hitch.
To release the lashing – untie the Clove Hitch, pass the working end back through the end bight, then pull on the working end to release the hitching.

Lashings and Bindings

Trucker's Hitch

The Trucker's Hitch, Trucker's Dolly, Waggoner's Hitch and many other names are attributed to this knot, which, despite it origins on land, can be very useful afloat too. It is favoured for lashing down loads because it allows the operator to apply a considerable amount of purchase, rather like a tackle without the blocks.

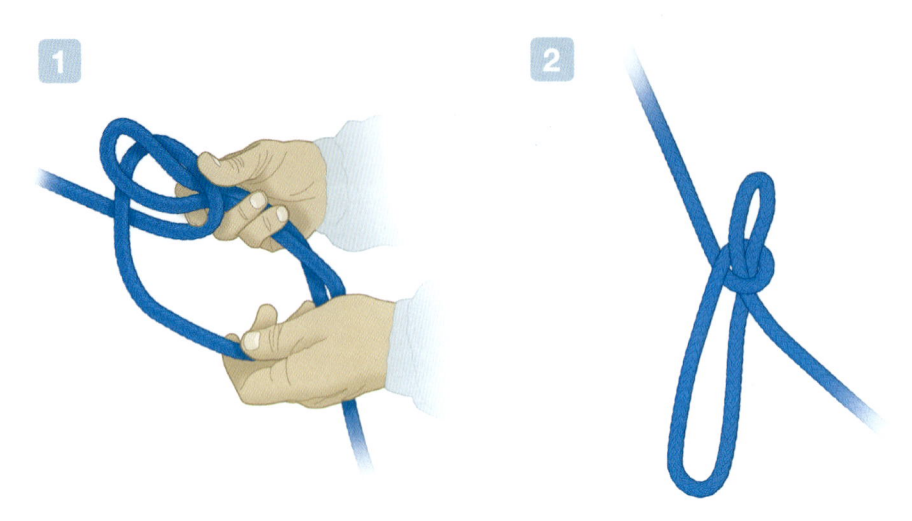

1

2

Make a closed loop in one hand then, using the standing part put a Half Hitch around one end of it.

3

Put a single twist in the lower part of the loop and pass the working end around a suitable fixed object that will take the weight of your pull.

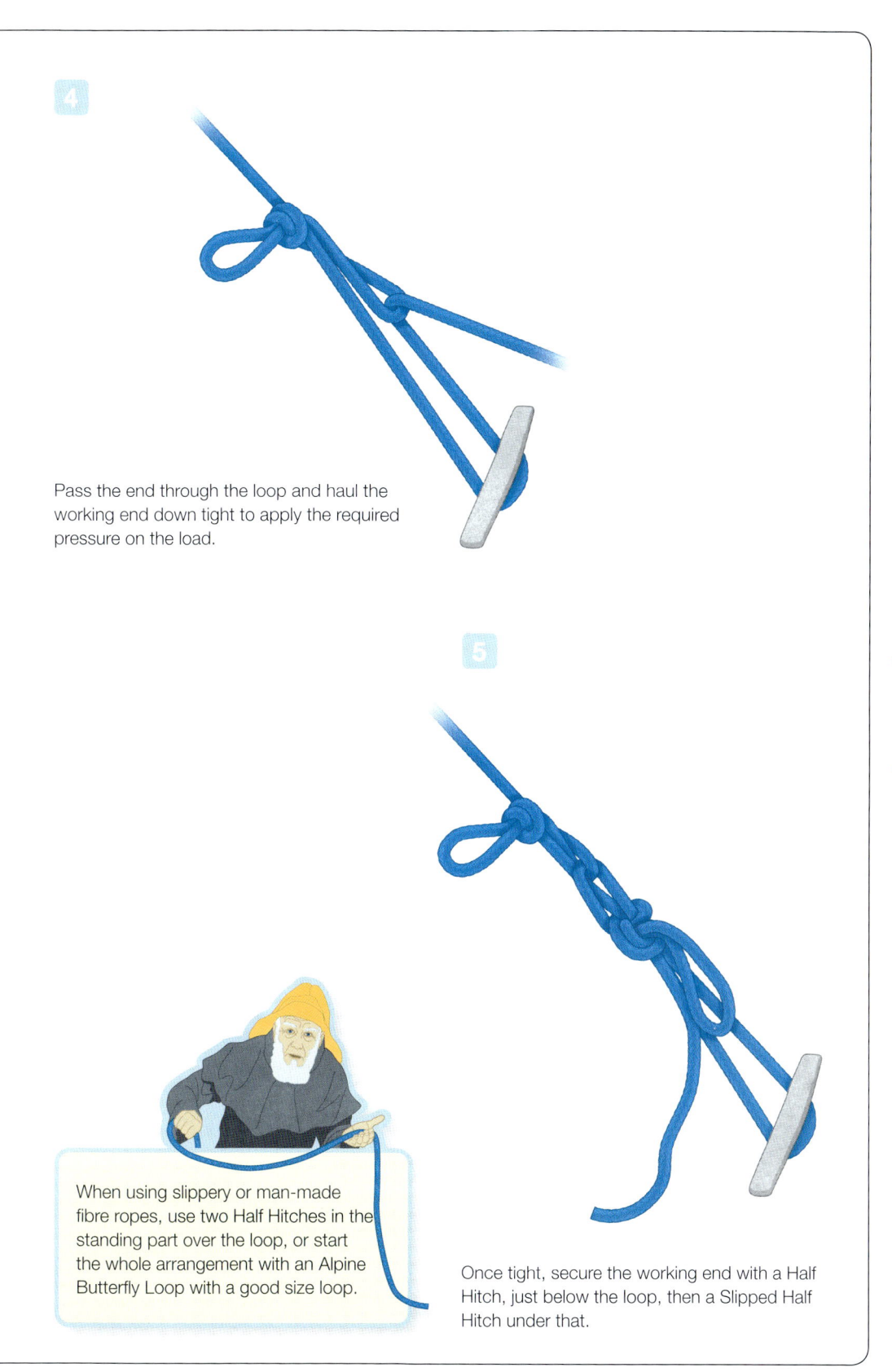

TRUCKER'S HITCH | 135

4

Pass the end through the loop and haul the working end down tight to apply the required pressure on the load.

5

When using slippery or man-made fibre ropes, use two Half Hitches in the standing part over the loop, or start the whole arrangement with an Alpine Butterfly Loop with a good size loop.

Once tight, secure the working end with a Half Hitch, just below the loop, then a Slipped Half Hitch under that.

Lashings and Bindings

Square Lashing

Square Lashing has many uses for jury and extempore rigging and is so named because the turns are laid on square. The diagrams here depict the lashing of two poles, however it can be used to lash just about any two objects together at right-angles.

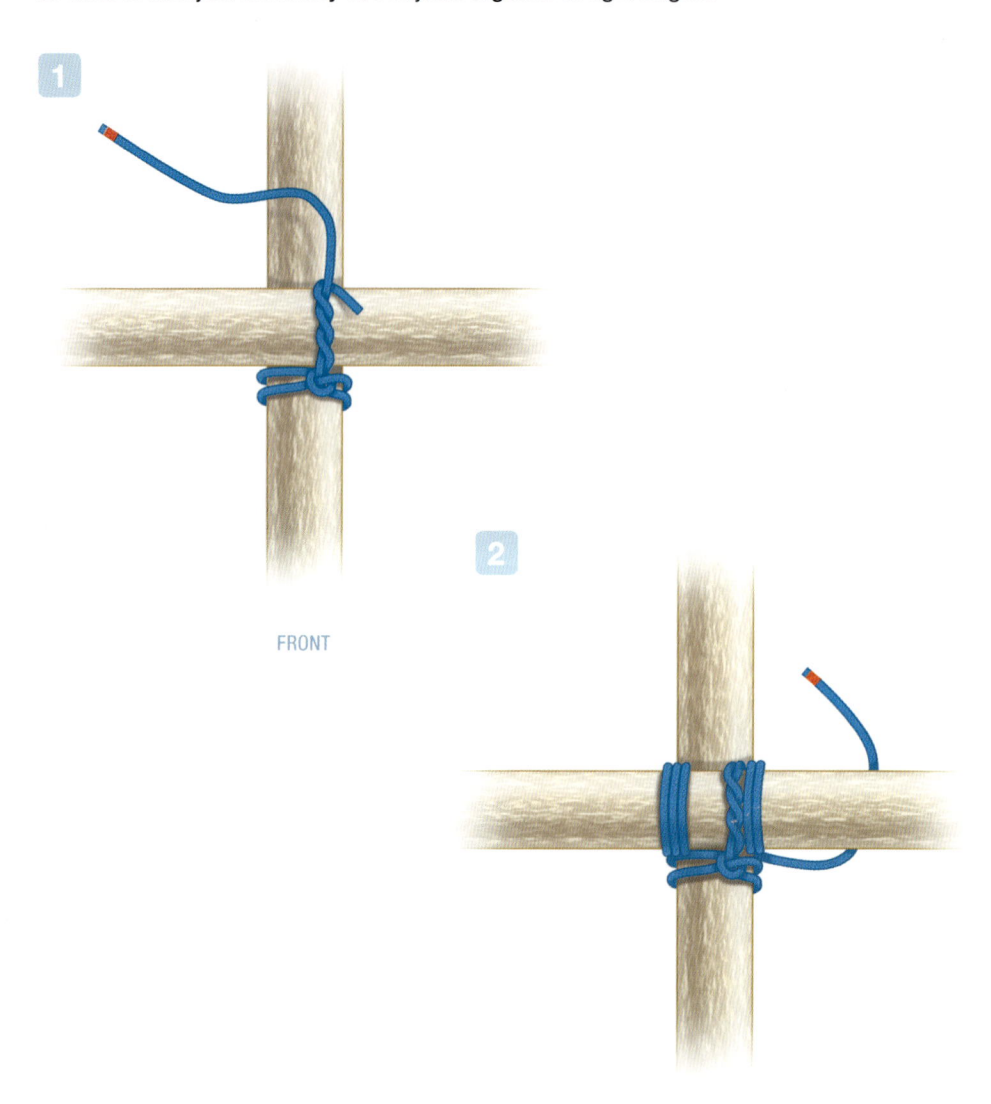

1

FRONT

2

FRONT

Lay the two objects together with the horizontal one in the front – it helps to support both a few inches above the deck. Tie a Clove Hitch around the vertical spar just under the horizontal one, leaving an end that can be twisted around the standing part and tucked out of the way. Pass the working end over the horizontal, around the back of the vertical, over the horizontal again then behind the vertical <u>above</u> the Clove Hitch.

SQUARE LASHING

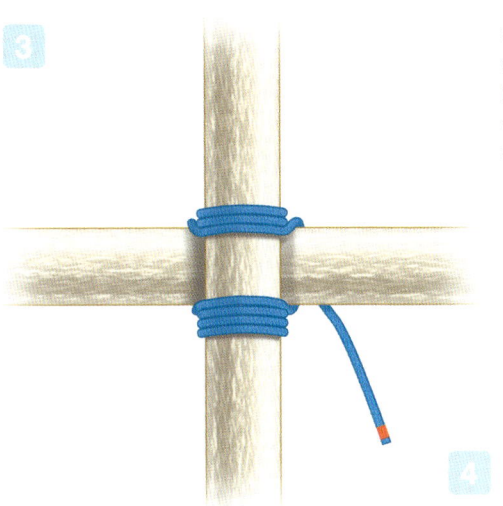

3

Continue for three turns, passing the working end <u>outside</u> the previous turns around the horizontal spar and <u>inside</u> the previous turns on the vertical spar. Pull each turn up as tight as possible.

REAR

4

Apply two or three 'frapping' turns around the lashing between the two spars – pulling them really tight to apply more pressure on the lashing turns. Secure the frapping turns with a Half Hitch as close to the point of exit from the lashing as possible on the horizontal spar (start on one end on the other), then complete with another Half Hitch to form a Clove Hitch.

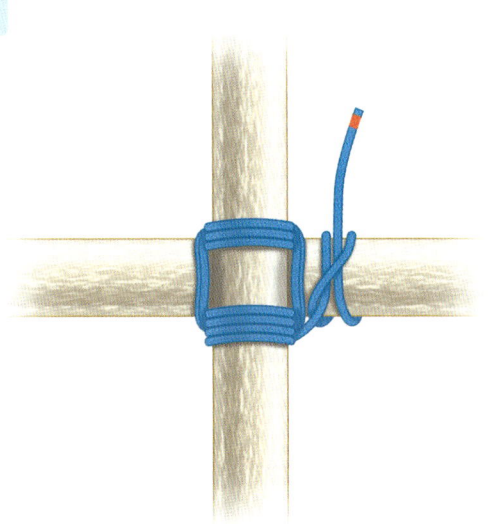

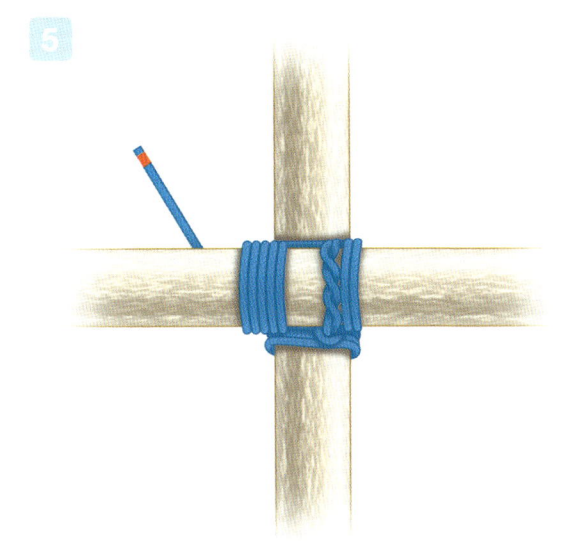

REAR

5

FRONT

If you are making a framework, or need to clamp the two spars together – use the Transom Knot (p140) as a temporary lashing.

Diagonal Lashing

The Diagonal Lashing is normally used on the braces of temporary structures and is more suitable (because the turns are laid on diagonally) for lashing objects that are not at right-angles.

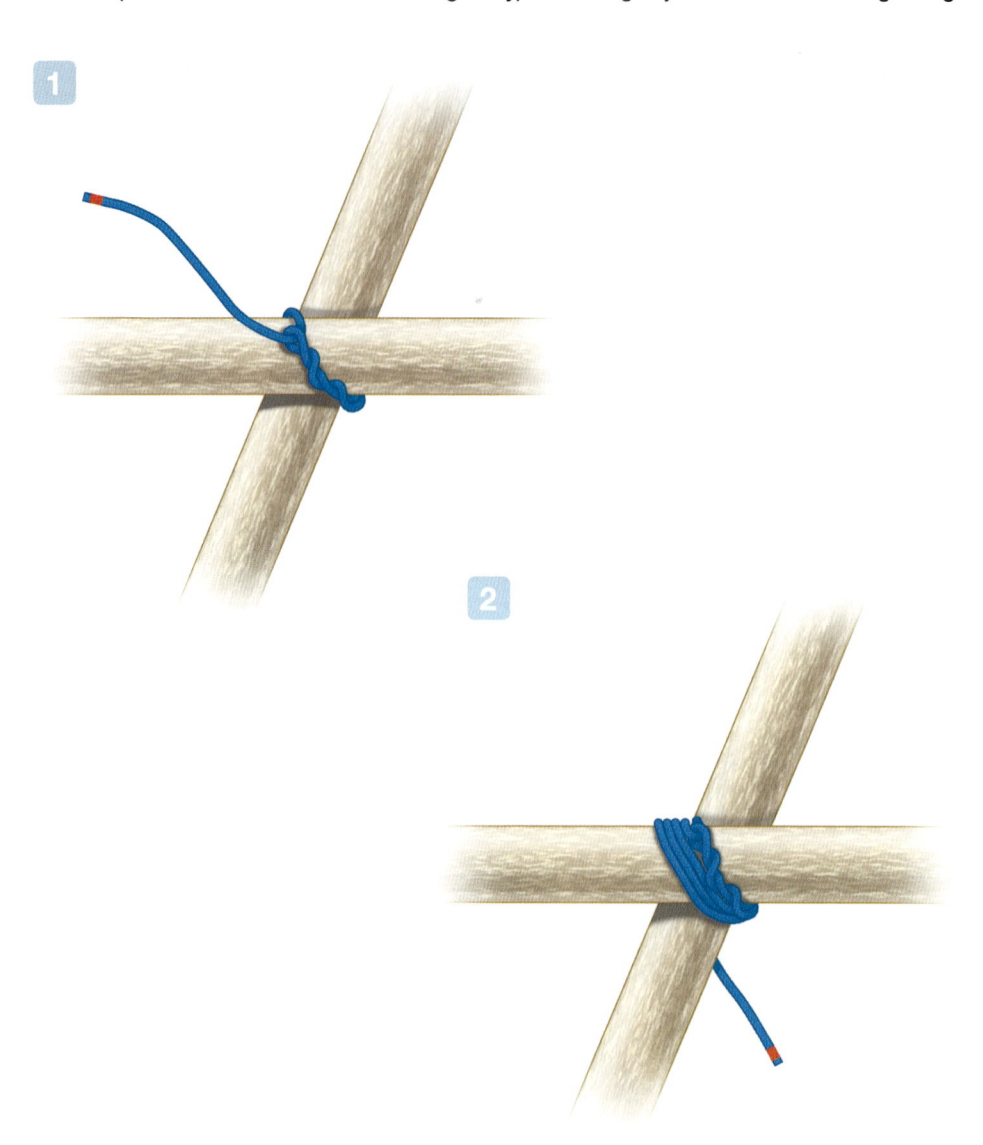

1

2

This lashing starts with a Timber Hitch which is placed across the two spars in the largest angle between them. Pull up firmly then continue to pass three turns around the two spars.

DIAGONAL LASHING | 139

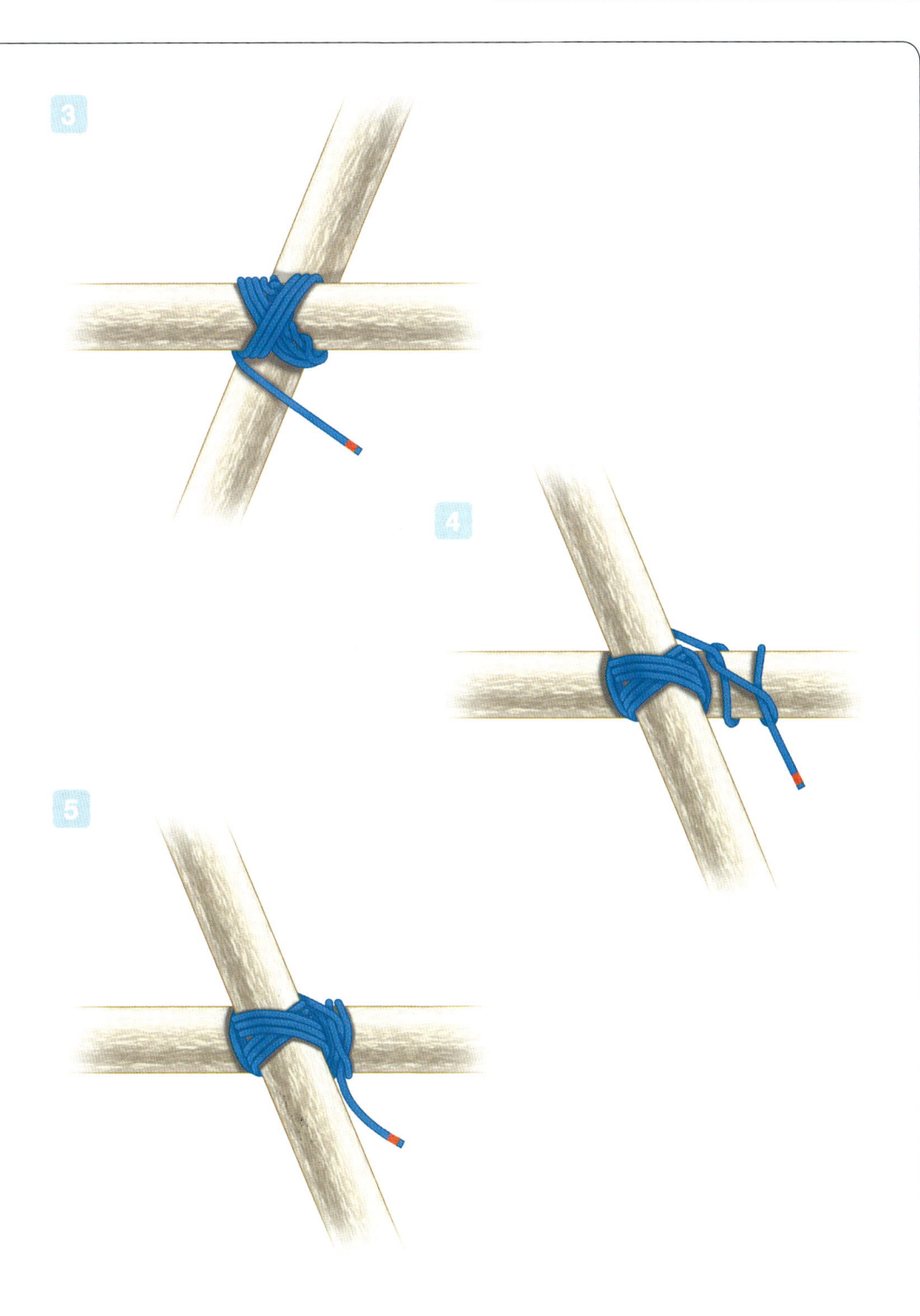

Change direction and pass three turns round the spars and in the smallest angle between them. Choose a point where you can now lead the working end directly into at least two frapping turns around the lashing. Tie off as close as you can to where the last frapping turn meets a spar, with a Half Hitch, followed by a further Half Hitch in the form of a Clove Hitch.

Transom Knot

This handy lashing knot, which is a variation of the Constrictor Knot but thought to be of Japanese origin, is an ideal temporary lashing for small diameter poles, or as a snake lashing when building a pole raft, decking, shelves or racks.

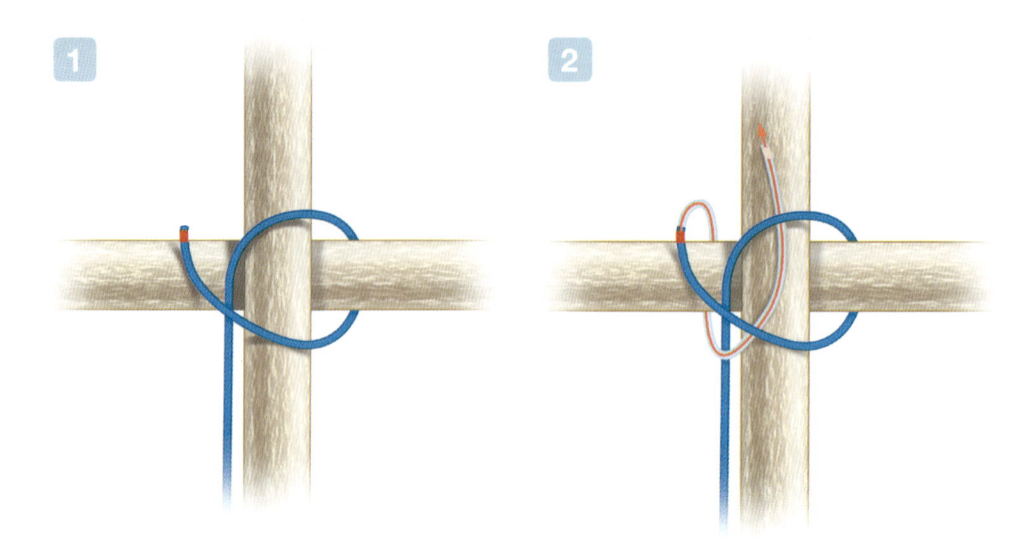

1

2

Lay the two poles at right-angles, pass the line from the top, under the horizontal pole to the right of the vertical pole, then diagonally across the vertical then under the horizontal pole to the left of the vertical. Complete the knot by passing the working end over the standing part, then tucking it to form an Overhand Knot. Pull tight and the knot will lock. For added strength, a second knot can be added on the opposite side.

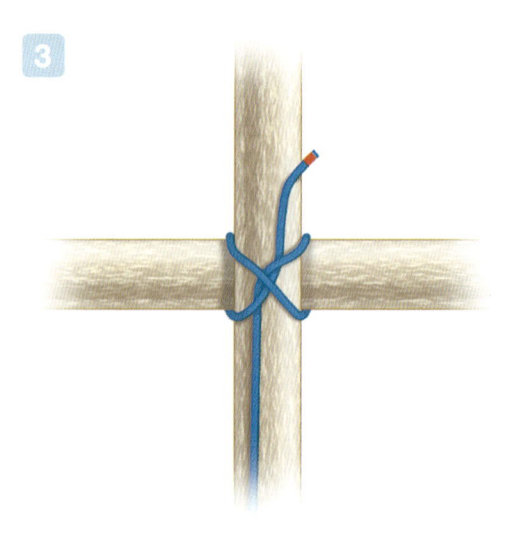

3

Rope Stopper

When transferring a fibre rope from a winch or the hands of multiple crew members to a belay device it is necessary to temporarily take the strain of that rope with a stopper. The stopper is made up from a short length of fibre rope (pre-stretch polyester is ideal) attached to a shackle, with which it can be secured to a ringbolt.

The stopper is laid on the rope in the direction of the load, starting nearest the deck fitting, with a Rolling Hitch then twisting the tail around the rope (with the lay if it is three strand rope) then held by one person (or stopped to the rope) while another transfers the end to the belay device and makes fast.

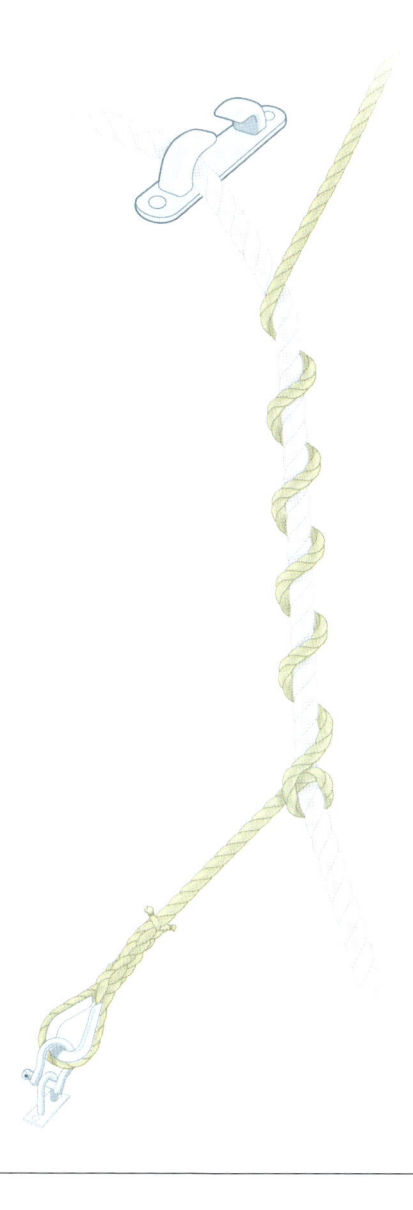

Chain Stopper

When the load on a wire hawser has to be taken up temporarily to transfer it from a winch to a belay device, a chain stopper has to be employed. The chain stopper is made up with a short length of chain which is shackled to a deck fitting, the chain is laid alongside the wire in the direction of the load then a Half Hitch applied with the chain around the wire WITH the lay of the wire – a further Half Hitch can be applied, however make sure there is some distance between this and the first one, otherwise they may slip and jam. The chain is then wound around the wire AGAINST the lay of the wire rope, then hand held or stopped to the wire.

CHAPTER 10:

SPLICING, SERVING & SEIZING

THREE STRAND BACKSPLICE

THREE STRAND TO CHAIN SPLICE

THREE STRAND EYE SPLICE

THREE STRAND SHORT SPLICE

THREE STRAND LONG SPLICE

MULTIPLAIT EYE SPLICE

MULTIPLAIT SHORT SPLICE

MULTIPLAIT ROPE TO CHAIN SPLICE

HALYARD BECKET OR BACK SPLICE

BRAID ON BRAID EYE SPLICE

BRAID WITH CORE EYE SPLICE

REDUCTION SPLICE

HOLLOW BRAID EYE SPLICE

YACHTSMAN'S ROLL SPLICE

ROPE TO WIRE SPLICE

THREE STRAND ROPE GROMMET

Introduction: Splicing, Serving & Seizing

The joining of one end of a rope to another, to itself, back into itself, into chain or other hardware, to form a permanent bond, is termed a 'Splice'. All of these functions can of course be done using knots, but knots are not as secure or as neat as a splice and will not pass through blocks or fittings. Most important of all, knots are known to reduce the strength of the rope in which they are tied (as much as 70% in some HMPE fibres), whereas a good splice will retain most if not all the working strength in the rope.

The choice – to knot or splice - has to be a practical one, taking into consideration:
- Rope construction (not all ropes can be spliced).
- The urgency of the task – splices can take time.
- Is the job to be temporary or permanent?
- Is a splice suitable for the task, having considered safety, security and strength?

Stranded Rope Splicing. Stranded rope splices were originally devised for natural fibre ropes, but with slight modification they remain useable with most stranded man-made fibre ropes of today. Splicing three strand rope is easy to learn and can be executed with very few tools. Four strand and cable-laid ropes are a little more complicated, but specialist splicing books contain instructions which are easy to follow once you have mastered the three strand methods.

Multiplait Rope Splicing. Splicing multiplait (8 or 12 strand) rope is normally confined to an Eye Splice for mooring ropes, a Rope to Chain Splice for anchor cables and perhaps a Short Splice. These splices also require the minimum of tools, but the Eye and Short Splices will require a certain amount of patience and the strength to open the strands, which gets more difficult as you progress through the splice.

Braided Rope Splicing. The multitude of Braided Ropes available now, has led to the development of many different splices and although the principles are covered in this book, it is always advisable to obtain the manufacturer's instructions (which have been designed and tested to suit the materials and design of the rope) before splicing a braid rope – a badly done or unsuitable splice can be DANGEROUS. The tools required to execute these splices vary, but a Swedish fid, splicing needles, hollow fids, whipping twine, together with a needle and sailmaker's palm are the basic tools needed for most jobs. There are two degrees of difficulty with braid splicing, one is learning the splice, which can vary from simple to quite complicated – the other is the physical strength required to pull up the splice at the end, which can vary from light, to those requiring the use of a winch!

Serving and Seizing. Serving (a tight binding using small stuff, twine or wire) is sometimes used over a splice, especially wire splices, to bind the ends of the strands down into the lay; mainly to stop them from springing out when the rope bends. It also protects the user from being cut and it looks neat, but does NOT strengthen a splice. Serving can also be used to cover rope and rails as a safety grip, or even for decoration. Seizing is used to bind two ropes together, for example, to form a Clinch, an Eye, or to secure shrouds around deadeyes. Another series of knots which are an essential part of splicing are the various types of Whipping and Seizing. Temporary whipping is essential to prevent (often referred to as a 'stop') ropes and strands from unlaying during the splicing process; permanent whipping (covered in Chapter 5) is used to stop the end of a rope from unlaying, especially where a knot or Back Splice is not appropriate.

Knots Used in Splicing

Here are a few of the more common knots and rope endings that you will need to be conversant with before embarking on the splicing projects in this chapter. The Alpine Butterfly Loop, or the Artilleryman's Knot are commonly used when splicing braided ropes, firstly to stop the cover from travelling too far along the standing part and secondly as an anchor point when snapping the splice in.

The Constrictor Knot is used as a temporary whipping or 'stop' to prevent rope unravelling, normally at the neck of the splice, as too is the Common Whipping, which is more often used if the whipping is to remain on the job after the splice is complete. The Butane End Seal (note the flame does not touch the rope) can be used when a hot knife is not available to seal the ends of man-made fibre ropes; electrical, masking or cloth tapes are all equally suitable to temporarily stop the ends of rope, strands, cores etc from unlaying during a splicing job.

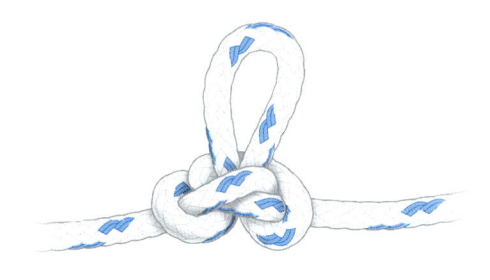

ARTILLERYMAN'S KNOT (p112)

ALPINE BUTTERFLY LOOP (p113)

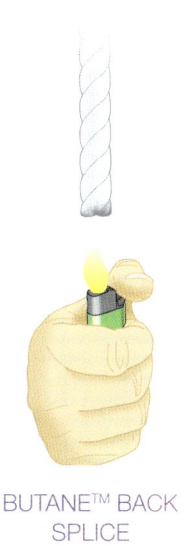

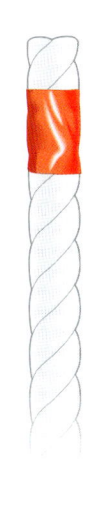

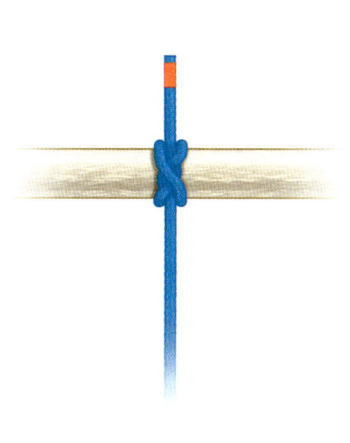

BUTANE™ BACK SPLICE

TAPED END

CONSTRICTOR KNOT (p51)

Three Strand Backsplice

The three strand rope Backsplice is used in the end of a rope to stop it from fraying. It provides a good end to handle, however it is bulky. Before splicing, check that any aperture it may have to be led through (like a block or thimble) is large enough to take it.

Tools required: knife (hot or blade), whipping twine, tape, and Swedish fid.

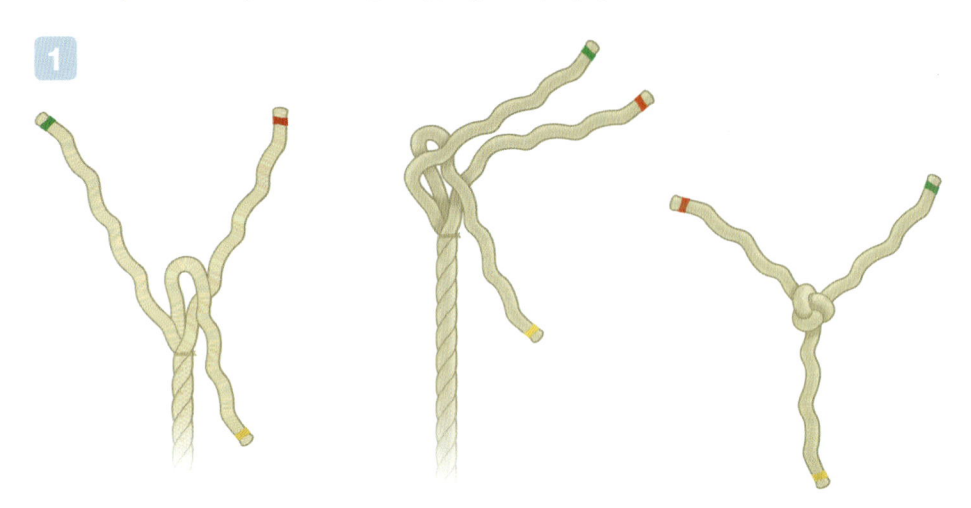

1

Commence by tying a temporary whipping around the standing part of the rope about four twists of one strand from the end. Unlay the 3 strands and tape or whip the ends. Tie a Crown Knot with the 3 strands – bring the centre strand from the rear and, leaving a small bight, lay it down in front of the standing part, take the strand on the left and cross it over the centre strand and on top of the right hand strand. Pass the right hand strand over the left hand strand and through the bight in the centre strand. Pull all three strands down tight onto the temporary whipping, which completes the Crown Knot.

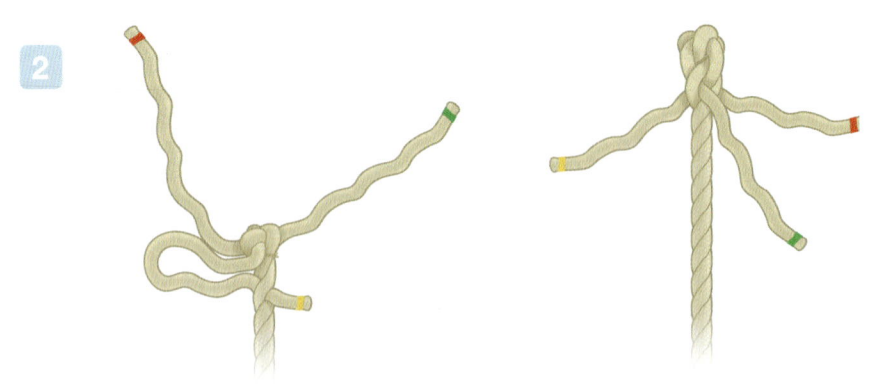

2

Take one strand, cross it over the standing part strand below it and tuck it under the next, working against the lay of the rope. Tuck the other two strands over one under one. Check that each strand emerges from under a different standing part strand, remove the temporary whipping, then snug each one up to the Crown Knot, completing the first tuck.

Make 2 more tucks with each strand. The ends can now be cut off or if a taper is required, leave one strand, tuck the other two over one under one, then take one of those strands and tuck it once more. The three ends should now be spaced down the standing part and when cut off will form a neat taper.

Three Strand to Chain Splice

When a three strand rope has to be spliced to a chain, provided all three strands will fit in the end link, the Backsplice can be adapted to make the union.

Tools required: fid, whipping twine, and tape.

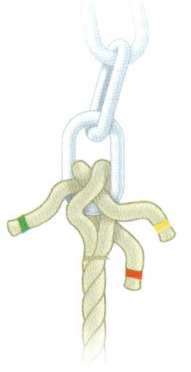

Put a temporary whipping about 30cm from the end. Unlay the three strands up to the whipping and tape the ends. Form a Crown Knot with the three strands, inside the end link of the chain. Splice the strands into the standing part of the rope like a normal Backsplice.

Three Strand Eye Splice

This splice is used to form an eye at the end of a three strand rope; more often than not a large soft eye in a berthing line or a small soft or hard eye to use as a becket. The method shown here depicts a small hard eye with a heart shaped thimble; to make a soft eye just omit the thimble details. Nylon rope will require 5 tucks, other man-made fibres 4 tucks and natural fibre rope 3 tucks.

Tools required: whipping twine, wood or Swedish fid, knife (heaving mallet – optional).

1

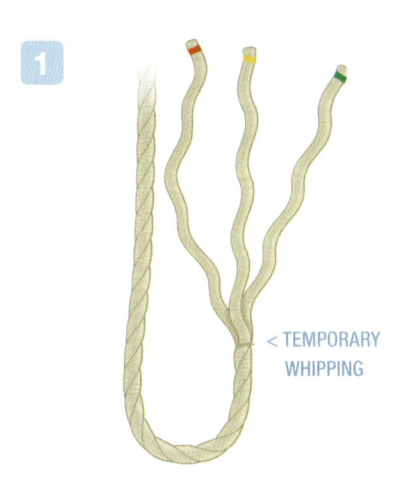

< TEMPORARY WHIPPING

Measure back from the end of the rope, enough to make the required number of tucks, plus a little working length – put on a temporary whipping at this point. Unlay the strands up to the temporary whipping and tape the ends.

2

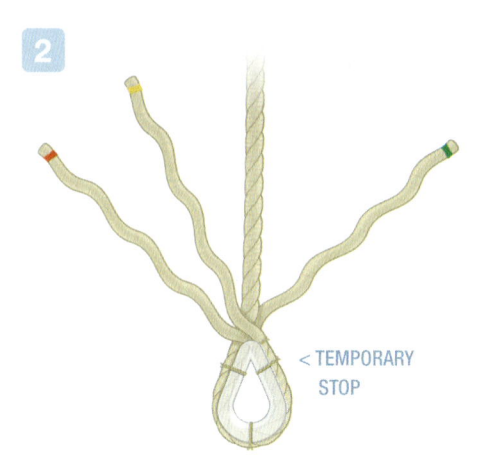

< TEMPORARY STOP

Make a bight the size of the eye required then insert the thimble, holding it in place with temporary stops, as shown. Lay the three strands so that the uppermost one (yellow) is in the centre, then one (red) to the left and one (green) to the right as shown.

3

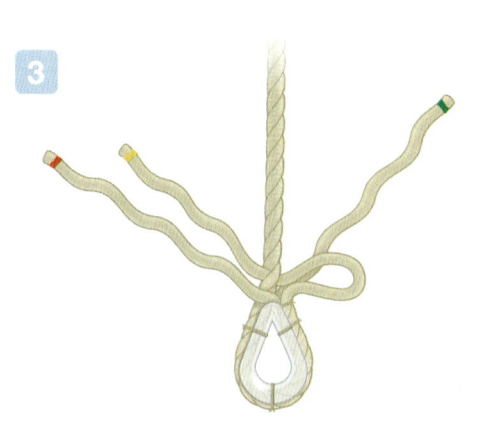

Pull the red strand tight up under the thimble, then tuck the yellow strand under a standing part strand as near to the thimble as possible. Pull up but not too tight yet.

4

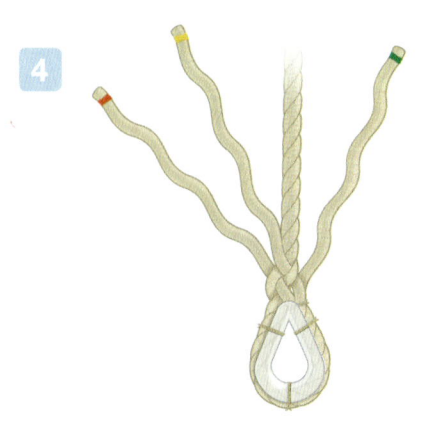

Tuck the left (red) strand over the strand the centre one is under, then under the next one and pull up.

THREE STRAND EYE SPLICE   149

5

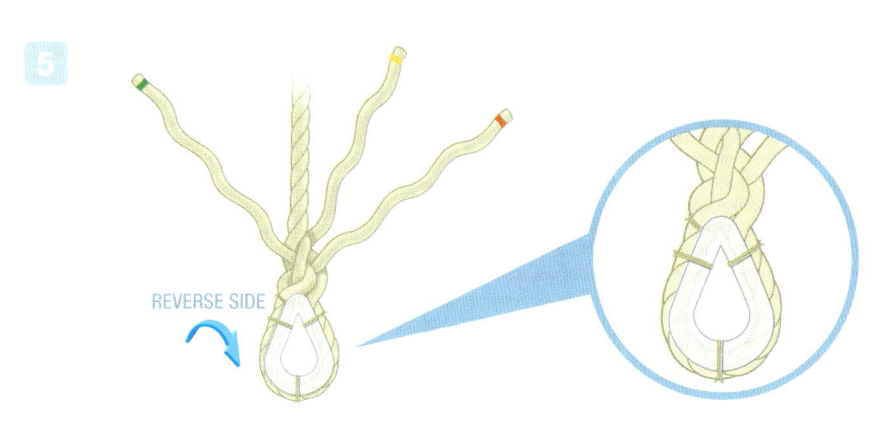

REVERSE SIDE

Now TURN the splice OVER – this is where most beginners find difficulty – and find the standing part strand which does not yet have a strand tucked under it; tuck the third (green) strand under from right to left as shown above. Pull up and now CHECK that the three strands each emerge from between two standing part strands, i.e. at 120 degree intervals.

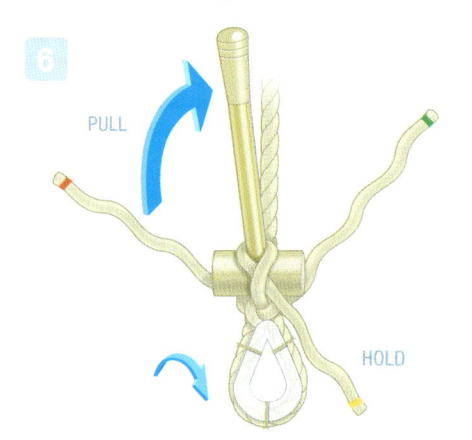

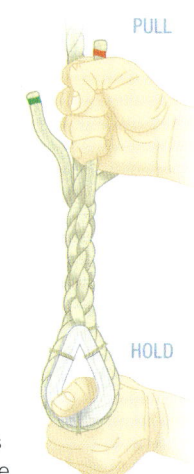

6

PULL

HOLD

PULL

HOLD

If you are laying in a hard eye remove the temporary whipping (for soft eyes in man-made fibres it is advisable to leave this on permanently), pull all three strands up as tight as possible – the ideal tool for this is a heaving mallet used as depicted above, but if you don't have one then pull up with the aid of a fid, marling spike, or by hand.

Continue tucking over one under one in sequence around the splice for the required number of tucks. Finish the splice using the methods described for the Back Splice or Short Splice or alternatively, especially if the eye is to be put under excessive loads, the ends can be 'dogged' – this is achieved by dividing each strand end into two then whipping one half of one strand to half the adjacent strand over the top of the standing part strand between them.

Hard eye splice with ends 'dogged'

Soft eye with ends 'dogged'

TIP FROM THE BOSUN'S LOCKER

If you tuck the first strand over/under/over/under – i.e. 2 tucks instead of one – you can achieve a much better purchase on the second strand to pull the thimble in tight.

Splicing, Serving and Seizing

Three Strand Short Splice

The Short Splice is used to join two identical three strand rope ends, if the extra diameter caused by the splice is of no consequence; usually as a temporary repair in a broken line.

Tools required: knife, fid, tape, and whipping twine.

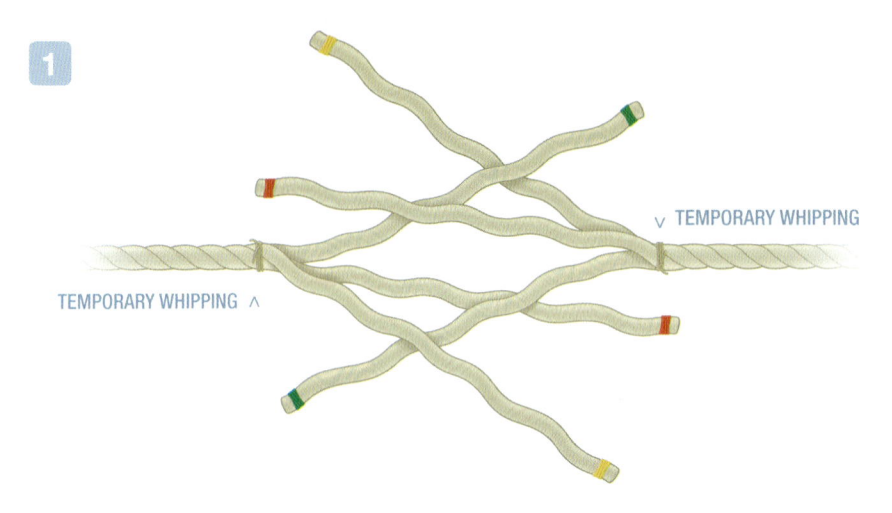

1

v TEMPORARY WHIPPING

TEMPORARY WHIPPING ∧

From the end of each rope, measure enough to lay in up to five tucks and add a hand width for good measure – put a temporary whipping on at this point. Unlay the strands and tape the ends. Lay the two ropes end to end and interlace the strands as shown.

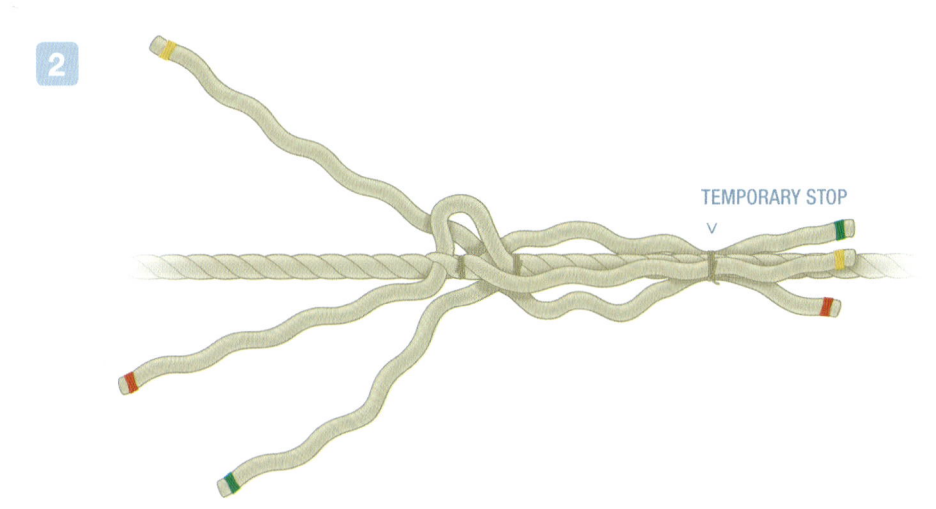

2

TEMPORARY STOP
v

Bring the two ropes up close and stop (Clove Hitch) the strands from rope B to the standing part of rope A. Commence tucking each strand of rope A into the standing part of rope B. Work against the lay tucking the strands in sequence, as you would an eye splice.

3

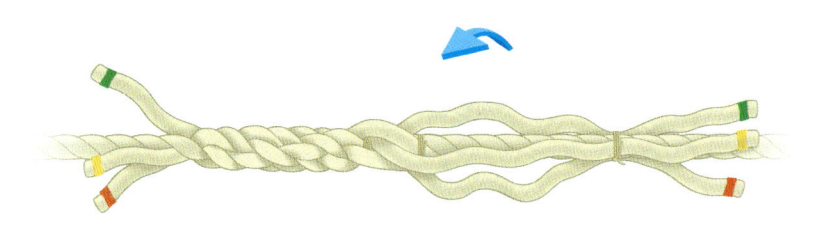

Continue tucking for the required number of tucks (3 tucks for natural fibre, 4 or 5 for man-made fibre rope).

4

Halve each strand then make a further tuck with one half, halve that again and make one more tuck, to taper the splice. Cut the ends neatly with knife or hot knife. Remove the temporary stop and whippings. Now splice the strands of rope B into the standing part of rope A, ensuring the junction is pulled up taut; finish the ends by tapering as you did before. Roll the splice in the hand or underfoot to bed the strands in and give the rope a round shape.

5

TIP FROM THE BOSUN'S LOCKER

When cutting the ends of strands that protrude from the lay of a rope or whipping – hold the knife blade up to the strand to be cut, then move the strand back and forth until it parts. This prevents the knife damaging the rope or the whipping.

Three Strand Long Splice

The Long Splice is used primarily to make a repair in a broken rope or to form a long loop where the splice will have to pass through a block or over a drive wheel. Even in natural fibre ropes this is the weakest of the splices and should be used with care; in man-made fibres, especially in soft laid rope, this splice may be difficult to execute and will need more distance between the three splice points. Note: the diagrams show only short spaces between the three splices; this is to fit the diagrams on the page – the text instructions regarding lengths should be followed.

Tools required: knife, fid and tape or whipping twine.

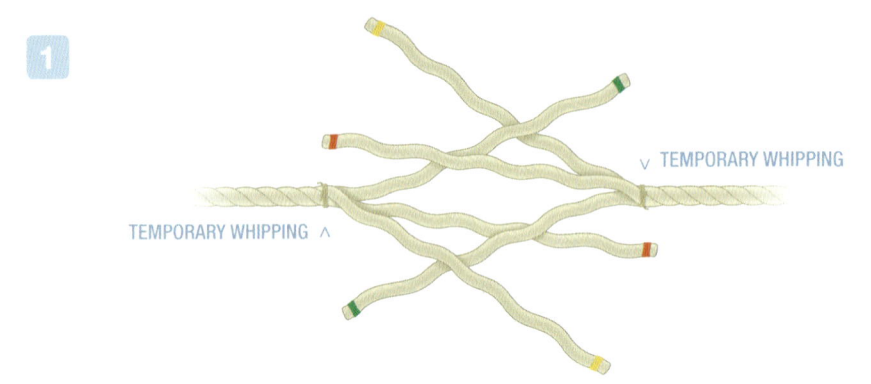

1

TEMPORARY WHIPPING

TEMPORARY WHIPPING

Count 10 crowns from the end of each rope end and put a temporary stop on both. Unlay the strands and marry them up to the stops as you would for a short splice, interlacing each of the opposite strands.

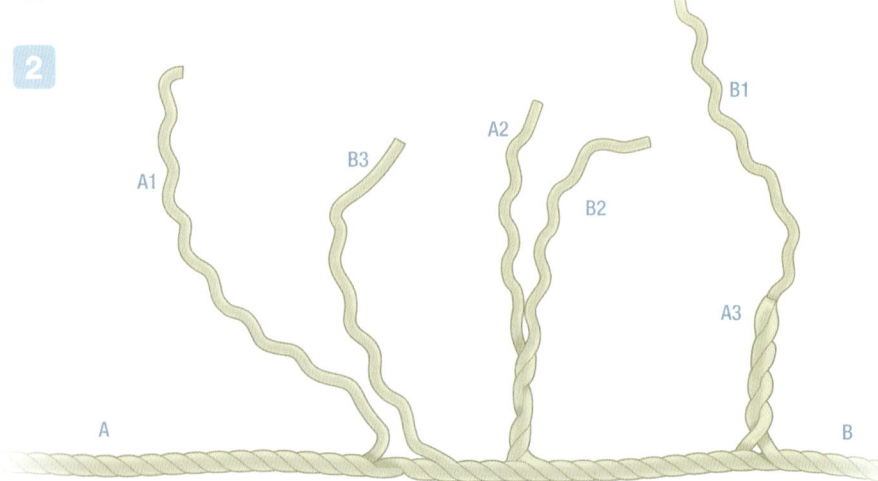

2

Match a strand from rope A with a strand from rope B at the point where if one is unlaid the other will naturally fall into its place – remove the temporary stops and twist these (A2 & B2) together as shown, to later become the central splice. Take the next two matching strands and unlay one (B1) from rope B back along the rope about 7 or 8 crowns - replacing it by laying in the strand (A3) from rope A – twist and lay this strand so that it fits snug and tight. Twist these two together as shown.

THREE STRAND LONG SPLICE

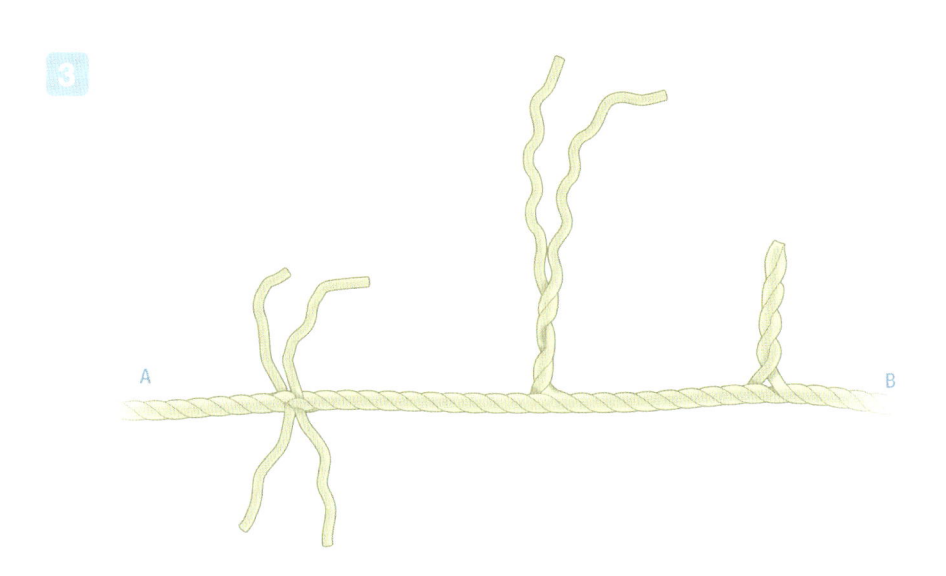

3

Having completed laying A3 into rope B, repeat the process with the remaining strand (B3) from rope B, into rope A. At each splice, divide the ends of both strands into two. Using the two uppermost halves, tie a Half Knot (left over right) and pull it tight down over the other two halves and into the lay of the rope as shown at diagram 4. Repeat this process with the two strands in rope B.

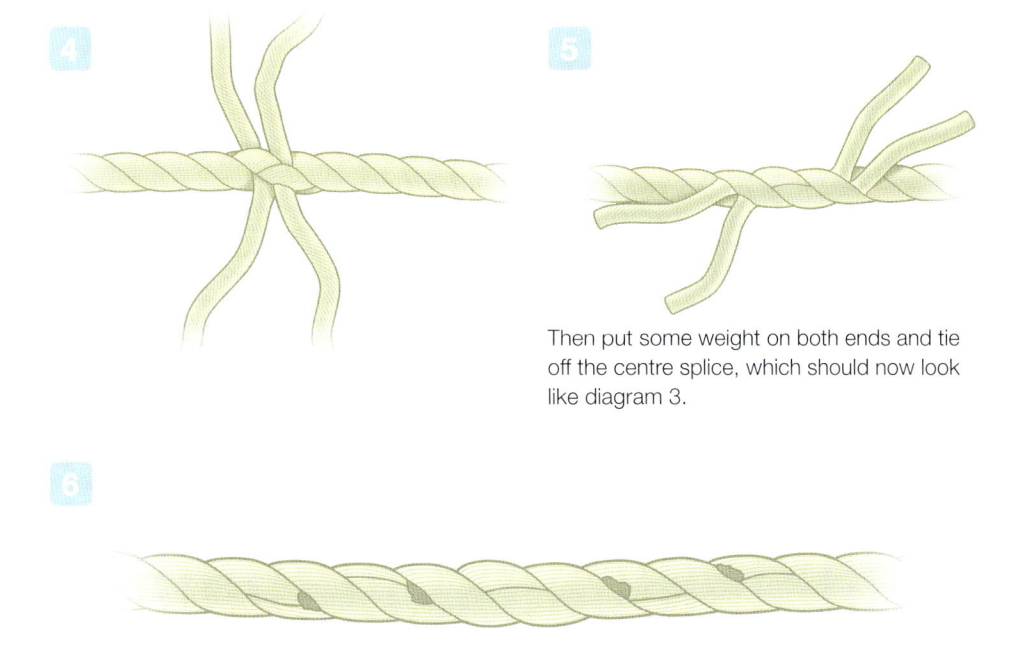

4

5

Then put some weight on both ends and tie off the centre splice, which should now look like diagram 3.

6

Having tied off all three splices, put the rope under strain and make sure each of the strands in both ropes is taking an equal load by adjusting the overhand knots as necessary. Now tuck the ends of each splice over/under/over as you would a normal splice, gradually removing yarns after each tuck to taper the splice. Roll in the hand or underfoot – the splice should be not much thicker than the diameter of the original rope.

Multiplait Eye Splice

This splice is normally used to lay a permanent soft eye in a multiplait berthing line. Before starting the splice, ensure you can identify the left and right hand laid pairs, as you will need to mark and identify the different strands as you progress through the splice.

Tools required: whipping twine, tape, Swedish fid, hot knife.

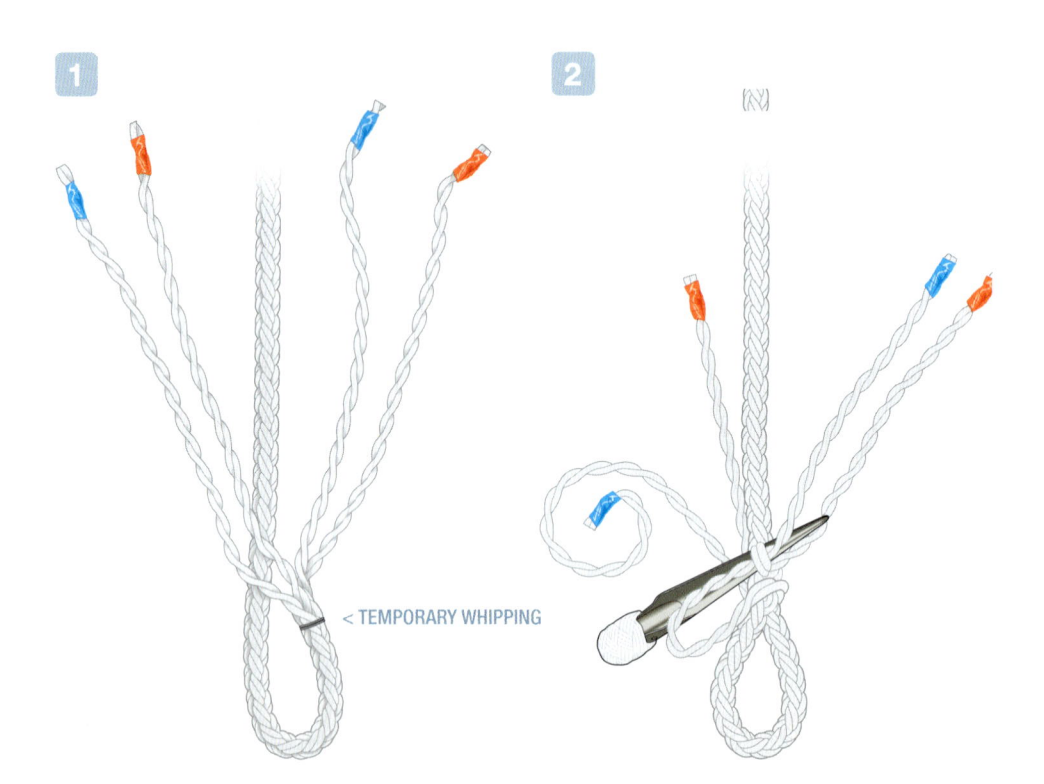

1

< TEMPORARY WHIPPING

2

Measure 30cm from the rope's end and apply a throat whipping (p67). Cut off the heat seal and unlay the strands up to the throat whipping. Keep the strands in their respective pairs by taping them together. In the diagram the right hand (Z laid) pairs have red tape and the left hand (S laid) pairs have blue tape. Create the size of eye required.

Using a Swedish fid, splice one of the Z laid strands under the Z laid strand of the standing part (keep them in their pairs) against the lay, turn the rope over and tuck the second Z laid strand under the other Z laid strand of the standing part. Repeat with the S laid strands, then pull all four pairs up tight. This completes the first tuck.

MULTIPLAIT EYE SPLICE | 155

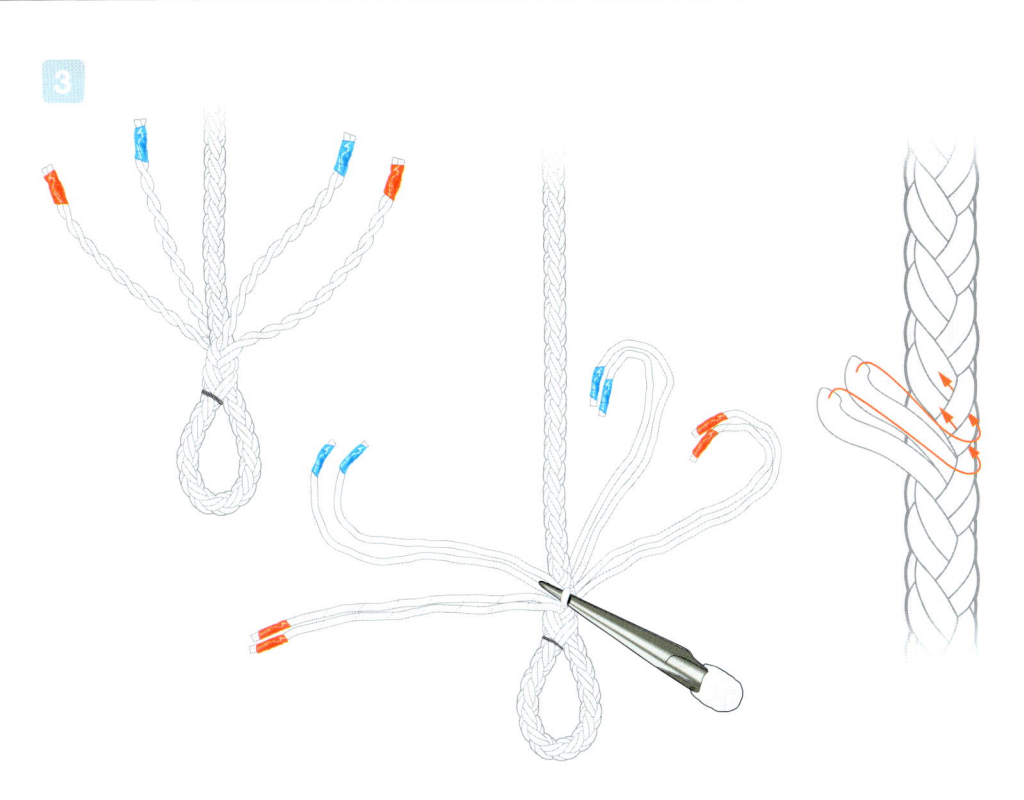

3

Remove the tape from the ends of the strands and take out the turns. Re-tape the individual strands, using the same colour coding for your tape. Now splice the single strands going straight down the rope over one under one. You do this with each strand four times.

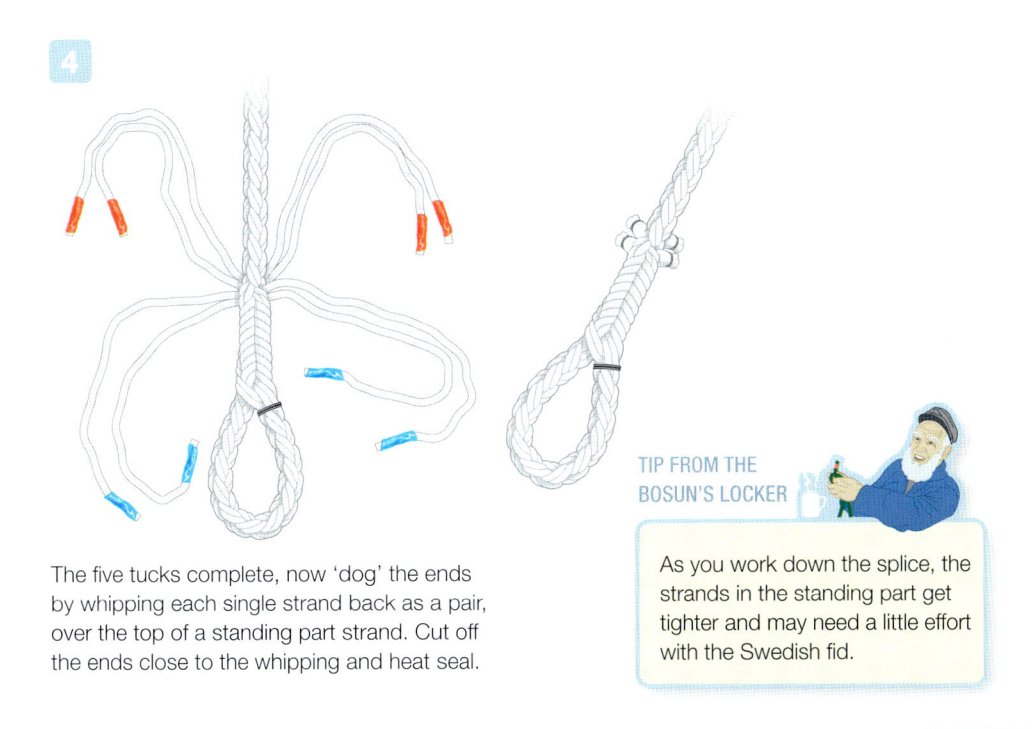

4

The five tucks complete, now 'dog' the ends by whipping each single strand back as a pair, over the top of a standing part strand. Cut off the ends close to the whipping and heat seal.

TIP FROM THE BOSUN'S LOCKER

As you work down the splice, the strands in the standing part get tighter and may need a little effort with the Swedish fid.

Splicing, Serving and Seizing

Multiplait Short Splice

Used for permanently joining two 8 strand multiplait ropes together.

Tools: Swedish fid, whipping twine, tape, hot knife.

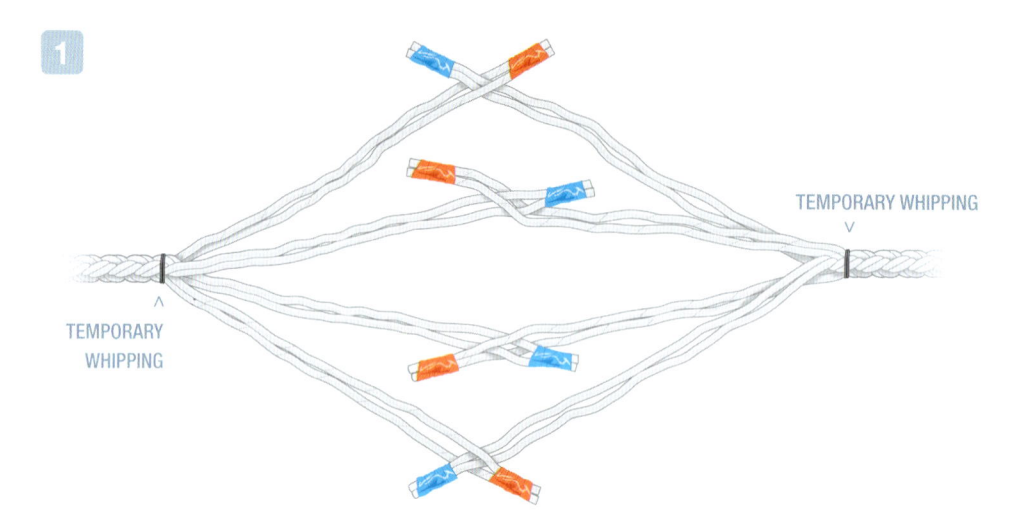

1

TEMPORARY WHIPPING

TEMPORARY WHIPPING

Measure 30cm from the end of each rope and put a temporary whipping on each one (Constrictor Knot p51). Cut off the heat seal and unlay the strands, keeping them in their pairs (2 Z laid – red tape and 2 S laid – blue tape). Interlock each pair of strands as shown in the diagram.

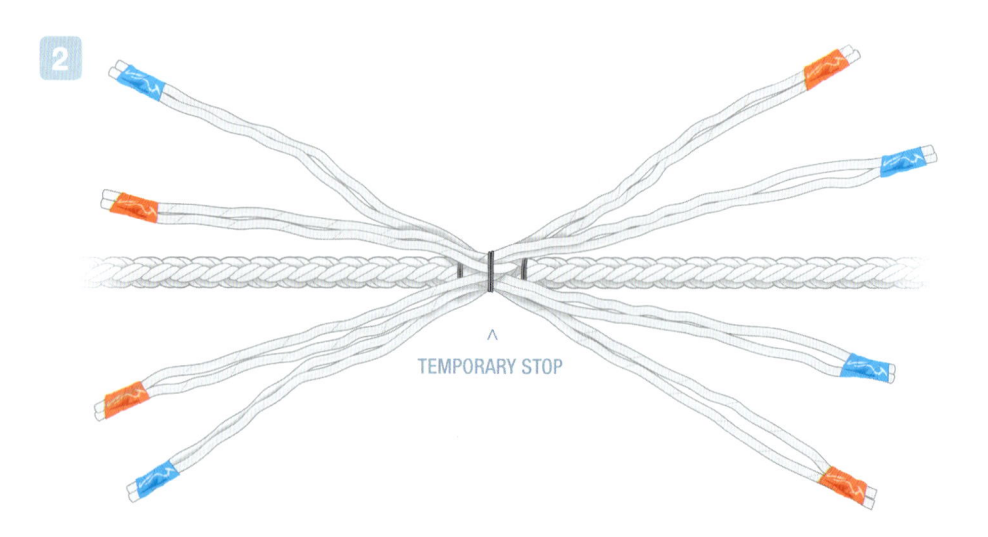

2

TEMPORARY STOP

Pull the strands tight. Put on a temporary whipping (Constrictor Knot) at the intersection, as shown.

MULTIPLAIT SHORT SPLICE

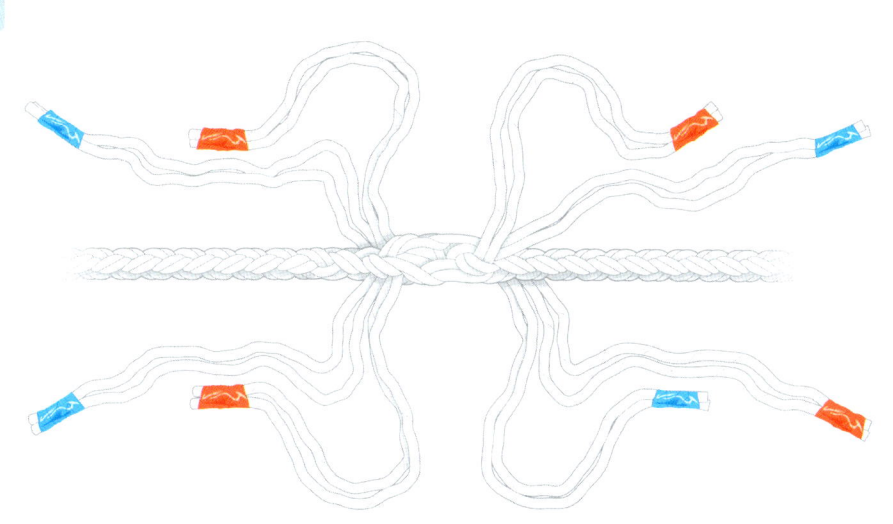

3

Commence splicing with one set of ends, the same as an eye splice. Complete 5 tucks along the standing part of one rope, then commence tucking the other. The temporary whippings can be removed after the first tuck is completed.

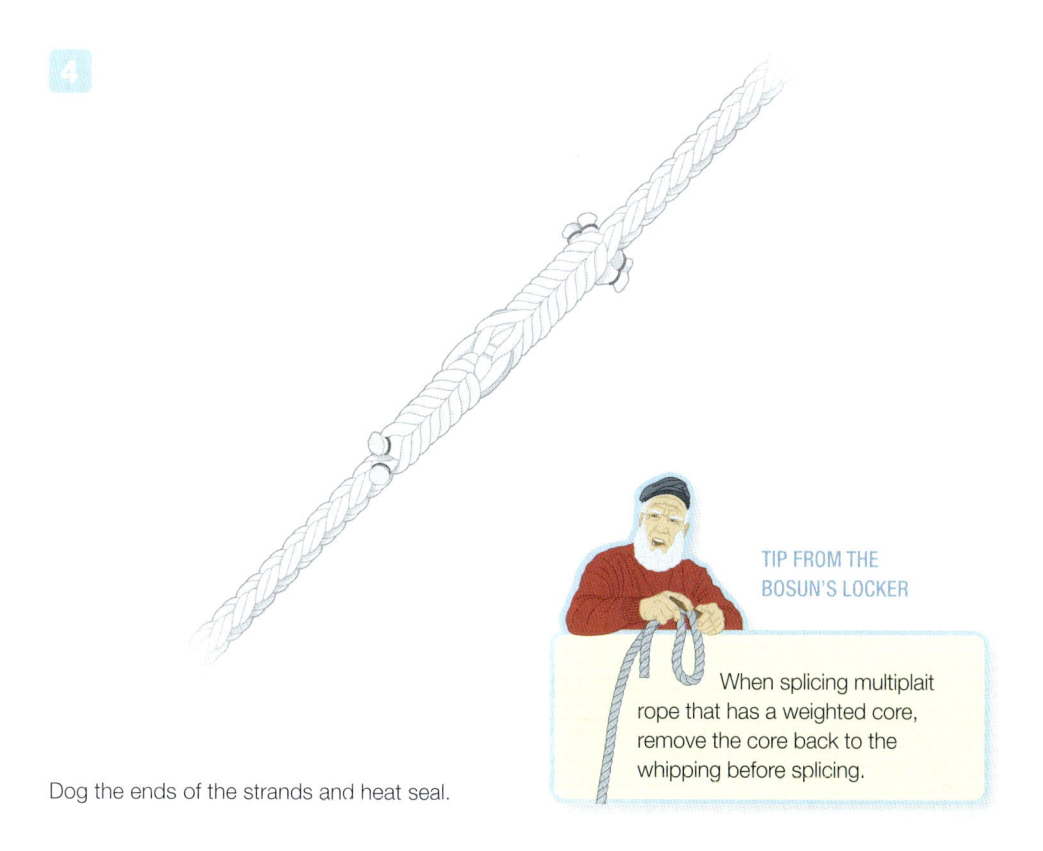

4

Dog the ends of the strands and heat seal.

TIP FROM THE BOSUN'S LOCKER

When splicing multiplait rope that has a weighted core, remove the core back to the whipping before splicing.

Splicing, Serving and Seizing

Multiplait Rope to Chain Splice

The advent of multiplait rope with its strength and flexibility now means that an anchor cable can be made up of both chain, to lay on the sea bed, and rope for easy handling and stowage inboard. To join rope to chain the eight strands of the rope are woven, one at a time through the chain links, then secured by dogging.

Tools required: hot knife, tape, whipping twine.

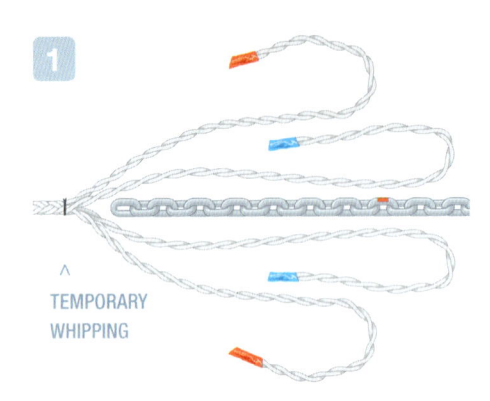

1

TEMPORARY WHIPPING

Mark the 15th link of the chain – lay the end of the multiplait alongside the chain so that it is about 20cm beyond the 15th link. Apply a temporary whipping to the rope alongside the first link of the chain. Unlay the 4 pairs of strands and tape the ends as shown.

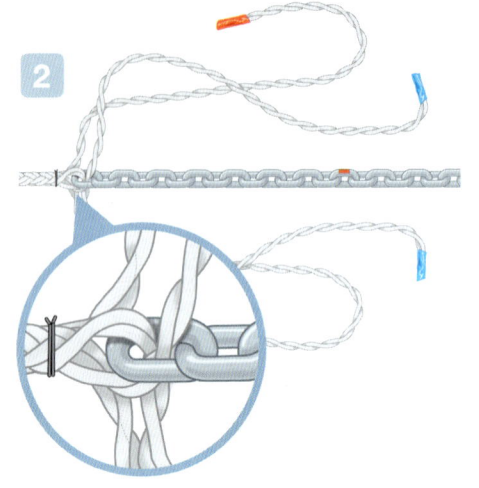

2

Take the right hand laid pairs and cross them over the middle of the left hand laid pairs. Pass the left hand laid pairs through the first link in opposite directions as shown.

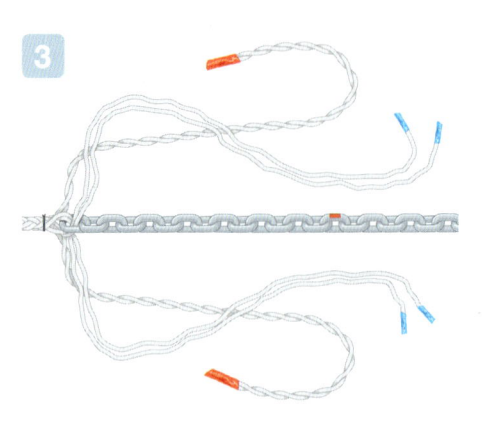

3

Now separate the left hand laid pairs and re-tape the ends.

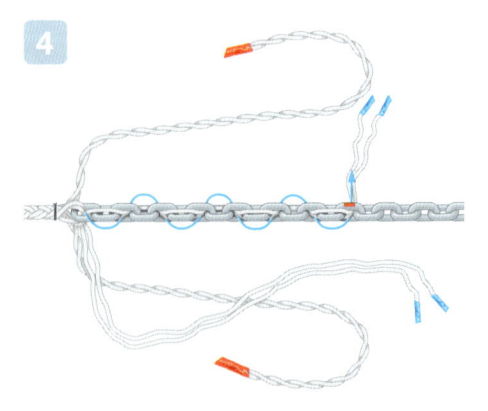

4

Take each single strand and weave it through the odd numbered links of the chain, one at a time until reaching the 15th link. Note how each pair has one strand on either side of each link.

MULTIPLAIT ROPE TO CHAIN SPLICE

5

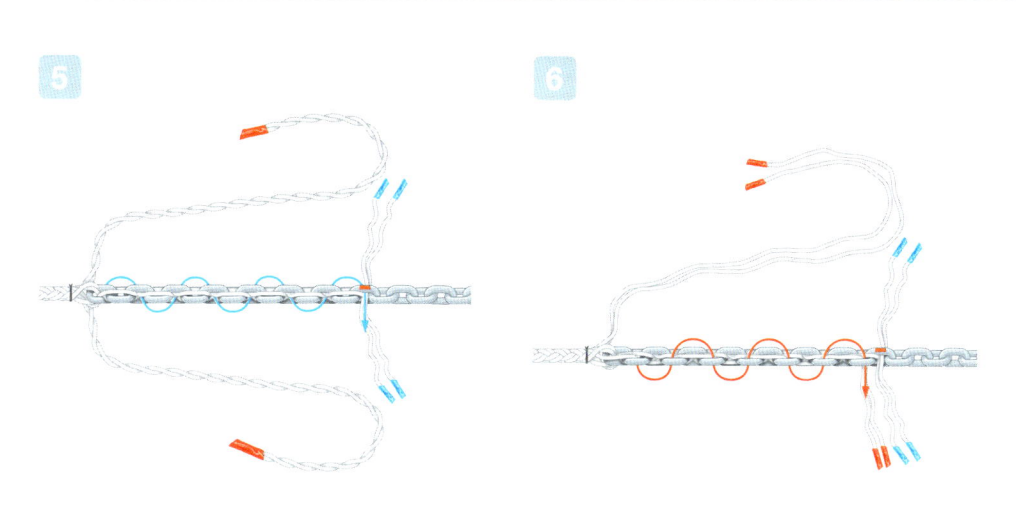

Now weave the other two left hand laid strands.

6

Repeat the process above with the right hand laid strand pairs, separating them and weaving them through the even numbered links of the chain, stopping at link 14.

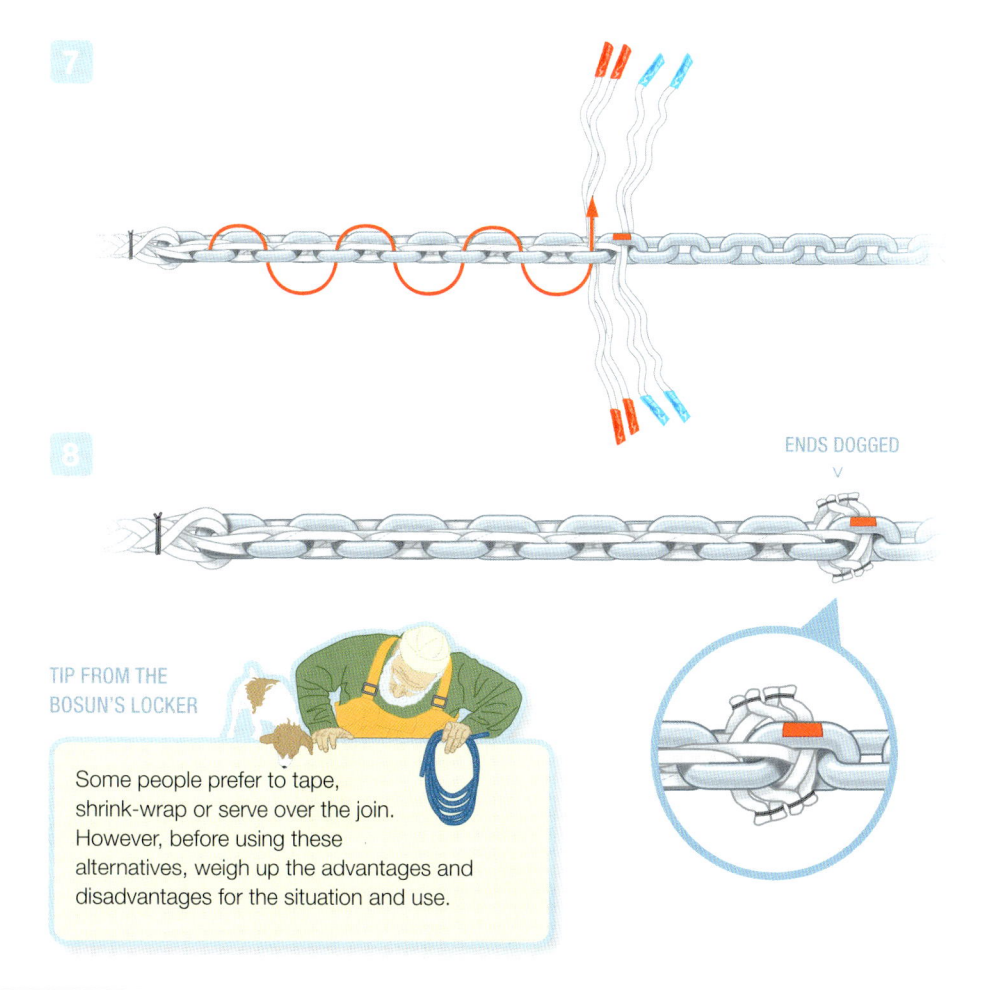

7

8

ENDS DOGGED

TIP FROM THE BOSUN'S LOCKER

Some people prefer to tape, shrink-wrap or serve over the join. However, before using these alternatives, weigh up the advantages and disadvantages for the situation and use.

Splicing, Serving and Seizing

Halyard Becket or Backsplice

A very useful Backsplice to make an eye or small becket in the end of a halyard. The eye can be used to secure a small line (or messenger) so as to reeve the halyard into the mast. As a Backsplice (eye pulled fully down into the cover) it can also be used to terminate the end of any braided line, instead of whipping. CAUTION: This is a VERY WEAK splice and the eye should only be used for light weights and lines.

Tools required: splicing needle, knife.

1

Apply a stopper knot (Alpine Butterfly) 3 metres from the rope end. Cut off the heat seal and pull the cover back to expose about 50cm of core. Cut off 40cm of core and discard.

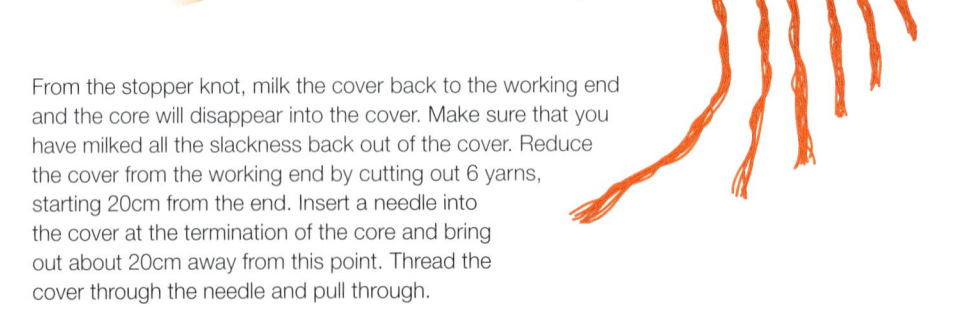

2

From the stopper knot, milk the cover back to the working end and the core will disappear into the cover. Make sure that you have milked all the slackness back out of the cover. Reduce the cover from the working end by cutting out 6 yarns, starting 20cm from the end. Insert a needle into the cover at the termination of the core and bring out about 20cm away from this point. Thread the cover through the needle and pull through.

3

Adjust the size of the eye by pulling the tail of the cover, or for a Back Splice, pull the becket down into the cover. Cut off the tail and milk end into cover. The cut end of the cover should now butt up against the end of the core. Sew locking stitches approx 10cm from the eye's end.

4

Braid on Braid Eye Splice

Used mainly to form an eye at the end of a halyard, sheets, or mooring and berthing lines. The Braid on Braid Eye Splice can be made up as a soft or hard eye. When learning this splice it is advisable to use the softer woven and new rope, not less than 10mm in diameter.

Tools required: hollow splicing fid and pusher, marker pen, tape and hot knife.

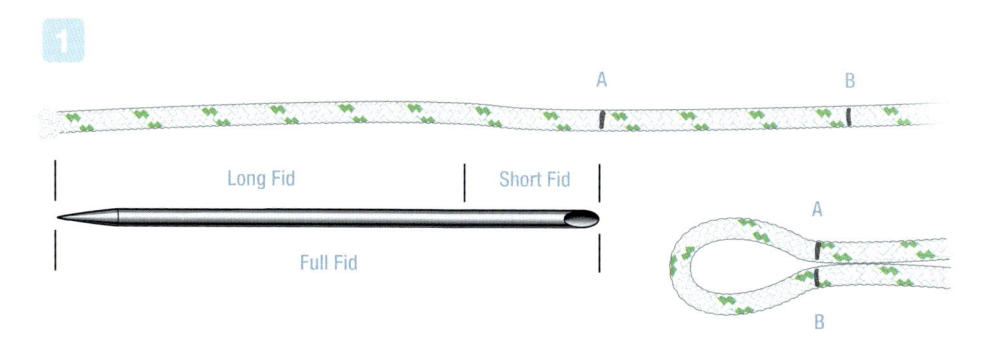

1

Tie a stopper knot 3 metres from the end (Alpine Butterfly Loop p113). Cut off the heat seal at the end and balance the core and cover, by milking the cover from the stopper knot to the end. Measure one full fid length from the end and mark 'A'. Form the eye and mark 'B' (see insert).

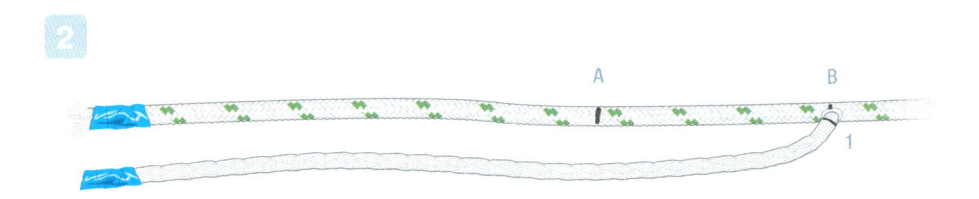

2

Make a small hole in the cover at 'B' with a fid and extract the core. Mark the core (1 mark) where it emerges from the cover mark 'B'. Tape the end of the cover and the core.

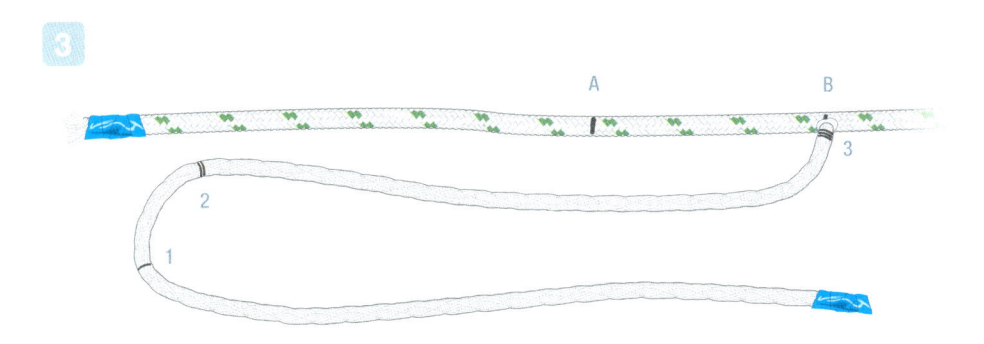

3

Pull more core out of the cover and measure from mark 1 one short fid length, mark this point 2. Pull more core out, then from mark 2 measure one full and one short fid length – mark 3.

162 | BRAID ON BRAID EYE SPLICE

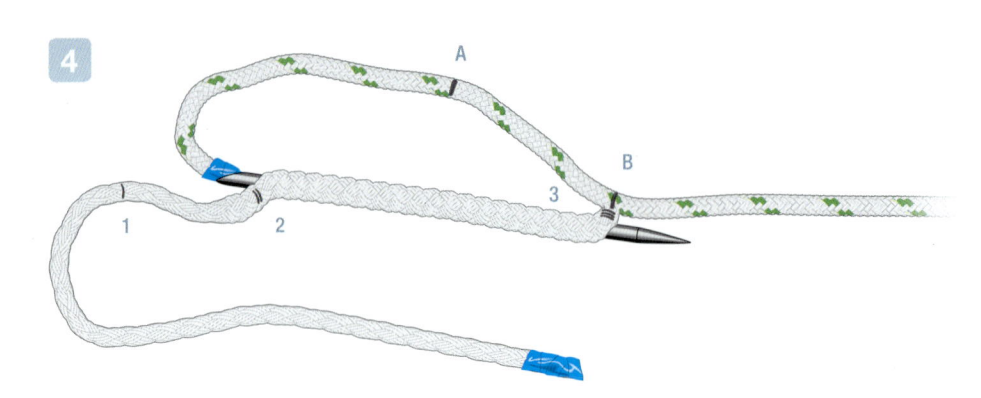

4

Insert the fid into the core at mark 2 and out at mark 3. Insert the end of the cover into the fid. Push the fid through and pull the cover out at mark 3.

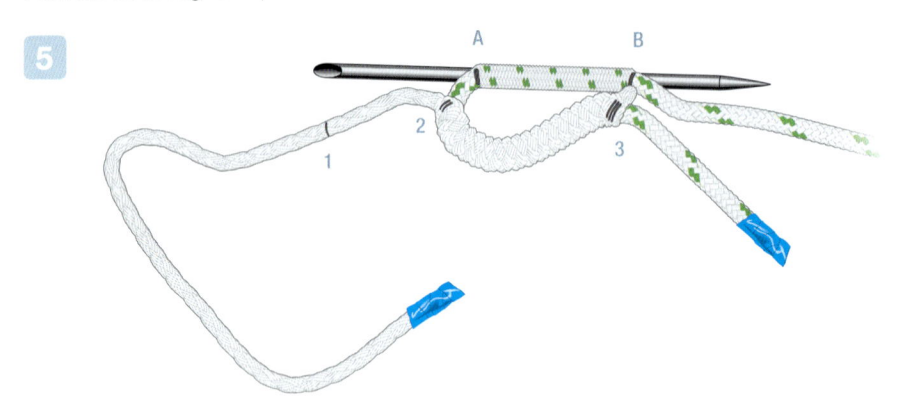

5

Insert the fid into the cover at 'A' and exit about 30mm past mark 'B'.

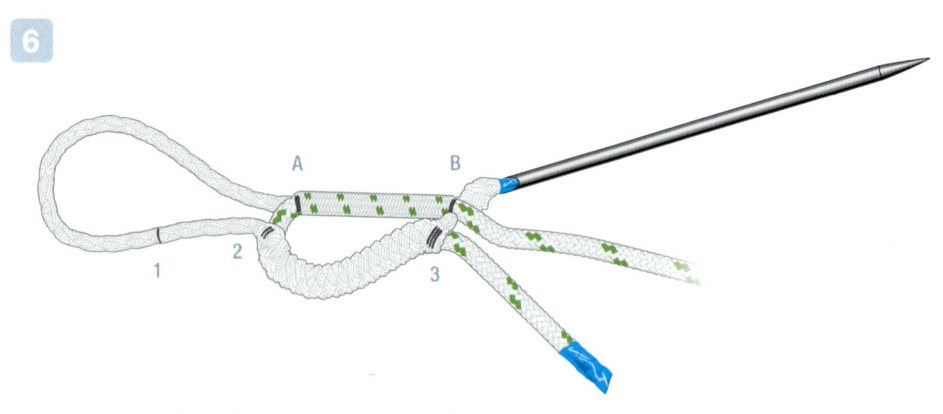

6

Insert the core end into the fid and push through.

Splicing, Serving and Seizing

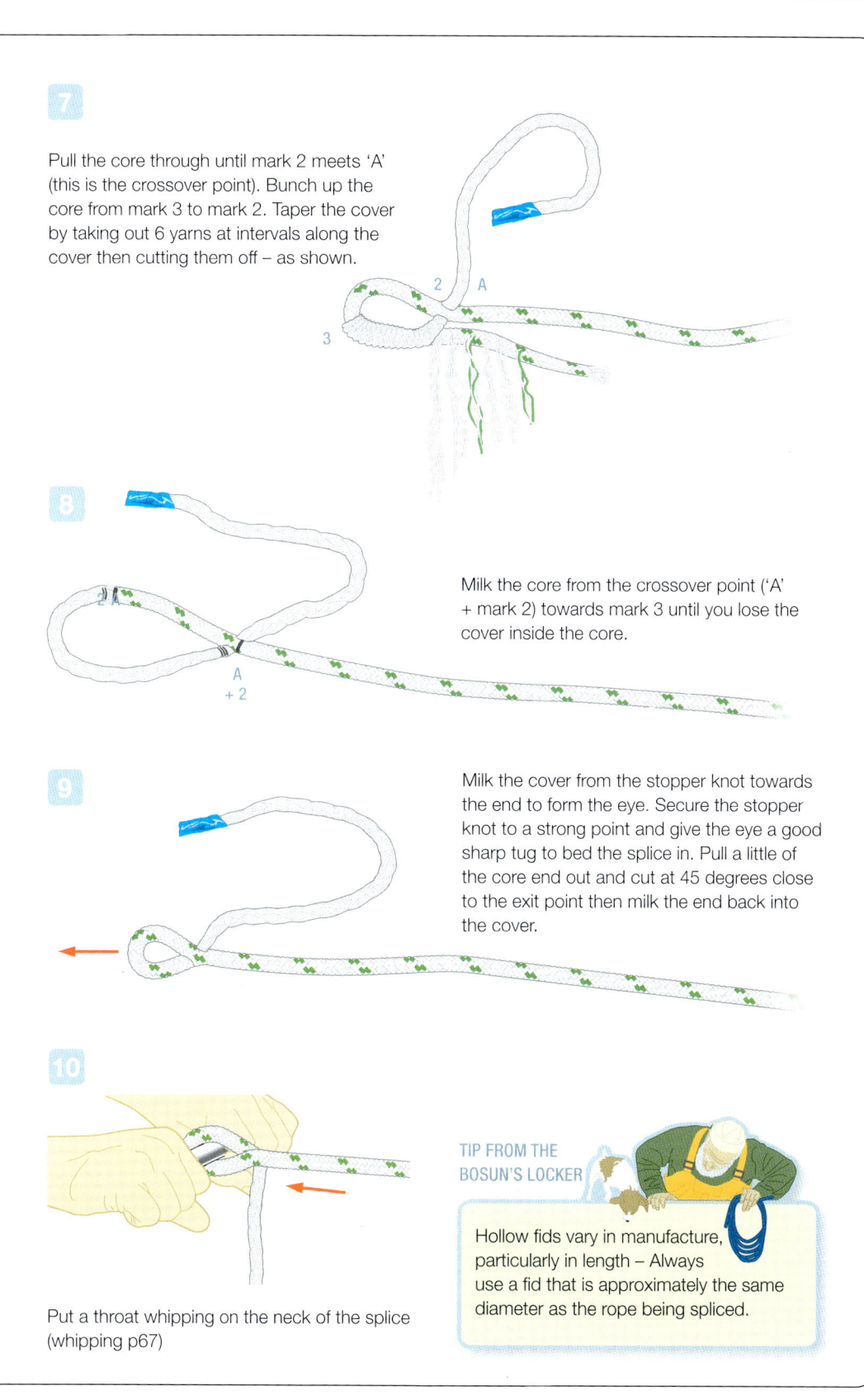

BRAID ON BRAID EYE SPLICE

7

Pull the core through until mark 2 meets 'A' (this is the crossover point). Bunch up the core from mark 3 to mark 2. Taper the cover by taking out 6 yarns at intervals along the cover then cutting them off – as shown.

8

Milk the core from the crossover point ('A' + mark 2) towards mark 3 until you lose the cover inside the core.

9

Milk the cover from the stopper knot towards the end to form the eye. Secure the stopper knot to a strong point and give the eye a good sharp tug to bed the splice in. Pull a little of the core end out and cut at 45 degrees close to the exit point then milk the end back into the cover.

10

Put a throat whipping on the neck of the splice (whipping p67)

TIP FROM THE BOSUN'S LOCKER

Hollow fids vary in manufacture, particularly in length – Always use a fid that is approximately the same diameter as the rope being spliced.

Splicing, Serving and Seizing

Braid with Core Eye Splice

Braid ropes with a three strand or parallel core should be spliced in accordance with the manufacturer's instructions, as they do vary depending on the way the core is constructed. Although at first sight, this splice looks easier than the braid on braid, it does need more practice to get the core and cover buried properly.

Tools required: splicing needle, tape, Swedish fid, marker pen, knife/scissors.

1

Tie a stopper knot (Alpine Butterfly Loop p113) 3 metres from the end. Cut off the heat seal. Expose 10cm of core and milk the cover back to the stopper knot – the importance of this will become evident when you need more slack in the cover later.

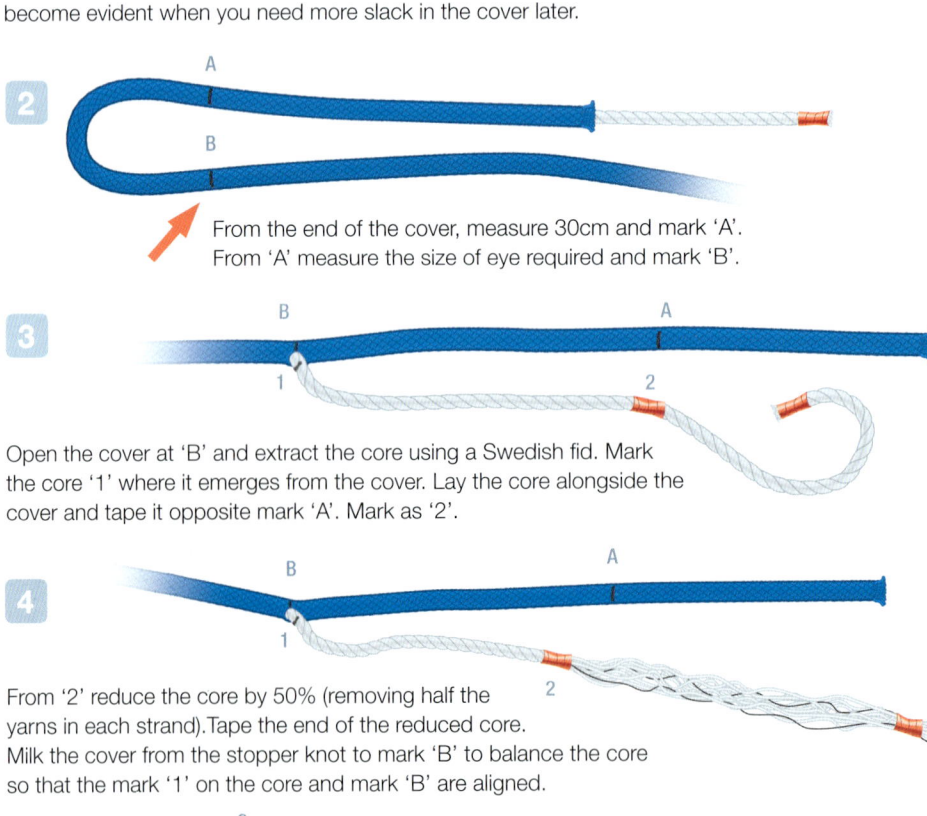

2

From the end of the cover, measure 30cm and mark 'A'.
From 'A' measure the size of eye required and mark 'B'.

3

Open the cover at 'B' and extract the core using a Swedish fid. Mark the core '1' where it emerges from the cover. Lay the core alongside the cover and tape it opposite mark 'A'. Mark as '2'.

4

From '2' reduce the core by 50% (removing half the yarns in each strand). Tape the end of the reduced core. Milk the cover from the stopper knot to mark 'B' to balance the core so that the mark '1' on the core and mark 'B' are aligned.

5

Insert a long splicing needle, 35cm along the standing part from mark 'B' and bring the end out at mark 'A' – taking great care not to snag the core. Thread the end of the core into the needle.

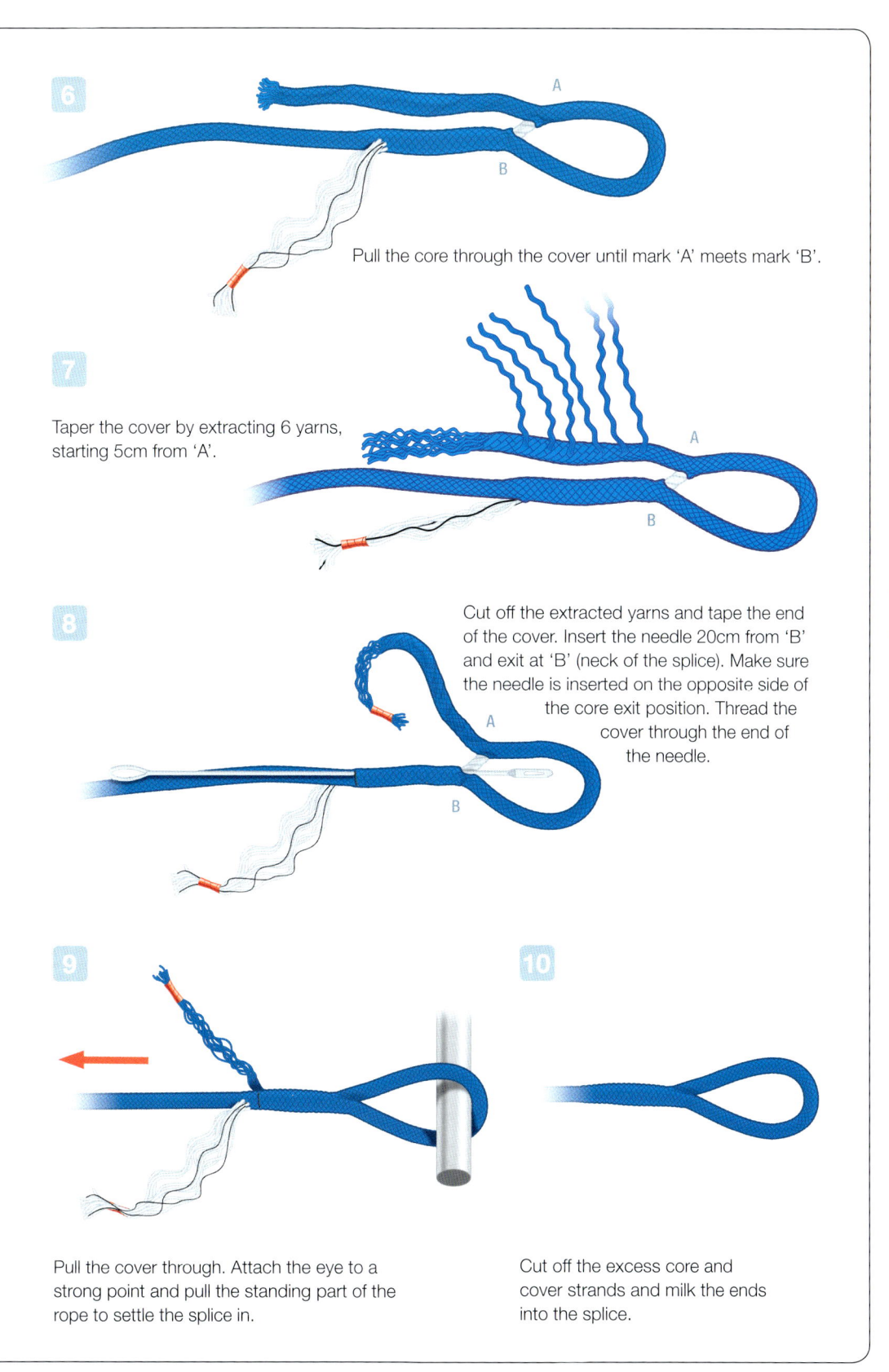

BRAID WITH CORE EYE SPLICE | 165

6 Pull the core through the cover until mark 'A' meets mark 'B'.

7 Taper the cover by extracting 6 yarns, starting 5cm from 'A'.

8 Cut off the extracted yarns and tape the end of the cover. Insert the needle 20cm from 'B' and exit at 'B' (neck of the splice). Make sure the needle is inserted on the opposite side of the core exit position. Thread the cover through the end of the needle.

9 Pull the cover through. Attach the eye to a strong point and pull the standing part of the rope to settle the splice in.

10 Cut off the excess core and cover strands and milk the ends into the splice.

Splicing, Serving and Seizing

Reduction Splice

The Reduction Splice or Taper Splice is used to secure the cover to the core of hollow braid lines such as Dyneema™/Spectra™ or Vectran™, when the cover is stripped from part of the line to save weight and enable the end to be spliced using the Brummel Splice.

Tools required: needle, whipping twine, knife or scissors, hollow fid.

1

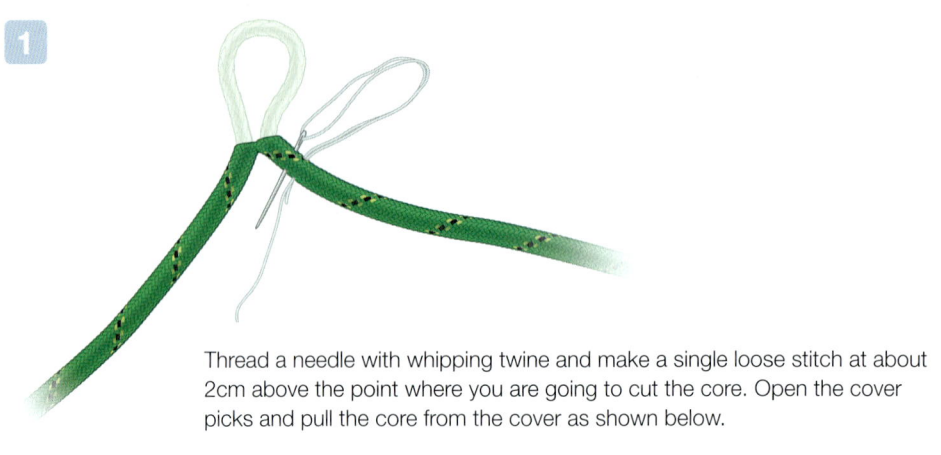

Thread a needle with whipping twine and make a single loose stitch at about 2cm above the point where you are going to cut the core. Open the cover picks and pull the core from the cover as shown below.

2

Cut the now hollow cover about 30cm from the lock stitch.

3

Insert a hollow fid into the core at the point where it enters the cover and out about 35cm along the core. Insert the end of the hollow cover into the needle and push it through until it exits the cover. Remove the cover from the hollow fid.

REDUCTION SPLICE

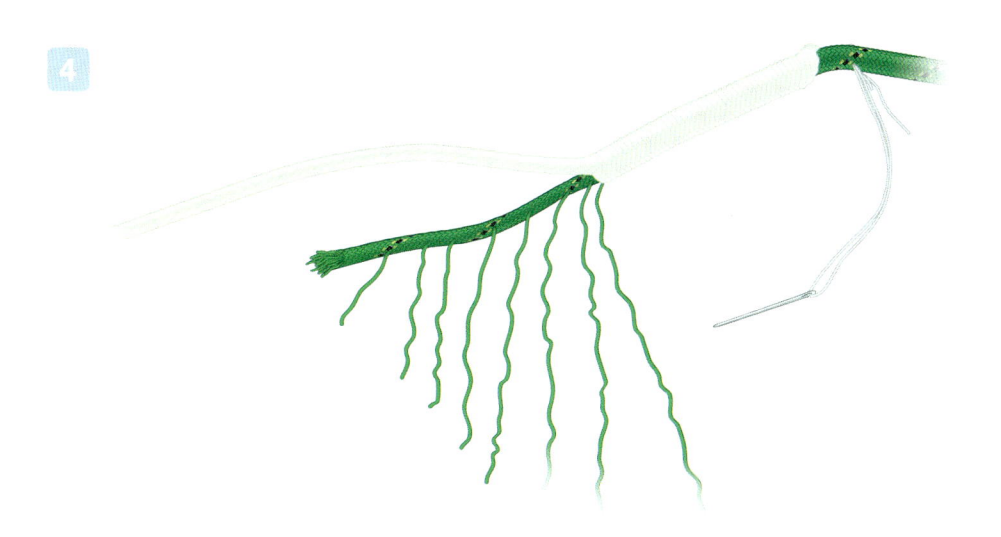

4

Bunch the core back to the lock stitch (hold with a needle if necessary) then taper the hollow cover back to about 20cm from the end. Cut the exposed strands then milk the core over the cover away from the lock stitch – this should now bury the hollow cover inside the core.

5

Complete the stitching at the join by adding another 3 stitches. Starting at the stitching, apply a Common Whipping, using whipping twine to cover the join.

6

Hollow Braid Eye Splice *(McDonald Brummel)*

The Hollow Braid Eye Splice shown here is the McDonald Brummel, so named by the American rigger Brion Toss, because it was developed by Margie McDonald. Developed for High Modulus rope, which is renowned for its weakness when knotted; this cross between a knot and a splice can be executed with the minimum of tools providing a fixed eye in any hollow braid, provided it is flexible enough to 'hockle'. It is also worth noting that this splice can be untied if necessary.

Tools required: hollow fid, whipping twine.

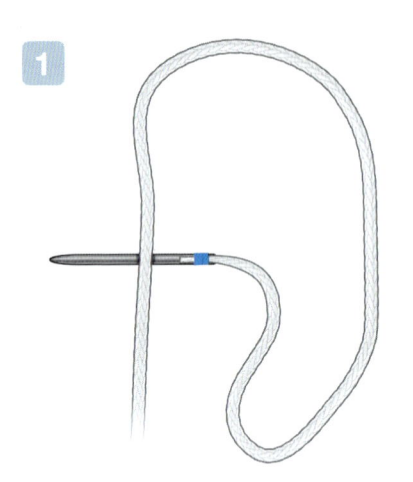

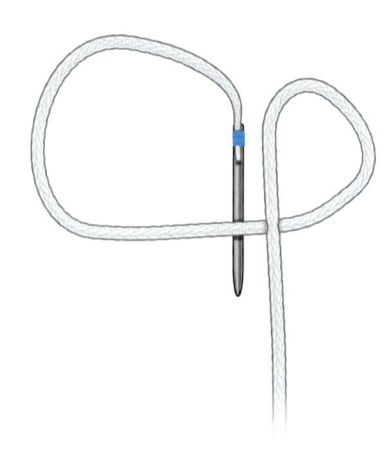

1

Secure the end of the hollow braid line into a hollow fid – or taper the end and use a Swedish fid to open the weave. Measure 72 times the diameter of the rope plus the eye and insert the fid at this point right through the braid. Pull through until the required eye size is formed. Insert the fid through the braid immediately adjacent to the exit point from the standing part.

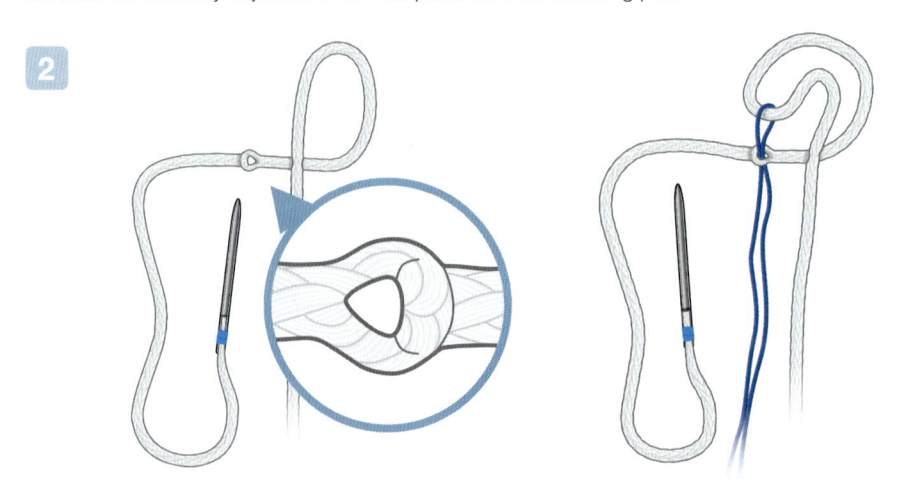

2

Hold the eye with one hand and pull the working end with the other to pull the loop right through itself until a hockle is formed; the rope may need a little massaging to complete this operation. Pull the top of the eye through the hockle – a short length of whipping twine makes this a little easier.

HOLLOW BRAID EYE SPLICE

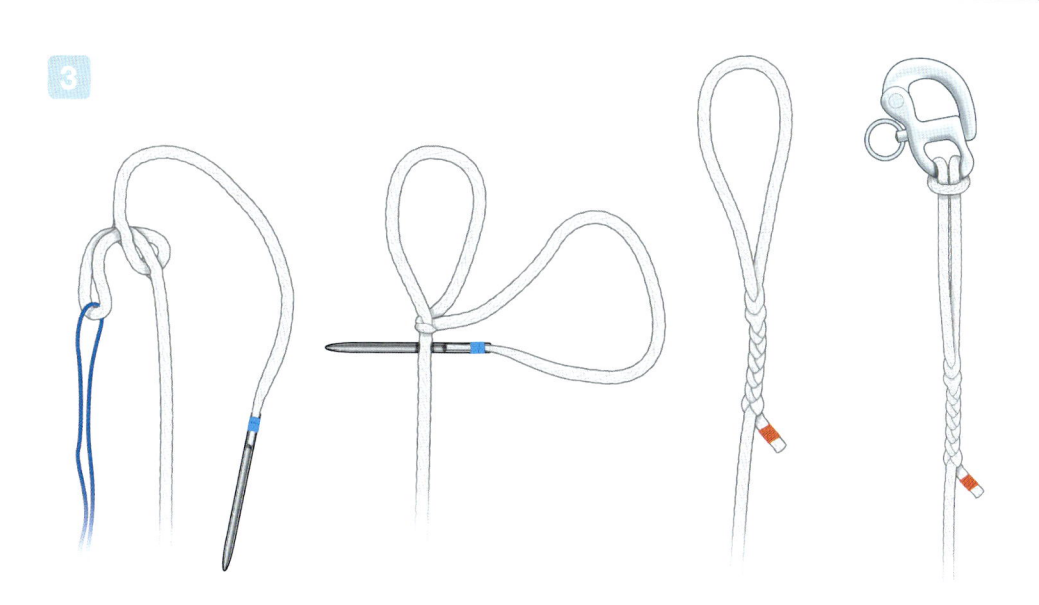

3

Pull the working end right over the eye onto the standing part where the hockle will undo itself and straddle it. Insert the fid immediately below this point and repeat to form a second and then subsequent knots. After the 5th tuck, tape the end cut off neatly.

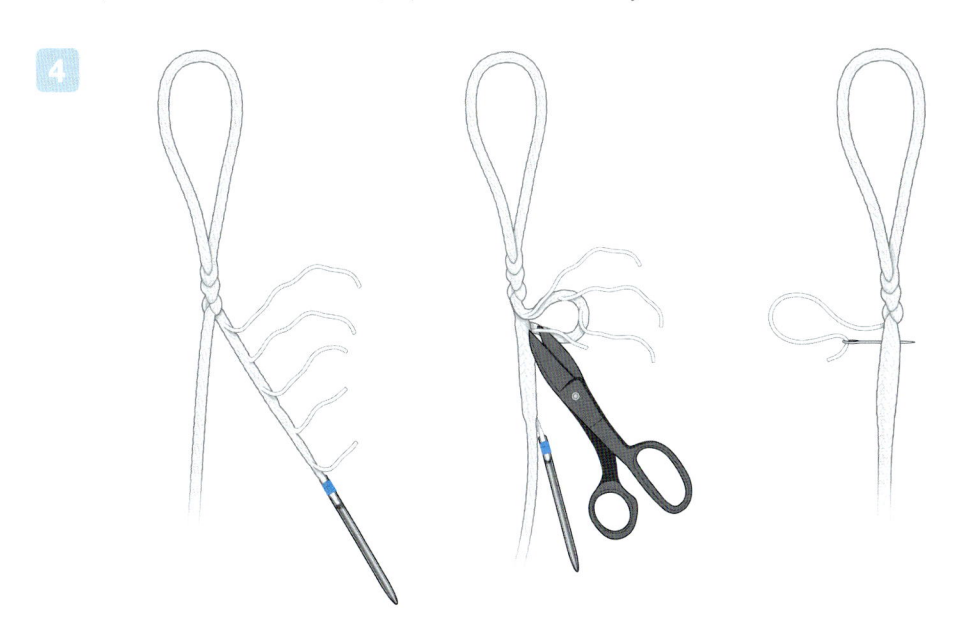

4

A variation on this splice, which gives a neater end and is more secure, is to make one or two Brummels then insert the end into a hollow splicing fid, reduce the working end to a taper by removing 5 or 6 strands at intervals, as shown above. Insert the fid down through the centre of the rope then, as each free strand bends back at the throat, cut it off then pull on the end, repeat until only the last strand is left. Pull the end gently, cut it off, milk it back into the braid then, using the last free strand, stitch the braid where the working end enters the centre of the braid.

Splicing, Serving and Seizing

Yachtsman's Roll Splice

Also known as a 'One Tuck Eye Splice' this neat and strong simple soft eye splice is very simple to execute in small 7 strand wire. The strength in this splice is in the laying up of the two sets of strands in the opposite directions. A single splicing tuck can be made with each of the 6 outer strands, but it does not add to the strength of the splice, neither, it should be noted, does the whipping over the throat; the main purpose of which is to prevent the ends of the strands from snagging and cutting fingers and sail cloth.

Tools required: wire cutters, tape, safety glasses, leather gloves, whipping twine, knife.

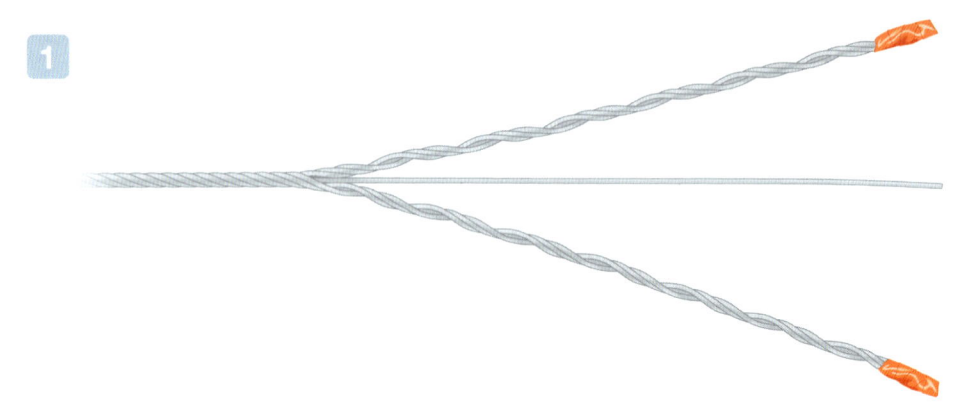

1

Cut the end of the wire clean and square. Take three adjacent strands and unwind them from the other three and the core – then separate the core and tape the ends as shown above. Unlay sufficient to form the eye required plus about 30mm. Tape the ends with insulating tape.

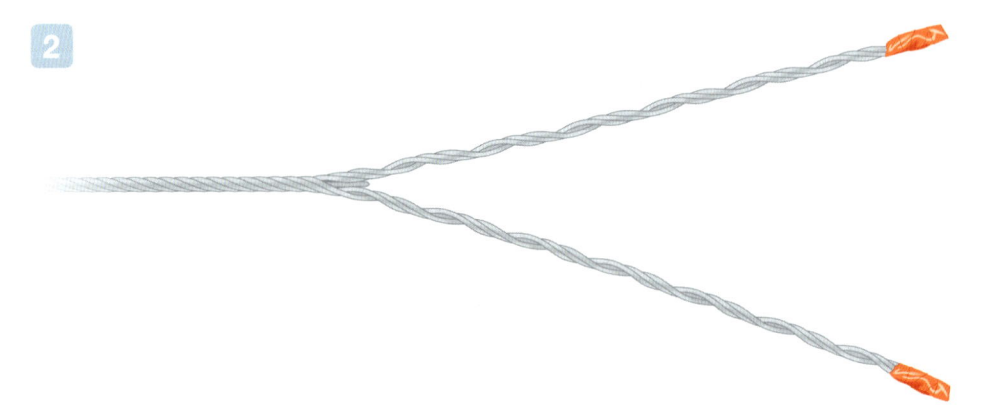

2

Cut the exposed core near the junction. Lay the two sets of three strands up again, so as to just cover the core end.

3

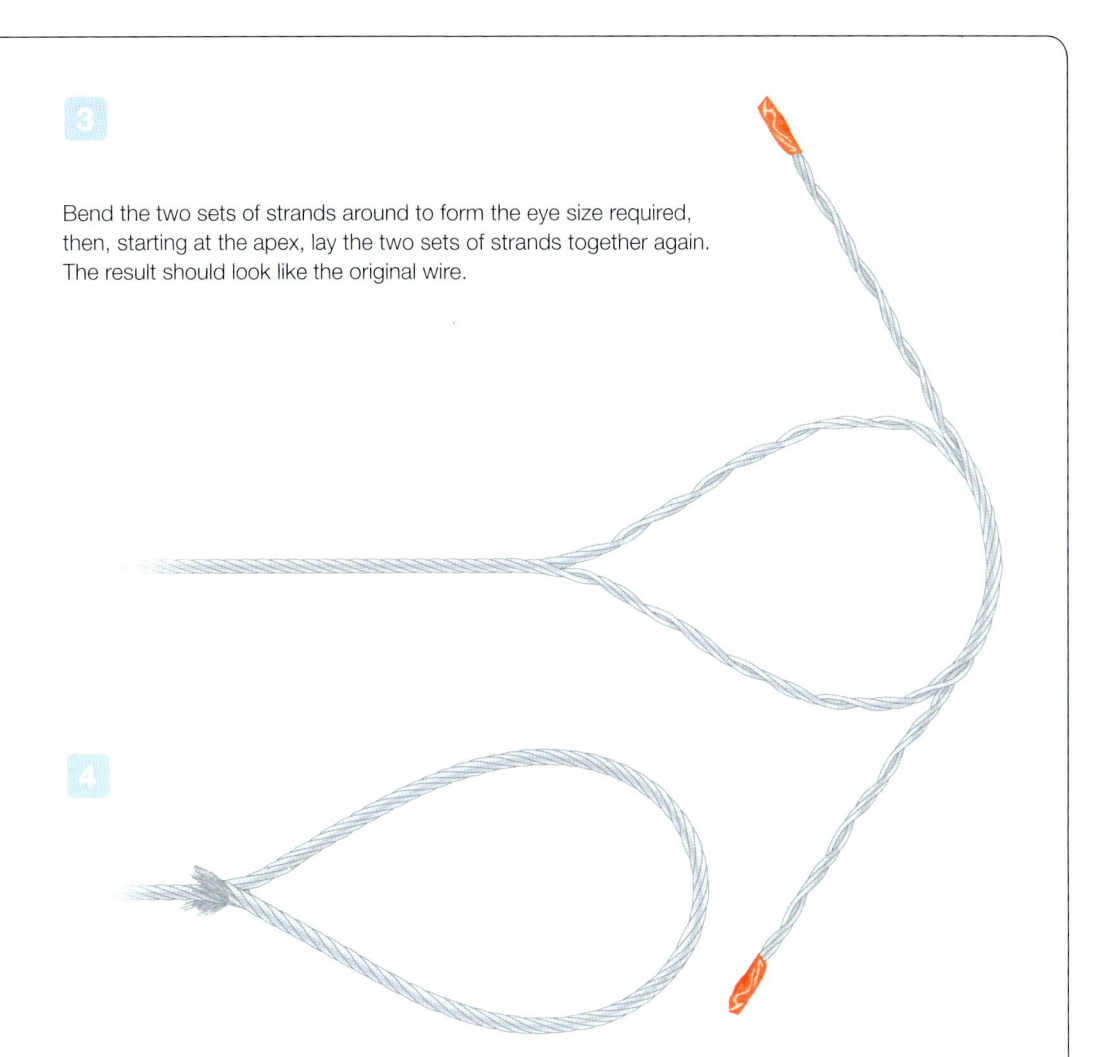

Bend the two sets of strands around to form the eye size required, then, starting at the apex, lay the two sets of strands together again. The result should look like the original wire.

4

Continue to lay up the two sets of strands until they reach the throat, where you should end up with one set on each side of the wire. Lay these flat along the wire and apply a Common Whipping over the ends and the throat as shown below.

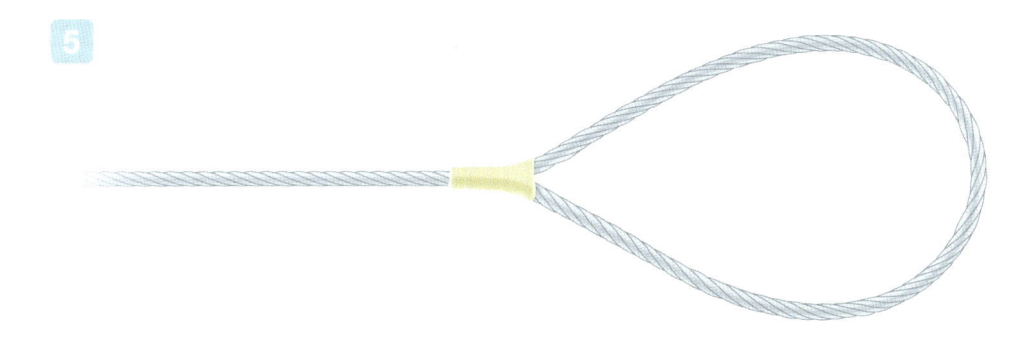

5

Rope to Wire Splice

Joining a rope to a wire halyard, so that it can be used in hand, sounds a daunting prospect; but if you can splice three strand rope, this is no more difficult. The rope, which can be braid on braid or braid with a three strand core, should have a diameter approximately twice the diameter of the wire. The wire shown here is 7 strand (6 preformed strands around a single core), if any other strand combinations are used they will need to be apportioned to suit the splice.

Tools required: wire cutters, (gloves and eye protection should also be used when working with wire) pliers, tape, Swedish fid, hot knife, tape measure, hollow fid, needle.

PREPARING THE WIRE

The first stage is to taper the end of the wire. Unlay and cut - one strand back along the wire about 18cm, the second strand 15cm, the third 12cm and the fourth 9cm; leaving two strands around the core to full length. Make sure there are no protruding filaments, then, using electrical insulation tape, cover the taper, taking care to bind over all the ends.

PREPARING THE ROPE

Tie a stopper knot (Alpine Butterfly) about 3 metres from the end of the rope – this prevents the cover from creeping too far back along the rope. Very lightly tape the cover just back from the heat sealed end of the rope, then cut off the heat seal. Hold the end of the core and push the cover back towards the knot until you have exposed about 60cm of core – put a needle through the cover and core to hold it in this position. Cut 15cm off the end of the core and tape the end. Now measure 40cm from the new end of the core and wrap a band of tape around it at this point.

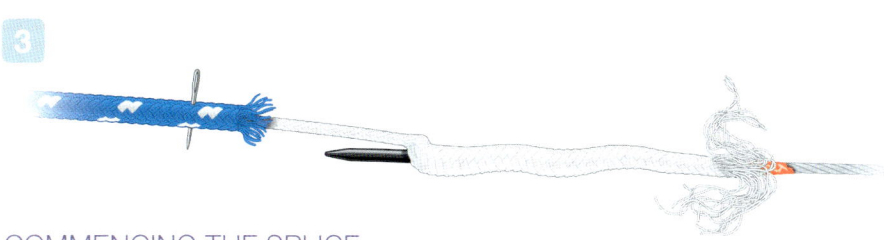

COMMENCING THE SPLICE

With a 3 strand core, untwist the lay near the 40cm tape and insert the end of the wire into the centre of the lay, then continue laying the wire, like a core, into the centre of the three strands to a point just past where the tapering began. Tape the core to the wire at this point and remove the end tape from the core.

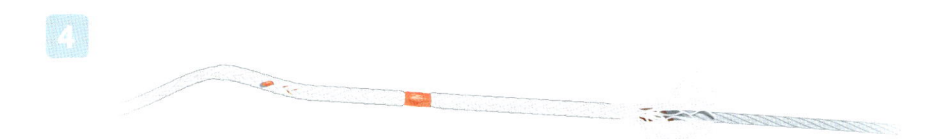

With a braided core, insert the end of the wire through the middle of the core, using a hollow fid, until it reaches the 40cm tape. Make sure the core is pulled tight down on the wire then tape it just past the point where the tapering began. Remove the end tape and unlay the core strands back to this tape. Divide the core strands into 3 groups (using adjacent strands – makes for a neater splice) and tape the end of each group.

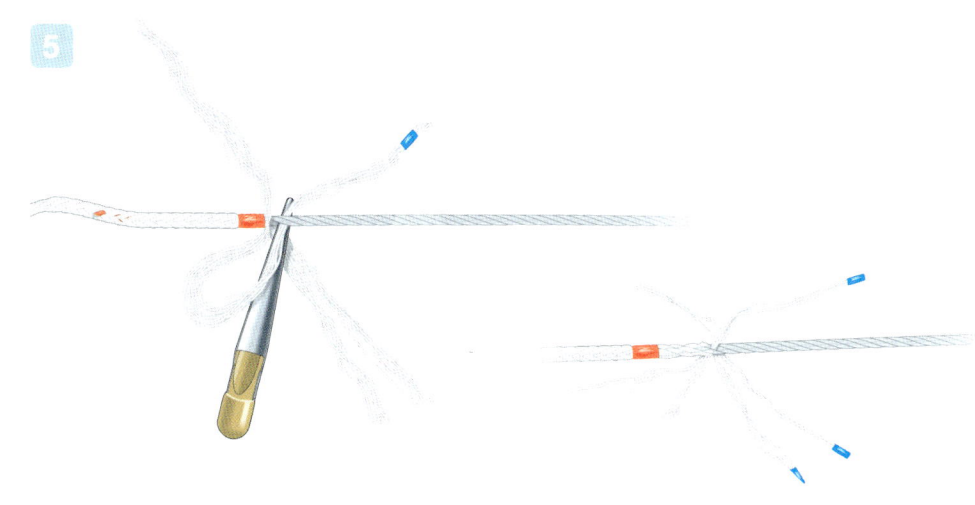

Splice the core to the wire, just as you would an ordinary three strand splice, except that you lay each tuck under two strands of wire. A Swedish fid, inserted between two strands then pushed down at an angle onto a hard surface will separate two strands fairly easily; if you are having difficulty clamp the core and wire end of the splice and using a pair of pliers/grips, gently untwist the lay until the fid goes in easily. Take GREAT CARE not to damage or catch any of the wire filaments or the core – if you don't have two clean strands of wire over your fid – take it out and re-enter the wire at a different point. Put in 5 tucks, tapering the last 3 by removing one strand from each tuck. Cut the ends off.

| ROPE TO WIRE SPLICE

6

COMPLETING THE SPLICE

Remove the needle holding the cover back, then starting from the knot, milk the cover down towards the wire (you may need to remove the end tape to allow it to pass over the first splice) until the end of the cover is at least 15cm past the core to wire splice. Put a Common Whipping on the cover where the core to wire splice ends.

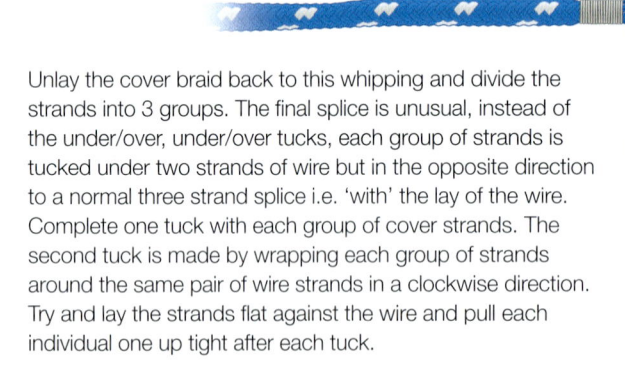

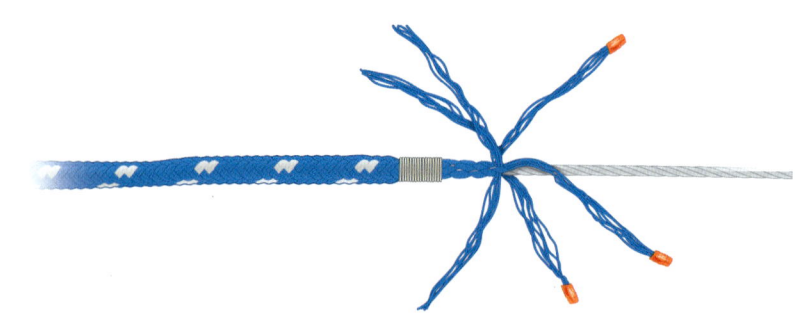

7

Unlay the cover braid back to this whipping and divide the strands into 3 groups. The final splice is unusual, instead of the under/over, under/over tucks, each group of strands is tucked under two strands of wire but in the opposite direction to a normal three strand splice i.e. 'with' the lay of the wire. Complete one tuck with each group of cover strands. The second tuck is made by wrapping each group of strands around the same pair of wire strands in a clockwise direction. Try and lay the strands flat against the wire and pull each individual one up tight after each tuck.

8

Make three more full tucks, then taper the splice as you go by removing one or two strands. The end result should be a tapered spiral. Cut the ends off up close, then, if you wish, lay a serving over the taper to make a nice neat end.

9

Three Strand Rope Grommet

Rope grommets are used for a number of secondary tasks in ropework. For deck games it becomes a quoit, for a sewn eye it is a foundation, around a wooden block it is a strop and no doubt you can think of many others. One note of caution, not all three strand rope is suitable to lay up into a grommet in this fashion – especially the softer laid man-made fibres, which do not hold their shape when unlaid. To make a 'set' of grommets, for sewn eyes or other small jobs, you will need to make them all the same size; this is done by marking a wooden fid along from the tip to where each grommet is pushed and the end knot tightened down. One strand of a three strand rope will make one grommet the same size as the rope.

Tools required: knife, Swedish fid (wooden fid), tape measure.

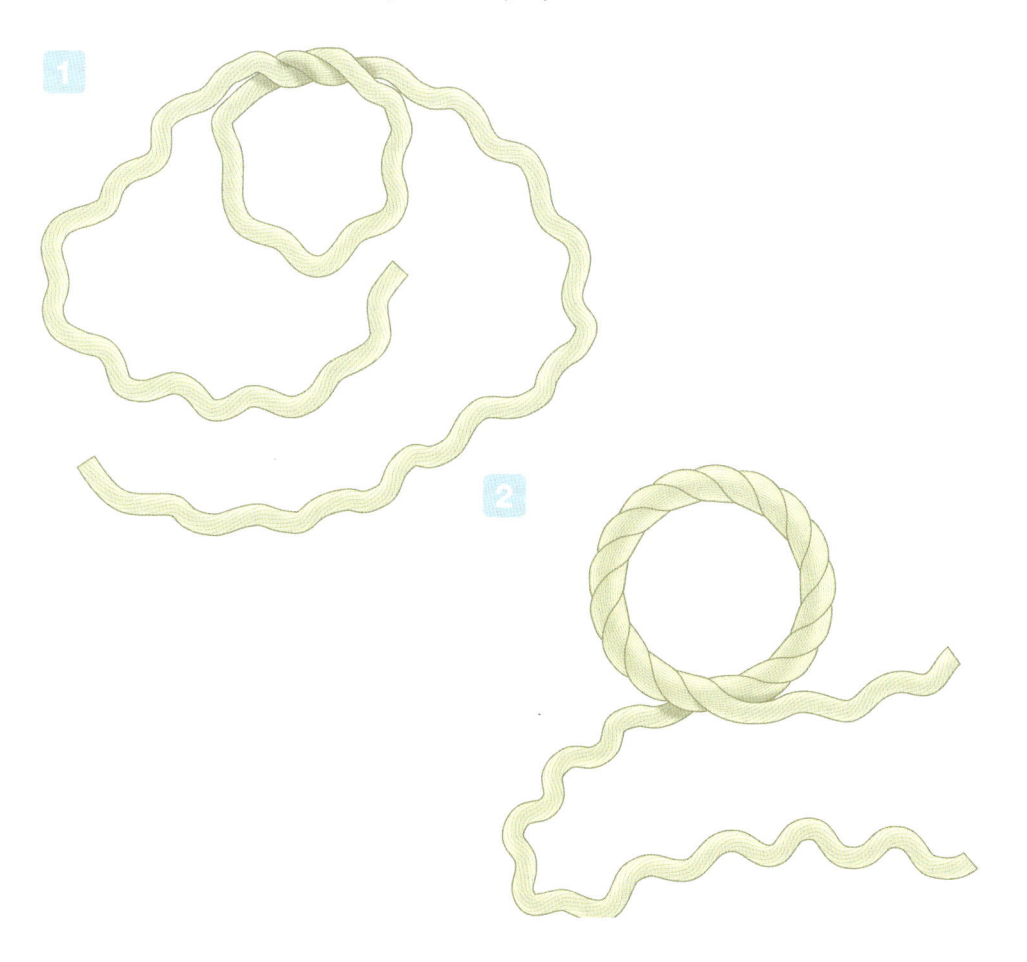

Cut the rope to the required length (three and a half times circumference of the grommet required) and unlay one strand from the rope. Centre the strand, then tie and overhand knot at the point which makes the grommet the size required. The left and right strands should bed into each other looking like 2 strand rope. Now lay one of the strands, all the way round the grommet. It helps to give the strand a twist as you lay it in. You now have a 2 strand grommet, into which the remaining strand will be laid.

THREE STRAND ROPE GROMMET

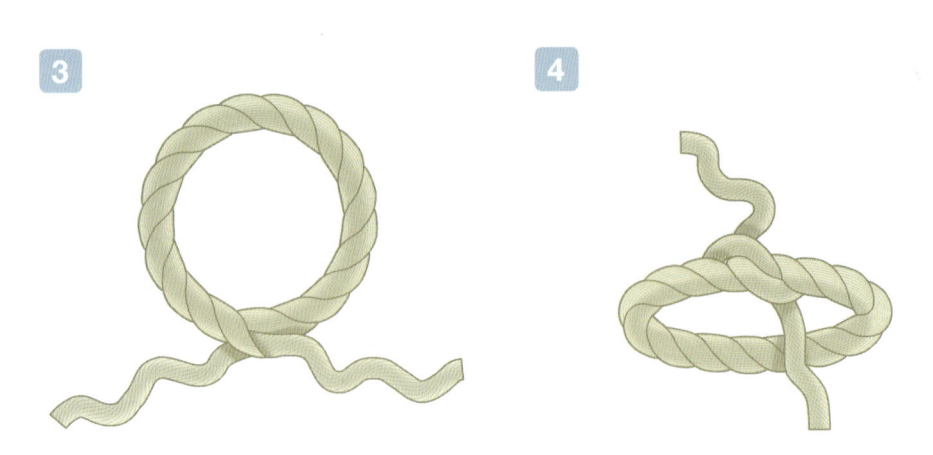

3

4

Lay the final strand in by twisting it up tight as you lay – the grommet should look exactly like the original rope with all three strands snug. You should end up with the two ends emerging in the same space in opposite directions. Tie a Half Knot (left over right) with the two ends then pull up tight so that they bed into the lay as shown in diagram 5.

5

6

Complete the join by splicing the ends over/under/over/under into the grommet – reducing the yarns as you progress.

TIP FROM THE BOSUN'S LOCKER

If the Half Knot join does not bed down into the lay at about the same diameter as the rope – halve each strand, tie the Half Knot with the two upper halves of each strand, pull up, then splice all four ends into the grommet.

Serving

A service is put on a wire or fibre rope (or even rails and handles), to protect the rope from wear, help in its preservation, stop wire strands from springing out of a splice, hand protection (and sometimes comfort) and, among other things, decoration.

There are four main elements to serving, the first is preparation for preservation (tar, preservative, lanolin etc), this is followed up by 'Worming', the process of filling the lay between the strands with yarns to avoid spaces (which could trap water) beneath the 'Parcelling' which is the next process whereby the rope and worming are now effectively bandaged, using canvas or tape – each of these processes are in turn treated with preservative. Finally the 'Service' is laid on and also treated with preservative (even hand rails should be either treated with a transparent water based varnish, (wood preservative also works on natural fibre ropes), or paint. There is a long established reminder that goes with serving – "Worm and Parcel with the lay, turn and Serve the other way".

Treat the rope with an appropriate preservative, then, using fibre rope yarns, lay as many as are necessary to fill the grooves between each strand, working with the lay of the rope – these too should be treated or pre-treated. Snug the worming down into the lay, just hand taut – it should not disturb the lay of the rope. Bandage over the worming using pre-treated strips of canvas or a cloth based tape, again working with the lay of the rope so as to work with the worming.

Having completed the preparation, serving can now begin – this can be from left to right or right to left, but, remember two more 'rules' – if the worming and parcelling turned to the right the serving must turn to the left, or vice-versa also when serving over a splice, work from the standing part towards the splice. Start by laying the end of the serving along the rope towards the direction you are going to lay the line on, put a couple of turns on by hand to hold it then offer up the serving mallet or board and wind the line on to it – over the head, round the handle, under the rope, over the head and up the handle – tighten the first two turns then proceed to rotate the mallet around the rope. For large jobs you will need someone to pass the ball of serving line around the work, for small jobs a hank (wound in an 8) with the line drawn from the centre can be managed by one person.

2

To finish the serving – make the last 6 to 10 turns over a Swedish fid or marlinspike as shown in diagram 2, but before making the turns, insert a length of 'heaving line' which is long enough to hold and pull on (blue line in diagram). Tuck the end of the seizing back under the last turns and pull up taut.

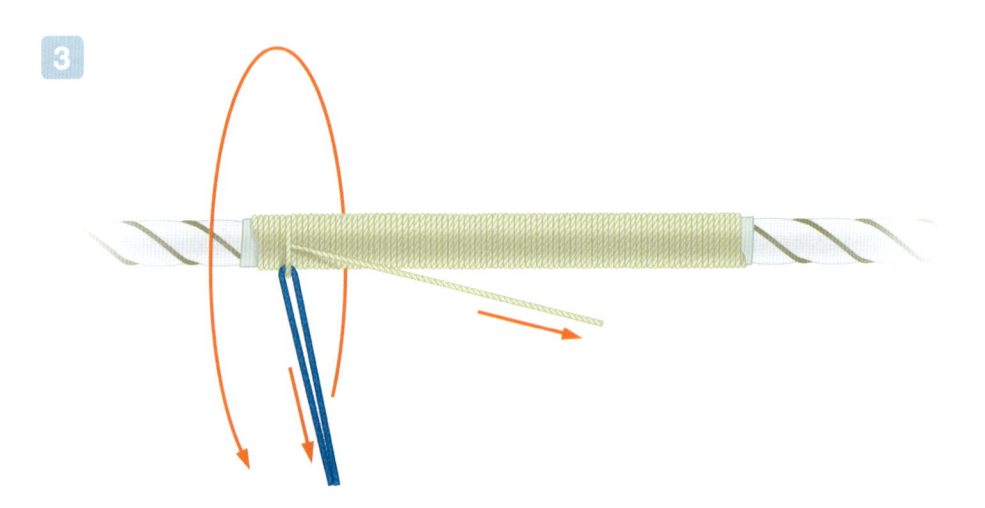

3

Now lay the last turns up tight by laying back on the 'heaving line' to tighten the turn, then rotating it around the rope. When complete pull on the end of the serving and cut it off up close to the turns.

4

Seizing

Seizing, not to be confused with whipping, is used to marry two ropes, where a splice is not possible or inappropriate. There are two commonly used seizings, the Flat Seizing which is for light work and has only one layer of turns and the Round Seizing for heavy loading, which has two layers of turns.

FLAT SEIZING

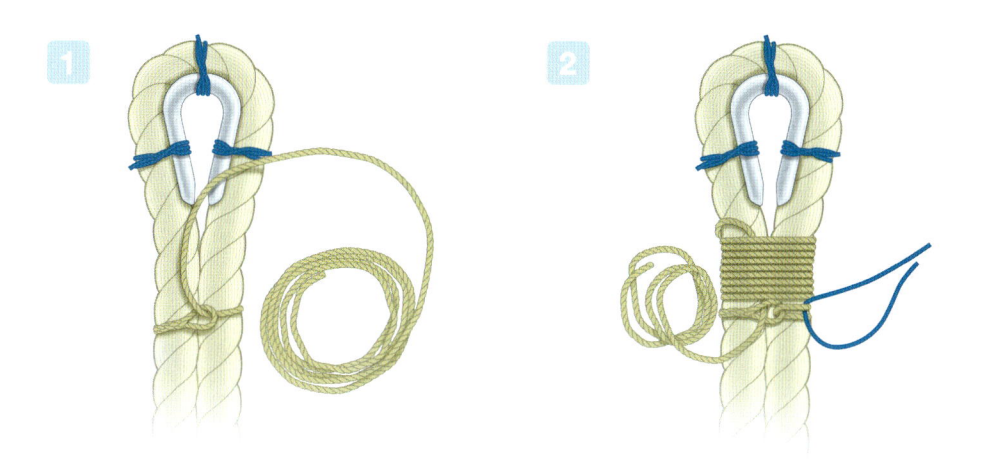

Make an eye (Splice or Timber Hitch) in the end of the seizing line and pass the other end through it around the two parts of rope to be seized. Loosely lay on sufficient turns (6 to 10 is normally sufficient) then tuck the working end under the turns and through the eye again. The turns are now pulled up as tight as possible – this can be done with a 'heaving line' in the same manner as used in Serving on page 178.

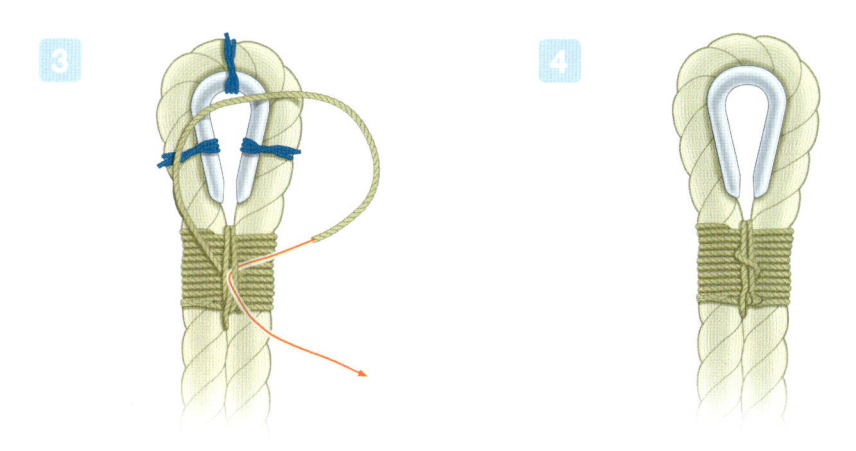

Pass two frapping turns tightly around the turns of the seizing and between the two rope parts. Secure the end with one or two half hitches around the frapping as shown.

ROUND SEIZING

1

2

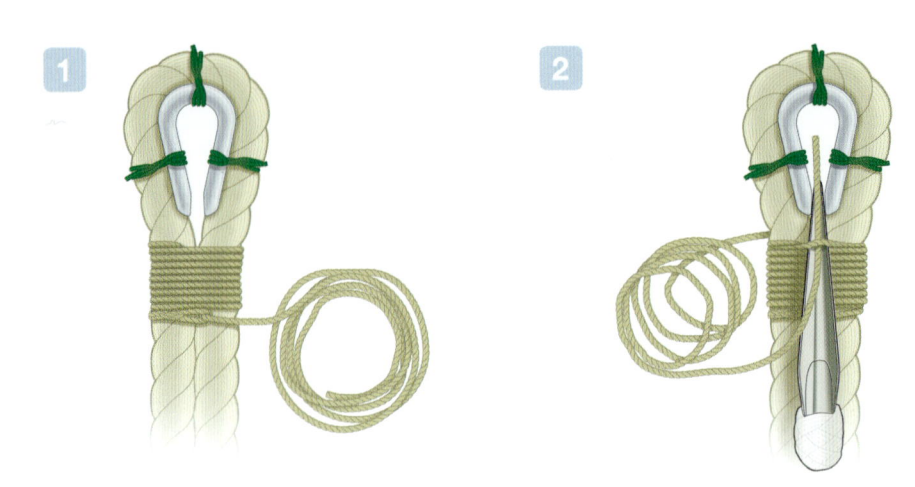

Start the Round Seizing using the same procedure as a Flat Seizing but this time with an ODD number of turns and ensuring they are very tight. The second layer of turns is laid on from the point where the working end is passed through the eye of the seizing, on top of the first layer, with an EVEN number of turns laying in the grooves between the lower layer turns. Pass the working end under the top lower turn before making two frapping turns between the two rope parts.

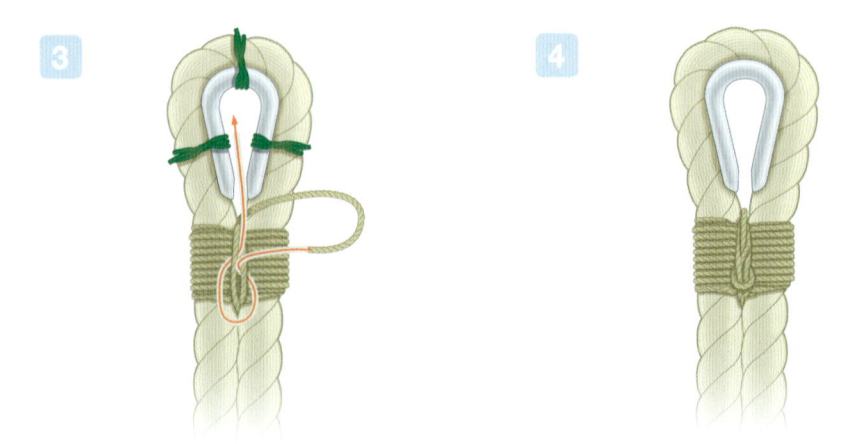

3

4

Secure the end with one or two hitches as shown in diagram 3, cut off the end and tuck it under the seizing.

CHAPTER 11:

MARLINESPIKE ROPEWORK

TURK'S HEAD KNOTS
STAR KNOT
DECORATIVE RAIL COVERINGS
KING-SPOKE TURK'S HEAD
TWO SHORT LANYARDS
KNIFE LANYARD
BINOCULARS LANYARD
SPECTACLES LANYARD
THUMP MAT
MAST DROPPER
CABIN STRINGS
OCEAN PLAIT MAT
SQUARE MAT
SIDE FENDER
DISC FENDER
BELL ROPE
BAGGY WRINKLE
LEAD LINE

Introduction: Marlinespike Ropework

This final chapter introduces some 'Advanced knotting' and is aimed at the accomplished knot tyer or enthusiastic learner. The selection of knots and projects featured are a mixture of those one frequently asks "How do I do….?", and one or two that are not featured in most available books but worthy of keeping alive. Starting with how to tie three Turk's Head Knots, a 'King Spoke' Knot, and the Star Knot, the chapter then continues with, 'how to make' some of those practical projects in rope and line (save your old rope and recycle it making some of these) that you wished you knew how to do, but don't; including, lanyards, rope mats, fenders, baggy wrinkle, a bell rope, boat lead line and a selection of decorative and traditional boat ropework.

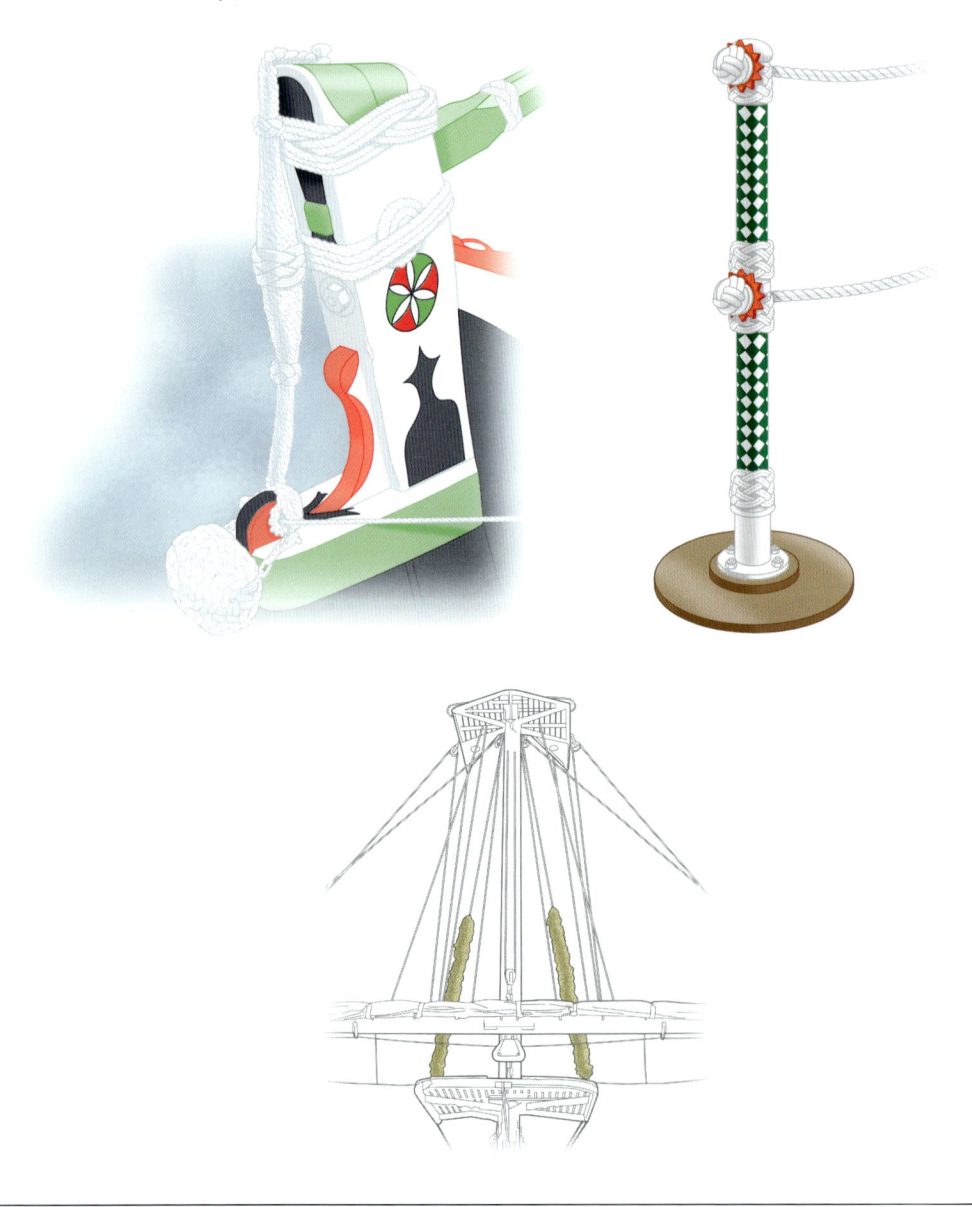

Turk's Head Knots

The Turk's Head Knot has practical applications as well as providing decoration or adornment and comes in many forms, each defined by the number of bights around its edge and the number of leads from one edge to the other – these in turn are multiplied with passes, usually two or three, but more passes are possible.

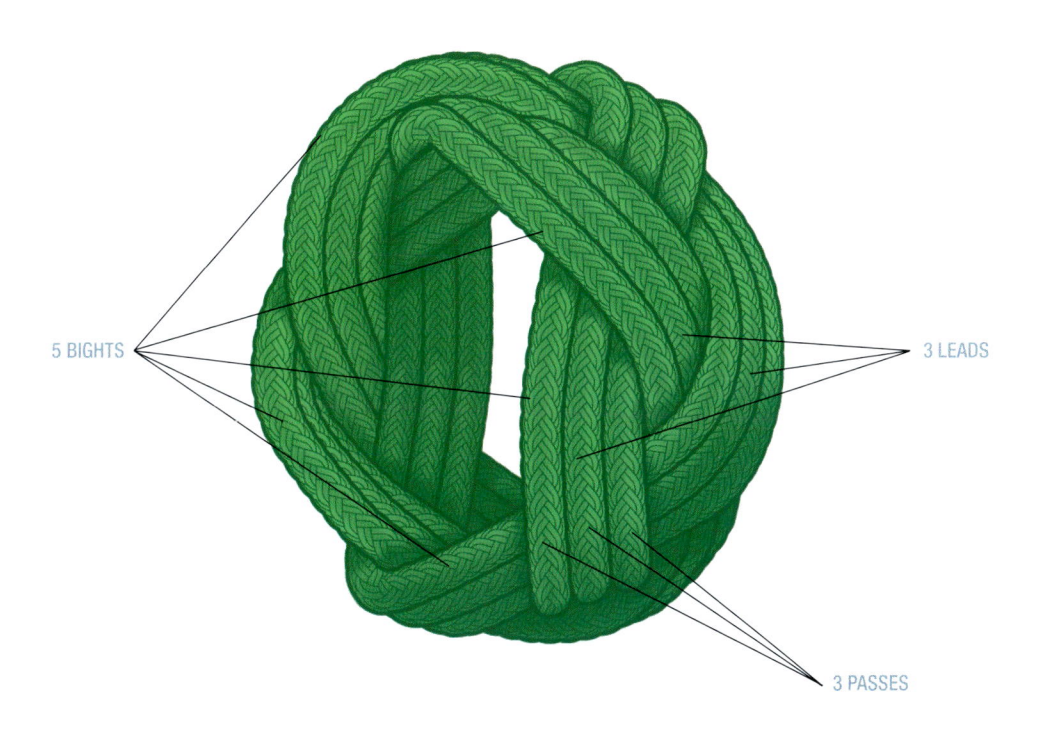

5 BIGHTS → ← 3 LEADS

3 PASSES

3 LEAD 5 BIGHT TURK'S HEAD

Turk's Heads are also said to be 'long' (more leads than bights), or 'wide' (more bights than leads). Two of the most commonly used Turk's Head knots, both of which are basic forms which can be enlarged and a third which starts the King-Spoke Turk's Head, are described in this chapter.

TURK'S HEAD - 3 LEAD 4 BIGHT

This Turk's Head is easy to learn and will provide a good grounding for beginners to grasp the over/under/over/under sequence of these knots. This one is the basis for a 'long' Turk's Head and can be increased by adding more leads (see 6 Lead 5 Bight Turk's Head).

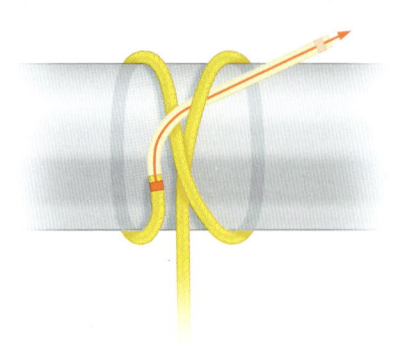

1

Start as if you are going to tie a Clove Hitch but instead of passing the working end under the crossover go over the top and under the right hand lead.

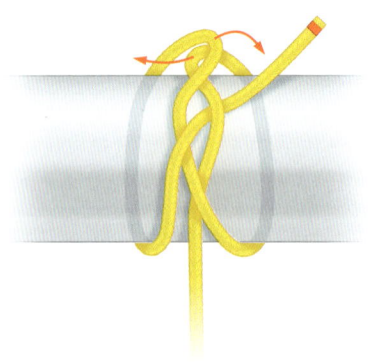

2

The first over/under sequence complete, pick up the top left hand lead and cross it over the right hand lead – to form two cross-overs beyond each of which is an aperture.

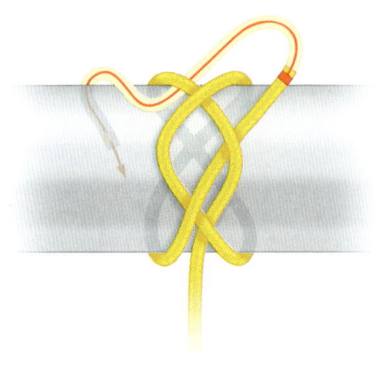

3

Tuck the working end down through the first by going over then under the standing part.

4

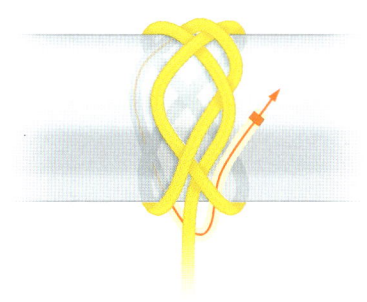

Then over and down through the remaining aperture over and under to emerge alongside the standing part to complete the knot.

5

Follow the lead around to make the second, then if necessary subsequent passes. Now tighten the knot gradually starting at one end, a little at a time taking care not to pull the outer bights too tight, or the knot will distort. The knot should be tight enough to hold the two ends concealed under the knot – gently pull them and cut up close so that they shrink back into the knot and are hidden from view.

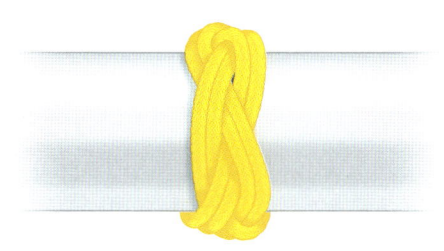

6

TURK'S HEAD - 3 LEAD 5 BIGHT

This basic 5 bight Turk's Head Knot can be developed into quite a large 'wide' knot to make a hat band or bracelet, simply by adding more crossovers in the initial sequence.

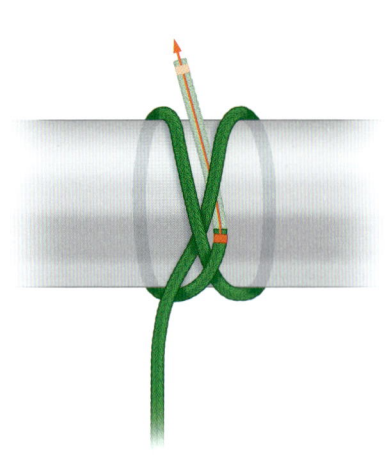

1

Start as if you were going to tie a Clove Hitch but this time go under the standing part and over the crossover then up under the standing part.

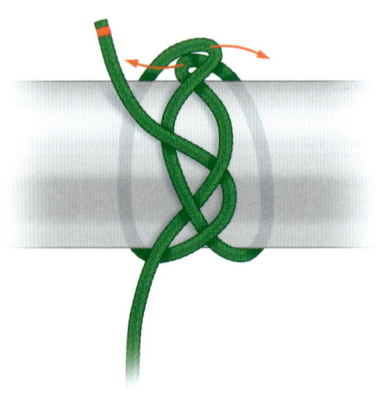

2

Take the top left bight and pass it over the right hand bight forming two new crossovers. Take great care not to lose the crossover at the back of the knot – it is very easy to do.

TURK'S HEAD KNOTS | 187

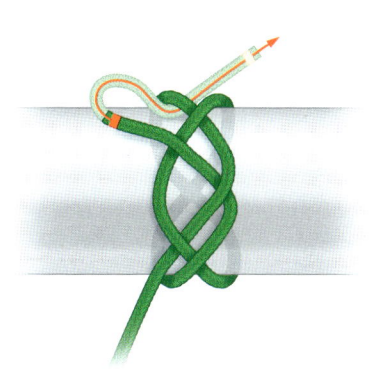

3

Continue the over/under/over sequence from left to right, right to left. This is the point at which more crossovers can be added to increase the size of the knot.

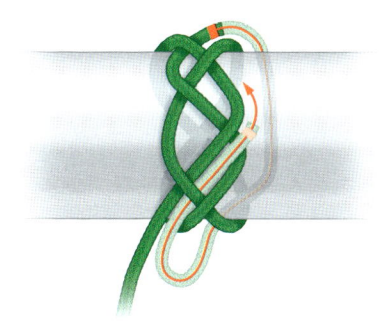

4

The working end should now emerge alongside the standing part to commence the double or triple passes.

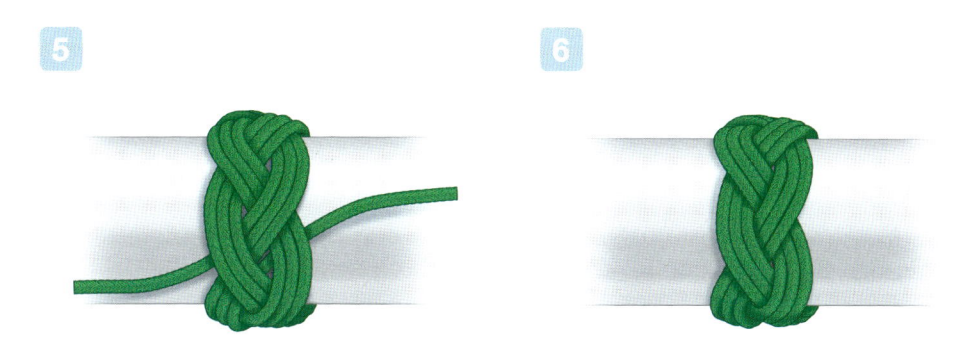

5

6

Tighten the knot gradually from one end taking care not to pull the outer bights too tight. Make sure the ends are securely tucked under the knot and emerge from the bights, cut them off so that they shrink back into the knot.

TURK'S HEAD - 6 LEAD 5 BIGHT

A slightly more complex knot, which has been drawn so that you can study the construction and follow the first pass around more easily; using the standing part as a reference point for each lead. You will of course have to spread the crossovers around the mandrel before tightening the knot. This Turk's Head is also the basis for tying the King-Spoke Turk's Head described later in the chapter.

To estimate the length of line required, wrap the line around the mandrel loosely 6 times the number of passes you are going to put in the knot and add 4 turns for handling – in this example 6x2=12+4 =16 turns.

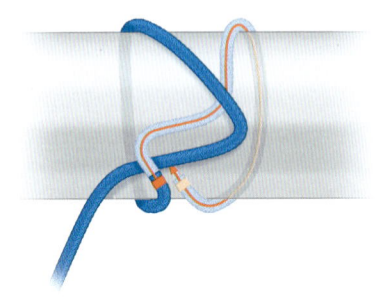

1

Using a cylindrical mandrel, or your hand, tie a Half Knot around it and shape the standing part as shown above. Bring the working end back round to meet the standing part in front of the mandrel (pass 1).

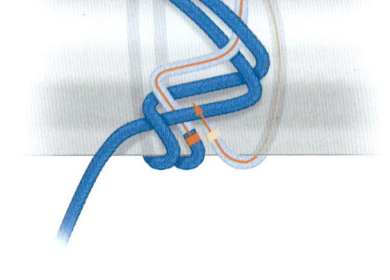

2

Pass 1 went over the standing part so this one goes under/over, then over/under and round to meet the standing part again.

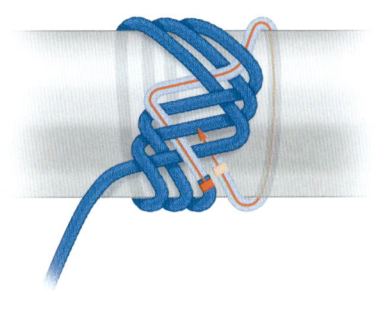

3

You can now see the over/under pattern beginning to build up and a regular sequence being followed by the working end through the knot. The last lead went under, so for this one, pass 3 goes over/under/over/under/over/under and round to meet the standing part again.

4

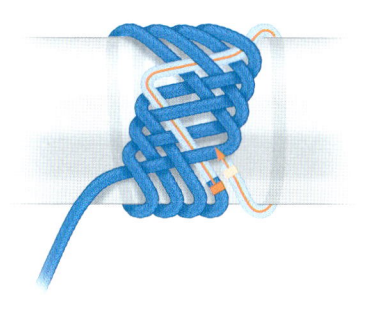

The last pass 3 went over the standing part so for this one, pass 4 goes under/over/under/over, then over/under/over/under and round to meet the standing part again.

5

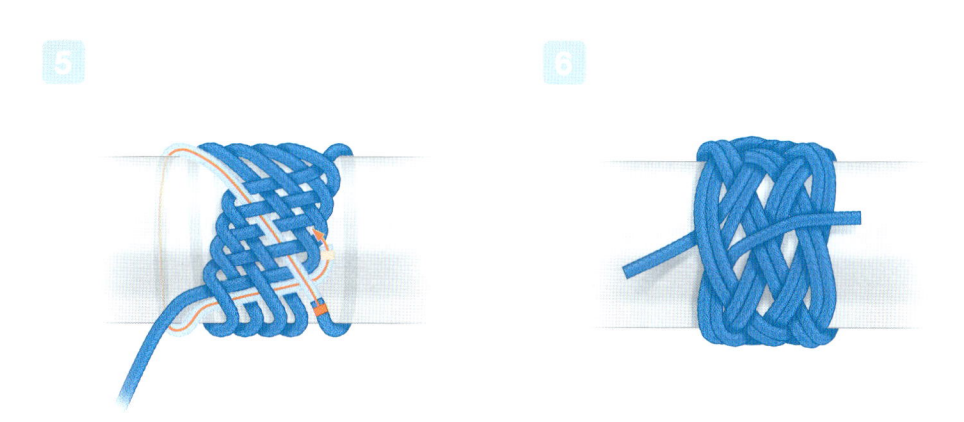

The final lead goes over the standing part then under/over/under/over before emerging beside the standing part, ready to make the second pass through the knot, as shown.

6

The completed knot of two passes. Further passes can be added, to bulk the knot out, or different colour line inserted between or outside of the two initial passes.

7

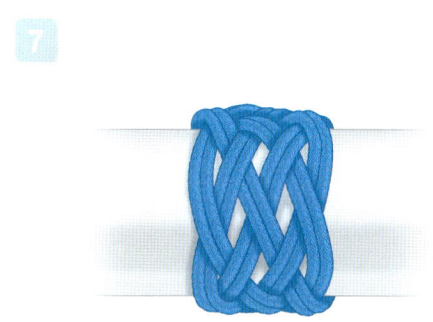

Star Knot

This, perhaps the king of decorative knots, is used to end or break up a sequence of braiding or to increase or decrease the number of lines being used in decorative cords; almost any number of cords can be used, but more than six will require a core. Its most common use is in the stem of a Bell Rope. Do not be frightened by the apparent complexity of the weave, just keep it small and neat, work round the knot in sequence and you will soon master it. Shown here is a five point knot, which is a manageable number to begin with.

Tools required: knife, whipping twine, Swedish fid.

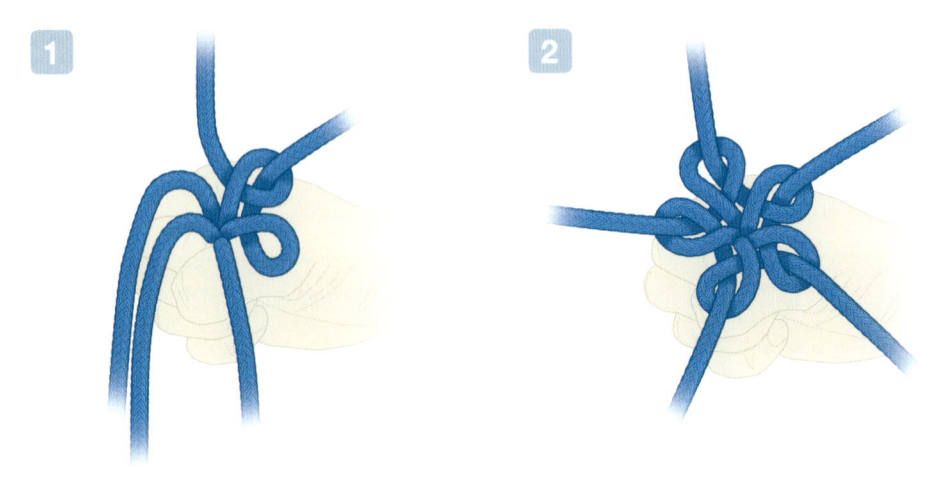

Bundle together 5 pieces of cord and tie a Constrictor Knot around them about 30cm from one end. Hold the bunch in a closed fist with the thumb and index finger uppermost to form a flat surface to work on. Make a small underhand loop with one cord, and again with the next adjacent cord – pass the working end through the previous loop, as shown in diagram 1. Continue round the knot in sequence until you arrive at the knot in diagram 2.

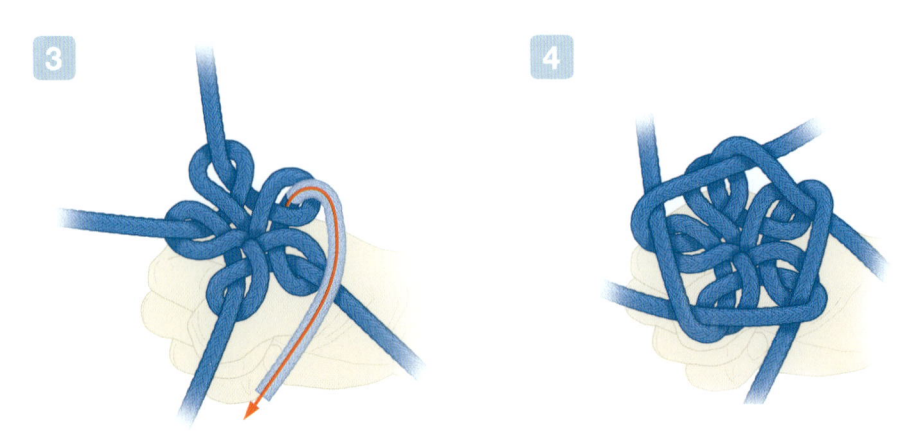

Next, crown each of the cords back over itself as shown in diagram 3, until you arrive at the knot in diagram 4 – at this point, tidy up the knot so that you have a symmetrical, equally spaced knot, because from now on it is easy to get lost.

Turn each cord back until it meets the one to its right, then follow that cord through the knot and down through the loop that it emerges from. Tuck it into your hand with the bunch so as not to confuse it with those cords not yet used. Follow on round the knot until you have all the cords in your fist. Release the cords you have just tied and the result should look like diagram 6.

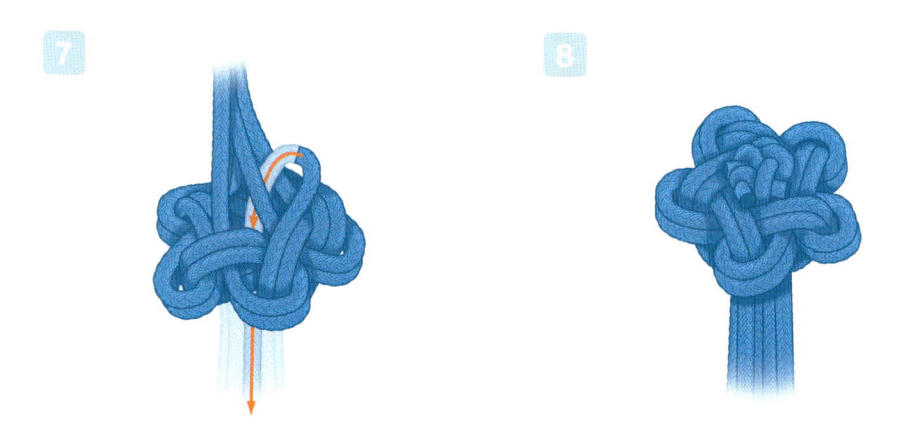

The final tuck is made by turning the knot upside down and passing each of the cords over its neighbour to the right and down through the centre of the knot.

At this point your knot is ready for dressing into its final shape. Start where one cord comes from the core and follow it round the knot, pulling it up gently – continue round the knot in sequence until you arrive back at the first cord, now adjust each cord so that the knot looks symmetrical, neat and fairly tight (not too tight or it is likely to distort). You can now continue using the cords to make a braid, or if the knot is to end a piece of work, tuck the ends back through the centre of the knot again and crown them as shown in diagram 8 and then push them down into the centre.

Decorative Rail, Spar & Stanchion Coverings

Here are 4 methods of covering cylindrical rails, boat hook handles, stanchions, hand holds and the like. They are all very easy to learn and execute but still need a degree of care in their pulling up – keeping the tension even. Wooden objects can be covered bare, although a coat of varnish should be applied first, metal objects should be covered with cloth tape, the type that climbers use on their fingers is ideal.

SERVING

Ideal for serving over handrails and tool handles, as it has a smooth finish. Apply using the instructions for Serving on page 177, but make sure that the line is laid on really tight.

FRENCH HITCHING

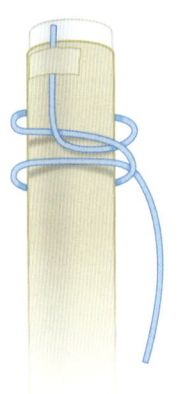

Tape the end of a single line to the object to be covered (wither as shown here or under the turns) then proceed to tie Half Hitches, in the same direction all the time, pulling each one up tight and back against the previous hitch. Lay on the last 6 hitches over a hollow fid or spike, pass the end back up into the hitching, tighten the last 6 turns as tight as possible then pull the end alongside the spiral (so that it does not show so much) and cut it off. The resultant spiral will be to the right or left depending on which way you lay on the hitches.

MOKU HITCHING

Moku Hitching results in a left and right spiral with crossings. Start with a Clove Hitch, then hitch the end from the right, to the right and the end from the left to the left. Lay the last 6 turns over a hollow fid or spike, pass both ends back up the hitching, tighten the last 6 hitches, pull the ends tight and alongside the hitching before cutting them off.

ST MARY'S HITCHING

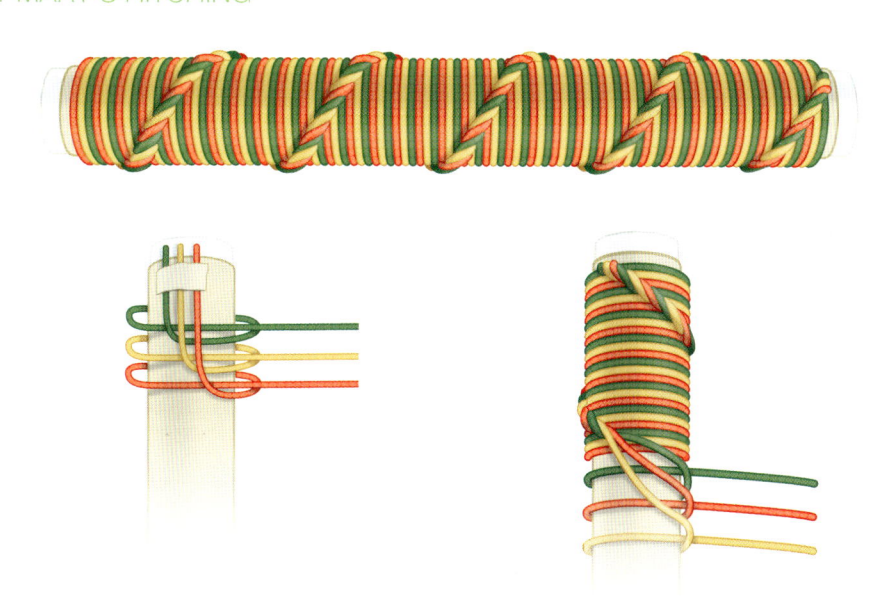

We have Brion Toss to thank for this beautiful spiral rope effect hitching. Tape three strands (shown here in different colours for clarity – but a single colour looks just as good) either outside the turns if you are going to put a Turk's Head on the ends, or under the turns. Half Hitch each one to the right (or left) as shown in diagram 1, i.e. Half Hitch cord 1, pass cord 2 over 1 and Half Hitch, pass cord 3 over 1 and 2 and Half Hitch. Pull all three hitches up tight together and back against the hitches above. Finish by laying the last 6 hitches over a hollow fid or spike, pass the ends back under the hitches, pull the last 6 up as tight as possible then pull the ends close to the spiral and cut them off.

King-Spoke Turk's Head

The 'midships', or 'king-spoke' of a helm wheel is usually marked as a reference for the helmsman. Here is a method which, although taking time and patience, will enhance your craft with a touch of handsome marlinespike knot-work.

Identify the king-spoke; then if the wheel rim is bare metal, make sure it is clean and dry, before applying a single layer of cloth tape around the rim extending about 2 inches (50mm), each side of the spoke.

STAGE 1   Tying the 6 lead by 5 bight Turk's Head 'former'.

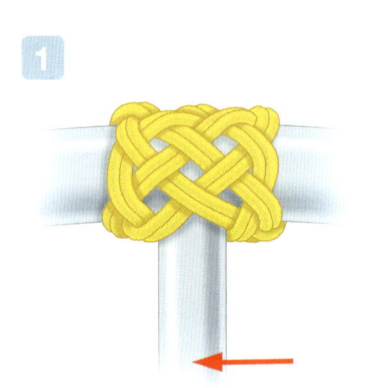

Using a piece of spare line 2.5m long and the about the same diameter as the line you have selected for the final knot, tie a 6 Lead 5 Bight Turk's Head Knot (p188) loosely on the wheel rim; passing the first turn over the wheel rim and to the right of the spoke, 2nd, 3rd and 4th turns to the left of the spoke and the 5th and 6th turns to the right again. On completion of the single Turk's Head, double the lead to the right of the original lead; taking care not to make the knot too tight – you will be laying in a further lead later, so leave plenty of room for it. Carry out a check that the pairs of leads go in an under/over/under sequence throughout the knot.

STAGE 2   Starting the King-spoke knot.

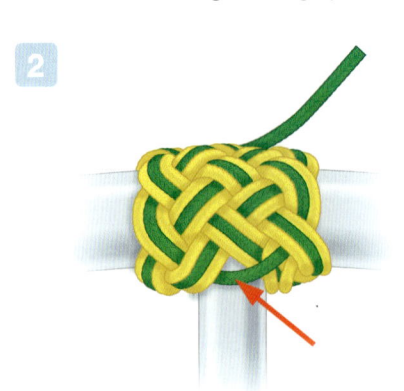

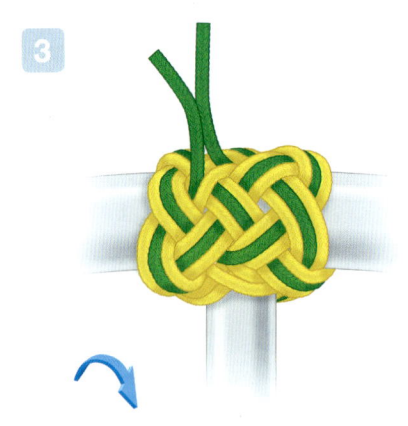

From the table (opposite), select the diameter and length of line to make the final knot. Locate where two pairs of the 'former' Turk's Head cross in the centre at the top of the wheel rim. Insert the end of your line between the pair that go under the crossing. Draw about half the line through. Continue through the knot between that same pair, until you get to the point where it is about to pass the king-spoke, then, instead of passing the spoke, bring the line in front of it and up into the same pair that came from the other side of the spoke (see diagram). You should now make one under tuck before crossing where you started. Continue laying the line between the pair of 'former'

leads until you reach the point where two pairs cross directly in front of the king-spoke on the other side of the wheel. Redirect your line across in front of the spoke and into the pair that pass under the pair you have just left. Continue between the pairs until you reach the point where you started, completing a modified Turk's Head of one pass.

Approximate rim/line measurements

WHEEL RIM DIAMETER	LINE DIAMETER	LINE LENGTH
19mm	2mm	2.0 metres
25mm	3mm	2.5 metres
32mm	3mm	3.0 metres
50mm	4mm	4.0 metres

STAGE 3 Final Stage

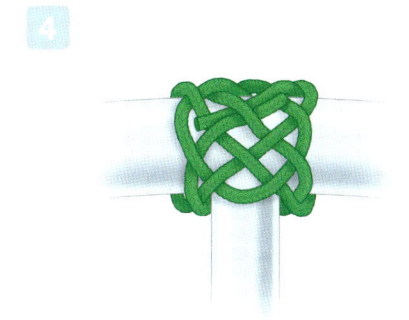

Carefully remove the 'former' Turk's Head completely. You are now left with the first pass of your King-spoke Turk's Head. Spread this out so that you are sure there is enough space to apply at least two more passes. Continue with the end you started with and start the second pass to the right of the original knot; when that is almost used up, take the other end and pass that back through the knot to complete three passes. Pass the ends under the knot and out under the bights on the rim. Massage the knot into as symmetrical a shape as you can, before gradually tightening it up a little at a time (you may have to do this 2 or 3 times) so that the leads lay nicely together and there is no bunching. Finally pull firmly on the ends, then cut them as close to the bights as you can; the end should shrink back under the knot.

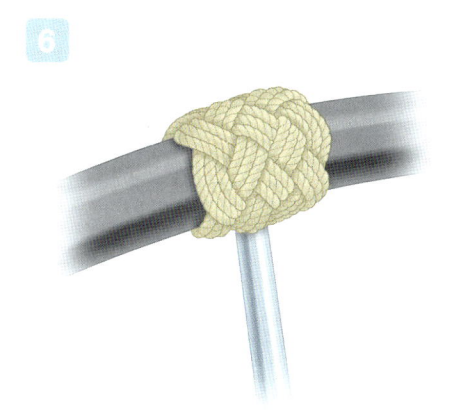

TIP FROM THE BOSUN'S LOCKER

If you are considering applying a preservative coat of varnish or lacquer to this knot:
1. Leave the excess tape on the rim until the coating is dry.
2. TEST the coating on an identical piece of line before applying it to your knot - some varnish turns natural fibre cordage black!

Two Short Lanyards

These two short lanyards are ideal for the release mechanism rings on snap shackles, for use as a short pocket knife lanyard which is housed in a belt holster, or even as a key fob. The first employs the so called 'Square Knot' used extensively in Macramé to form a flat cord, known as a Solomon Bar. The second is based on the Crown Knot and forms a round cord.

Tools required: knife (blade or hot) or scissors.

THE SOLOMON BAR LANYARD

Line: 2 – 4mm line is ideal and needs to be approximately 12 times the length of the required lanyard handle.

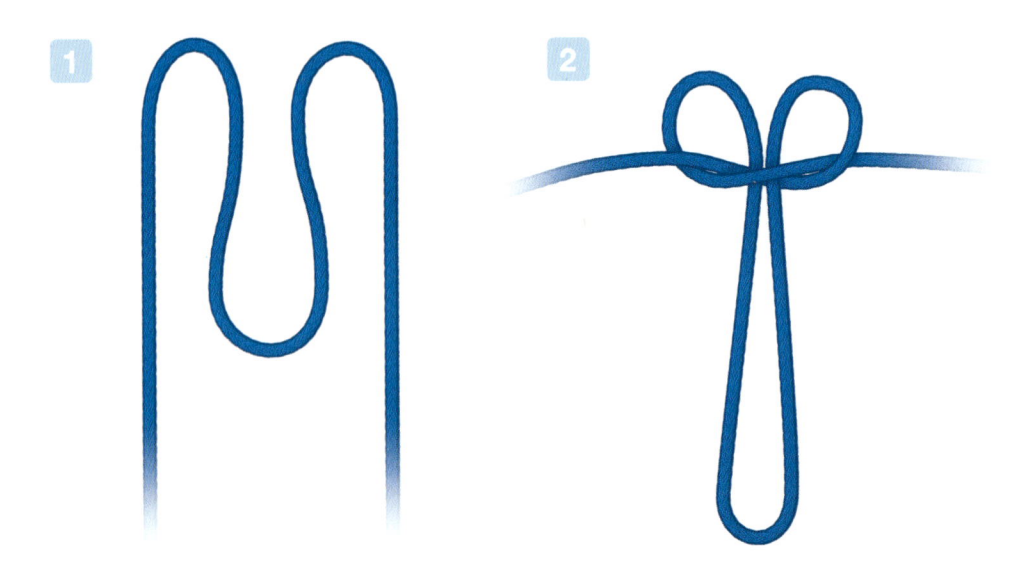

1

Fold the line in half, then 1.5 times the length of the lanyard bend the two ends down each side of a central loop, as shown.

2

Take the right hand cord and pass it behind the loop, now take the left hand cord over the right, in front of the loop then under the right hand cord again to form a Half Knot.

TWO SHORT LANYARDS | 197

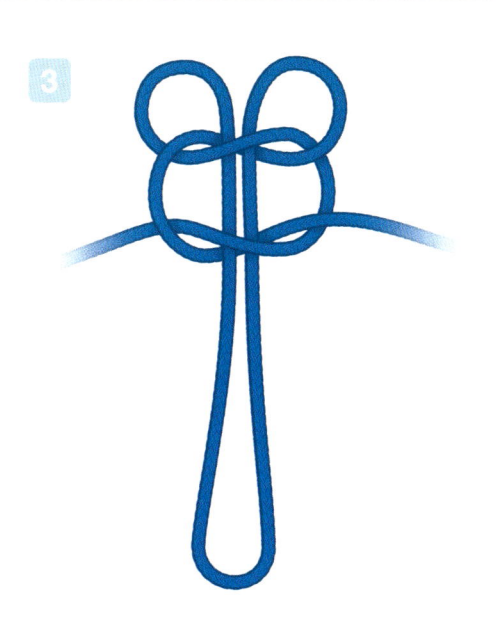

3

Take the two cords and make another Half Knot the other way round to form a Reef Knot structure around the loop.

4

Pull the first Square Knot (Reef Knot) up tight, taking care not to lose any of the loop length.

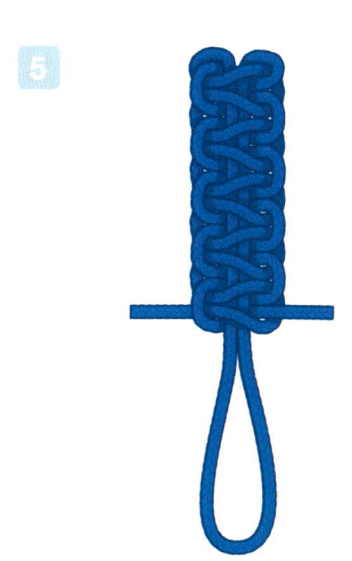

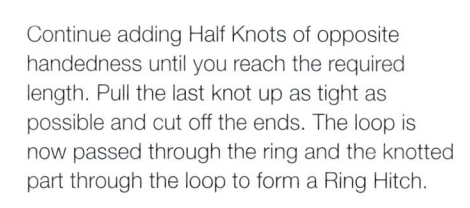

5

6

Continue adding Half Knots of opposite handedness until you reach the required length. Pull the last knot up as tight as possible and cut off the ends. The loop is now passed through the ring and the knotted part through the loop to form a Ring Hitch.

Marlinespike Ropework

THE CROWN SINNET LANYARD

Line: 2 – 4mm line is ideal and needs to be approximately 20 times the length of the lanyard handle. For example – a 10cm handle will require 2 metres of line.

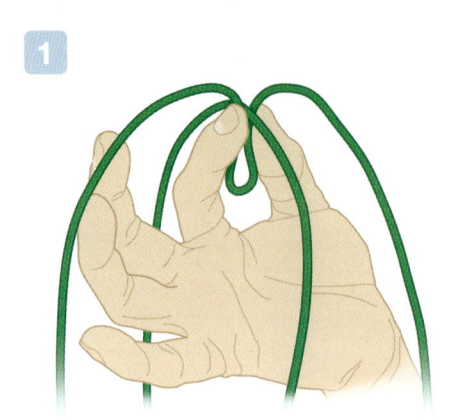

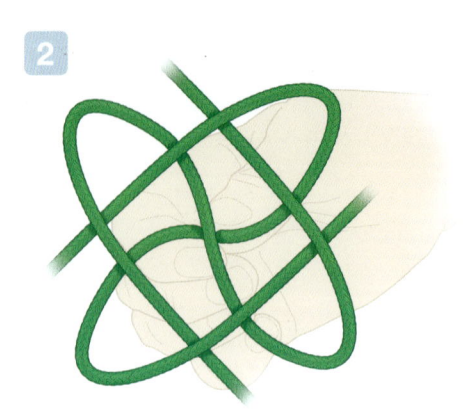

1

Cut the line into two equal lengths, fold one in half and form a bight (about 50mm long). Then lay the second line centre across the bight and hold them both between the thumb and forefinger.

2

Crown each lead to the right – over the one to its right each time. Hold the bight and the second line firmly, then pull up the Crown Knot, taking care not to pull out the bight or pull through the second line.

3

4

Continue crowning in the same direction pulling up each knot with even tension. If you crown to the right, tighten the knot going round to the left – so that you pull down one lead on top of the next one to be tightened. Cut the ends off and heat seal or glue them.

Knife Lanyard

No tools should be used above deck level without some form of lanyard with which to prevent them from falling from aloft, or over the side. This simple lanyard can be used with any tools that have a hole in the handle or a shackle or ring attachment, especially your pocket knife. The lanyard has two loops, one which is fixed and used to form a Ring Knot on the tool, the other is adjustable so that it can be worn around the wrist or waist, tied to a rigger's bucket or tied to a halyard for hoisting aloft.

Tools required: knife and whipping twine.
Materials: 1.5 to 2 metres of 4 to 6mm three strand cord.

About 30cm from one end of the rope, put on a temporary whipping, then unlay the three strands back to it. Make the first tuck of an Eye Splice, pulled up snug to the whipping. Crown the three strands around the standing part, then wall them on top of the crown – forming a Diamond Knot. Follow each lead around the knot making three passes, then gradually tighten the knot up until it is snug around the standing part - tuck the ends down through the knot and cut them off close to it. The result should look like a Turk's Head.

Put another temporary whipping 30cm from the other end and unlay the three strands back to the whipping. Take a short length of whipping twine and, using a Constrictor Knot, bind the point that is whipped to the standing part to form a loop. Tie a Diamond Knot around the standing part then remove the Constrictor Knot. You should now have a sliding knot around the standing part.

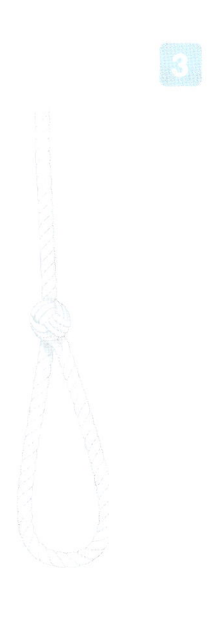

Binoculars Lanyard

This binoculars lanyard will ensure that your pair will be both handy and safe around your neck – as well as looking seamanlike. Two knots are employed; the 6 strand French Half Round Sinnet and the Diamond or Pineapple Knot.

Tools required: fid, whipping twine and knife.

Materials required: 6 lengths of 3 or 4mm cord, each 2 metres long, 2 stainless steel split rings.

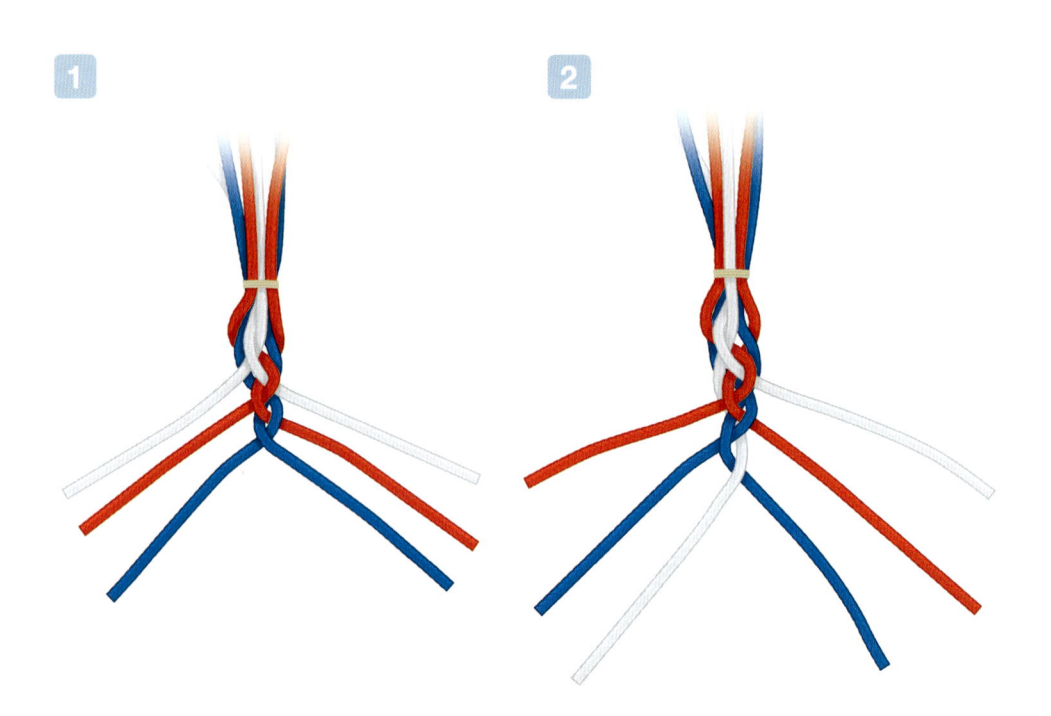

Bundle the 6 cords together then put a temporary stop (using a Constrictor Knot) 30cm from one end. Divide the cords into two groups of 3, then cross the two cords in the centre (white), maintaining 3 cords each side before taking the new top left hand cord and passing it under 4 and back to the left (red). Take the top right hand cord under 4 and out to the right (red). Then the new top left under 4 and out to the left – top right under 4 and out to the right. The first set of plaits completed, now take the top left under 4 and out to the left, top right under 4 and out to the right and so on in sequence, until you have completed 1 metre of plait. Put a temporary stop on this end of the plait.

BINOCULARS LANYARD | 201

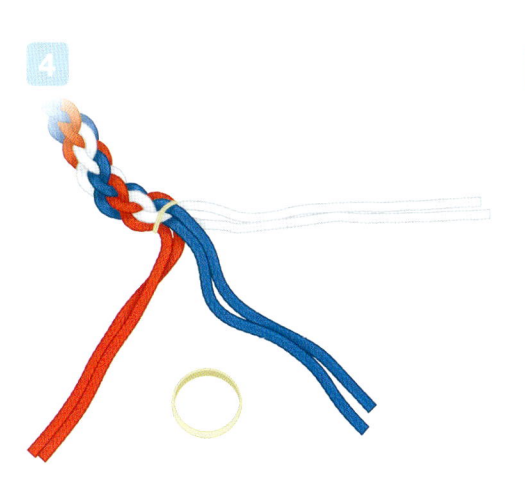

4

Divide the cords of one end into 3 sets of pairs (tape the ends together), then crown them over a split ring as if it were a rope to chain splice (p158). Pull up reasonably tight.

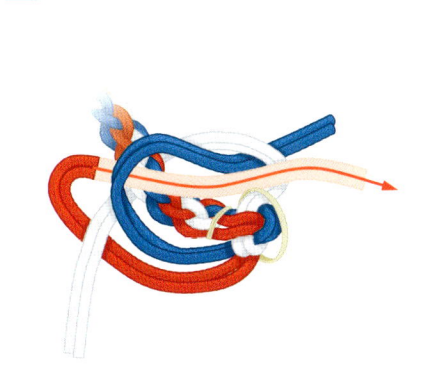

5

Next take the three pairs and wall them above the crown.

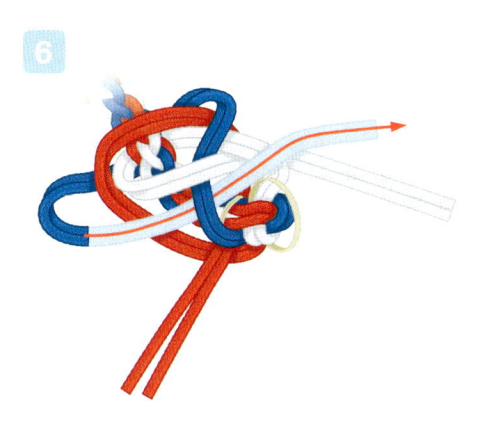

6

Complete the knot by taking one pair, passing it to the left, around the sinnet, over its neighbour and under itself. Work the knot up tight and cut the ends off. Repeat the same process at the other end of the sinnet.

7

8

Attach the lanyard to the binoculars using the split rings through the lugs on the frame.

Marlinespike Ropework

Spectacles Lanyard

Those of us that wear spectacles or 'shades', know the fear when afloat, that they might be knocked off and end up in the water. Here is a simple neck lanyard, fashioned from a length of line, which can easily be made up onboard for yourself or your guests.

Materials required: 2.5 metres of fairly soft cord about 2 to 3mm diameter.

1

2

Measure off 2.5 metres of cord. 30cm from one end make a slipped overhand loop (p39) to begin making about 40cm of Chain Shortening or Drummer's Plait.

Note: Make the plait carefully so that you always have the working end on the same side of the previous bight before pulling through the next one. Do not pull the bights up too tight – the plait should be soft and flexible, if it is stiff you are making it too tight, which will be uncomfortable and not 'sit' right on the neck. As with all decorative rope work, equal tension throughout the work is fundamental to a neat result.

3

Finish the plait by pulling the working end through the last bight.

4

Double the plait so that the two ends are together – cut the longest end to make both ends of equal length, then tie a Double or Triple Overhand Noose (p111), (keeping the end as short as possible) in both ends.

5

Pull the Overhand Knot up as tight as possible then trim and heat seal (or glue) the working ends. Place each noose over the spectacle arms, adjust for comfort then pull up tight.

6

Thump Mat

Thump mats are used to act as a buffer between blocks and the deck to prevent damage and unnecessary wear – apart from silencing the noise!

This mat is really a flat Turk's Head so the pattern can also be used to make an attractive two dimensional flat knot as a pendant for a necklace etc. The method shown here is suitable for tying the knot in-situ around a ringbolt with a block attached.

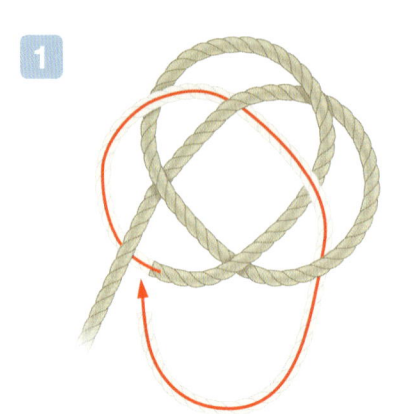

1

Make two overhand loops, one on top of the other as shown above, with the ringbolt in the centre of the knot. Complete the 3 Lead 4 Bight Turk's Head by weaving the working end under and over through the knot.

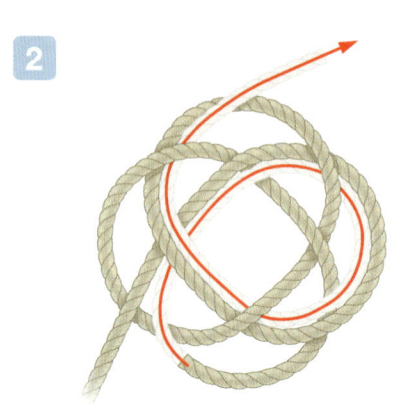

2

The first pass complete, now follow the lead round for 3 or more passes, depending on the diameter of the knot you require.

3

Make sure the two ends finally pass under one of the leads – on the deck side of the mat so that they will not show when cut off. Stitch the two ends to the standing parts alongside them.

4

Mast Dropper

Traditionally used on the towing mast of a horse drawn narrowboat – this decorative piece of ropework can also be used as a lanyard, handhold or decorative piece for your boat or bell.

Tools required: knife, Swedish fid, whipping twine, tape, measure.

Materials required: 1 metre each of 12mm, 3 strand rope and 3mm cord – white cotton is best but polyester is a suitable substitute.

1

Take 1 metre of 12mm cotton 3 strand rope - 10cm from one end put on a temporary whipping, tape the ends of the three strands to prevent them from fraying and then open the strands out, up to that whipping. With the end you have just prepared, splice a 25mm eye using three tucks as shown above.

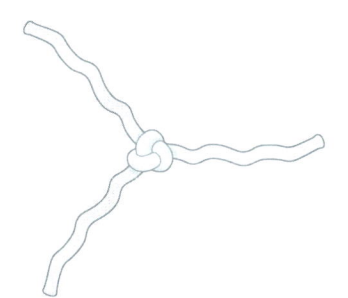

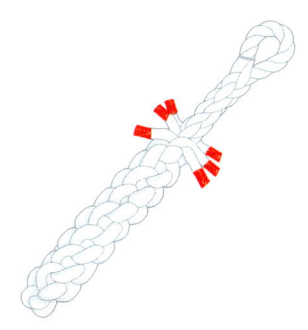

2

3

Measure 25cm from the top of the eye and put on another temporary whipping, tape the ends of the three strands and unlay this end up to the whipping. Hold with the eye downwards and tie a Crown Knot with the three strands, as if you were beginning a Back Splice, then continue crowning the three strands (to the left) up towards the eye until you have completed 14 rounds. Now tuck these three strands into the standing part as if you were splicing until they meet the strands from the eye.

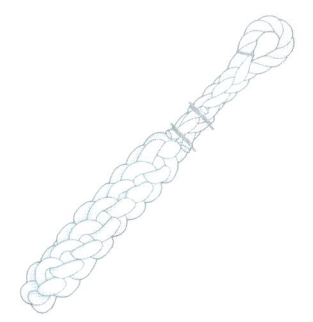

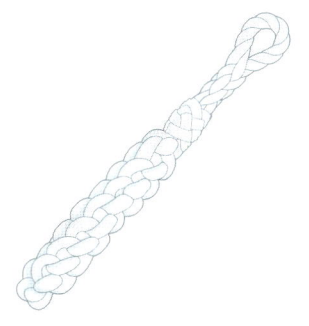

4

5

Remove the tape from the strand ends, fray them out, then lay them up and down the standing part – hold in position with two Constrictor Knots. Cover this join with a long Turk's Head – a 5 Lead 4 Bight is ideal or the 6 Lead 5 Bight on p188. Trim off any loose ends.

Cabin Strings with Three Drops

Ken Nelson provided this method of making a three drop Cabin String arrangement for a traditional English narrowboat. The strings are suspended on the port side of the cabin, aft; which is where the stove is situated. The tow or mooring ropes, when not in use would be coiled and secured to the cabin with these strings so that they dried, partly from the heat emitted from the stove and chimney.

Tools required: knife, whipping twine, fid.

Materials required: 17ft (5.2m) of ½ inch (13mm) diameter cable laid white cotton rope. Three strand polyester can be used as a substitute if cotton is not available.

CENTRE DROP

Cut one piece of rope 75" (1.9m) long, Put a temporary whipping on 9" (23cm) from one end, tape the strand ends and open up the lay.

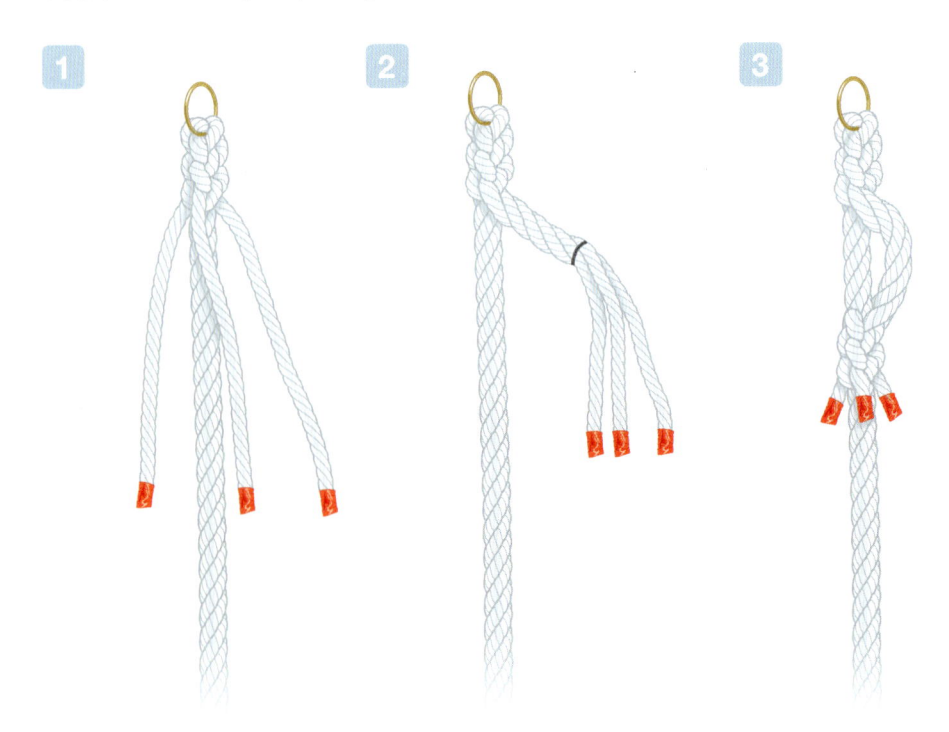

Next crown (a ring can be inserted at this stage to hang the strings by) and then back splice for two or three tucks (1). Now lay up the three strands back into a rope long enough to form a loop (2). Put a temporary whipping on, then splice back into the standing part using three tucks (3).

CABIN STRINGS WITH THREE DROPS

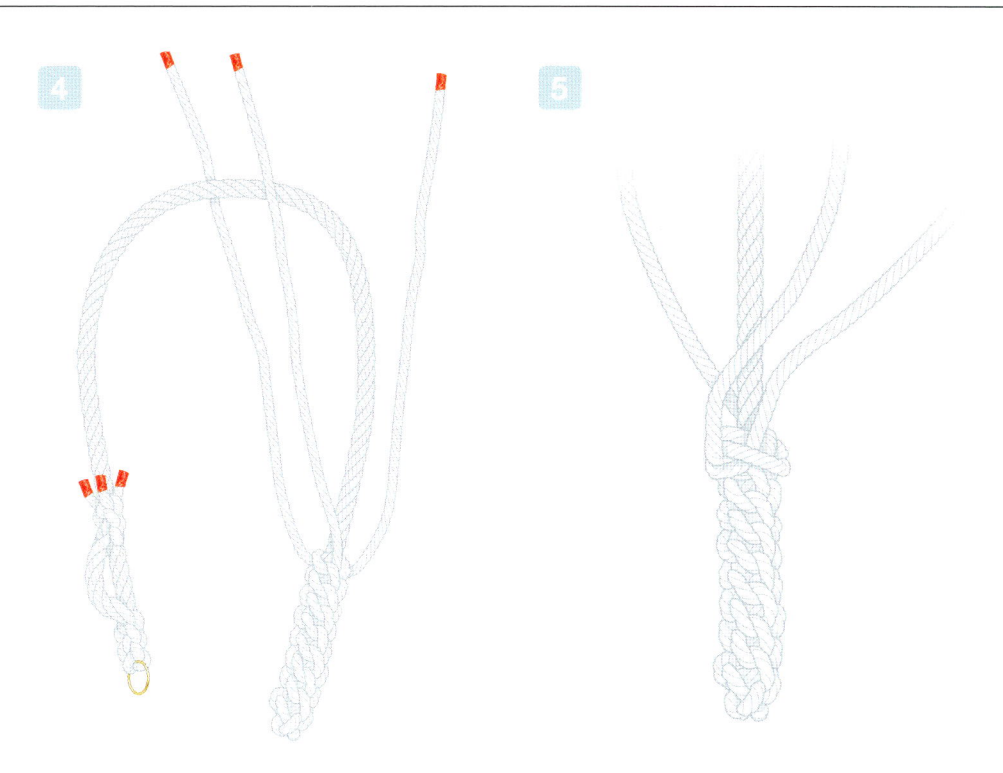

Next put a seizing on the rope 31" (78cm) from the spliced end, tape the ends and open the lay all the way back to the seizing. Now crown the strands and pull up taut. Hold the rope with the splice at the top and crown the strands back up the rope 15 times, then tuck the ends through the standing part as you would a splice (4). Now form a Diamond Knot - loosely crown, then wall and double twice, work out the slack and cut the ends off. Cover the ends of the splice at the top of the rope with a 3 Lead 5 Bight Turk's Head (p186) using Seine twine.

OUTER DROPS

Cut another piece of rope 10' 9" (3.3m) long and put a whipping on 36" (90cm) from each end. Pass one end through the loop in the centre drop - then repeat the crowning and Diamond Knot, as you did on the centre string.

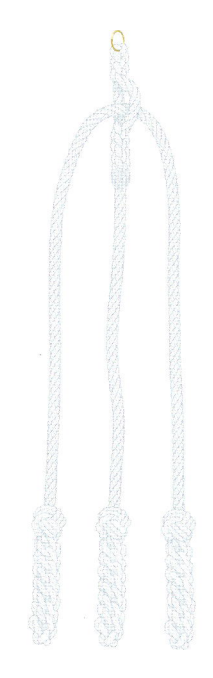

Ocean Plait Mat

'Green on Blue' is a familiar RYA slogan to many of you – well here is a way of recycling those old halyards, sheets and mooring lines; rather than polluting the water or filling up a landfill site. Make a handsome mat to adorn the deck at the bottom of a ladder, or even your doorstep at home. Just one word of warning, you do need a lot of rope to make a mat, but it is possible to join pieces on without them showing. This simple mat starts with an Half Knot, which progressively develops into a simple plait before being doubled, tripled or quadrupled as size and rope allow.

Tools required: palm & needle, whipping twine.

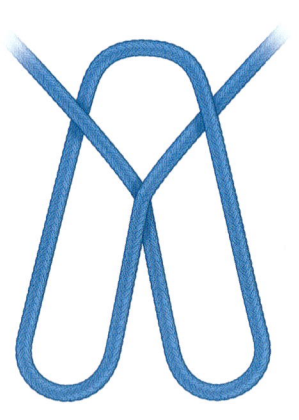

1

Middle the rope, then tie a simple Half Knot and lay it on a flat surface. Hold the belly of the knot with one hand and elongate the two sides by pulling gently on the bights of first one end, then the other. Make the two large bights about the same length that you want the mat to end up.

2

Put a right twist in both the bights – now follow one lead through and check that you have an over/under/over sequence throughout the knot.

OCEAN PLAIT MAT | 209

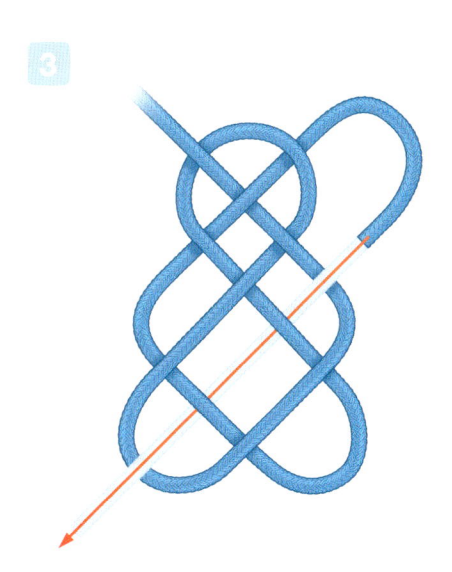

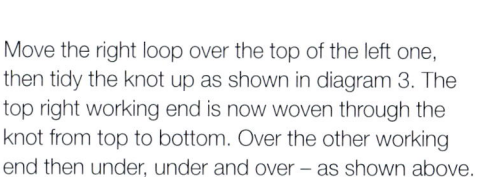

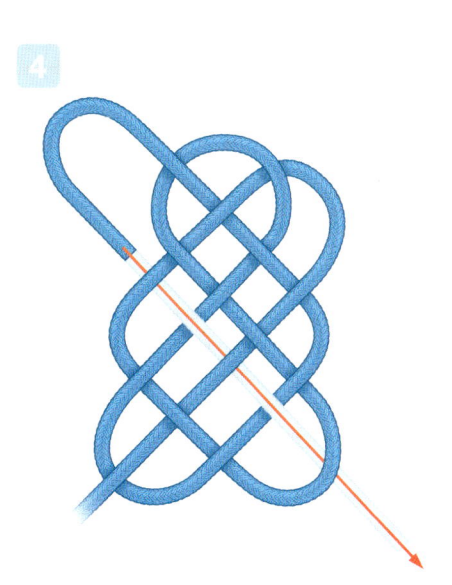

3

Move the right loop over the top of the left one, then tidy the knot up as shown in diagram 3. The top right working end is now woven through the knot from top to bottom. Over the other working end then under, under and over – as shown above.

4

Follow on with the top left hand working end down through the knot in an under/over/under sequence from top to bottom.

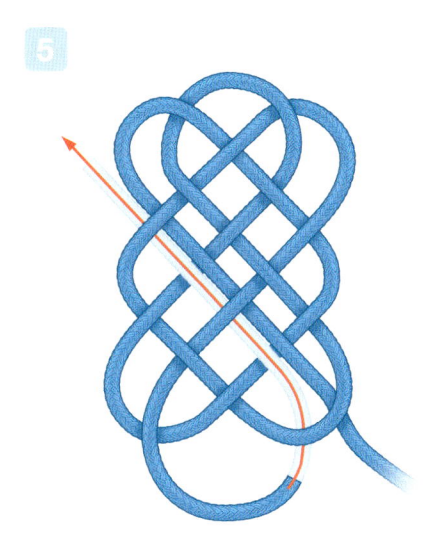

5

The basic framework is now complete and now needs to be adjusted to the size of mat required before following round with as many passes as will fill the knot or that you have rope available for – the choice must be yours.

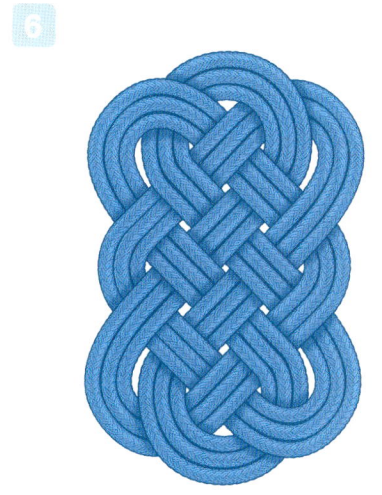

6

The two ends should stop opposite each other, and when the mat has been given its final adjustment to make it as symmetrical as possible, cut the ends off and sew them to the adjacent standing parts on the underside of the mat.

Marlinespike Ropework

Square Mat

This square, or very nearly square mat can be made up as a small table mat with 2 to 4mm line or a deck mat with 6 to 12mm (anything larger tends to be uncomfortable under foot). The dimensions of the mat can be varied too – limited only by the amount of line you have available. In this example the mat is made with 14 metres of 8mm rope and measures approximately 25cm x 30cm. Another advantage of this mat weave is that you can add more or different colour rope inside and/or outside the initial two or three pass weave; this is particularly useful if you do not have enough length in one piece of rope to complete the mat.

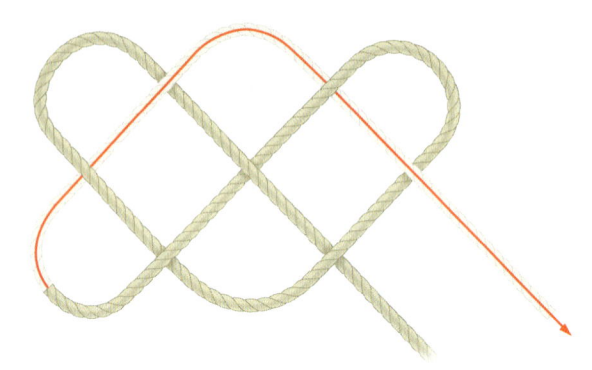

1

Find the approximate centre of the line and tie a large Half Knot – lay it on a suitable surface and form it into a heart shape, as shown in diagram 1. Take the left hand lead and weave it through the overhand knot under/over/under/over, to emerge alongside the right hand lead. The next stage is the first stage of expanding (at the moment you have a mat with two bights on the sides and three bights top and bottom) by increasing the mat by one bight on the top and bottom and one bight on the sides.

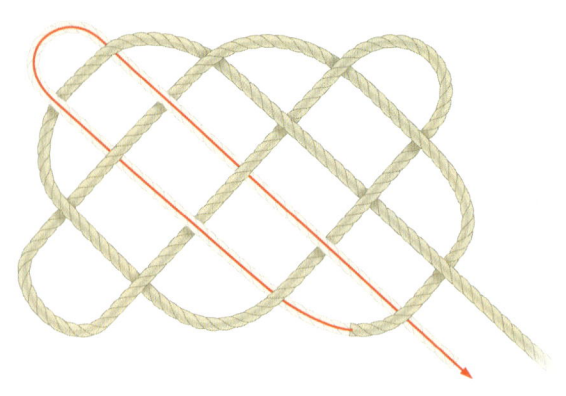

2

With the right hand lead, pass it under the left then follow the same over/under sequence as the left hand lead – under/over/under. Now go over the top left bight and back through the knot alongside the left hand lead under/over/under/over, then under itself. You now have four bights top and bottom and three bights each side, although one, the bottom right, is not yet made.

3

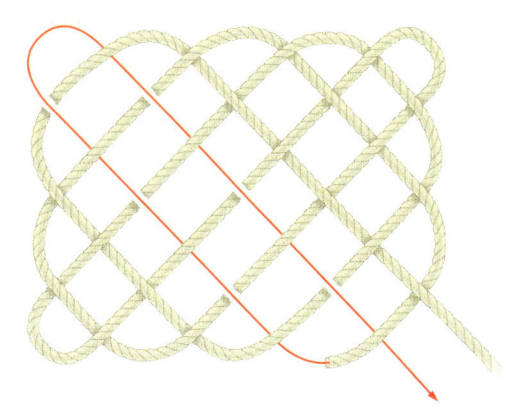

To increase by one more bight, separate the two leads you have just completed then insert another expansion bight as shown above. This expansion process can be continued until you have a mat the size you need. Remember to expand the whole arrangement to keep it in proportion and with enough space between leads to make another two or more passes around the knot.

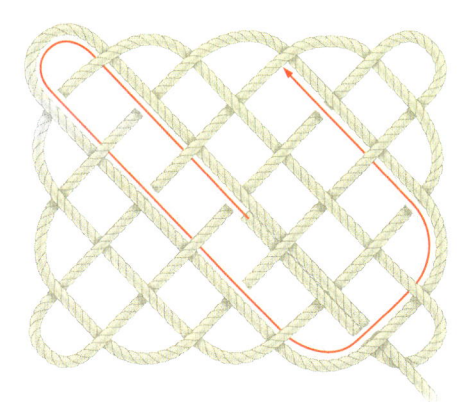

4

Having completed the expansion process, check that you have an under/over/under sequence throughout the mat. Now take one of the leads and commence the second pass around the knot, entering alongside the other lead – make sure you remain on the same side all the way round. When you run out of rope with this end, take the other and go round the knot in the opposite direction.

If you run out of rope, consider if it is time to start pulling the knot up snug or adding another piece (the ends need to be butted together so that you can pull the knot up snug); alternatively you may want to go back to where you completed two passes and then insert a different rope in between the first two passes, or one each side. To pull the knot up snug – start at one end and go all the way round the knot adjusting the lead so that all the spaces are equal and have enough room for the number of passes you are going to fill them with. When you get to the start point again, carry on round with the second lead, laying it alongside the first but in the opposite direction. To finish off, cut the ends of the rope opposite each other and sew them to the adjacent standing parts of the knot.

5

Side Fender

This simple fender can be made from old or new braid or stranded rope, either will serve equally well.

Tools required: knife, Swedish fid, whipping twine, Super Glue™.

Materials required: at least 12 metres of 10 or 12mm diameter rope.

1

Cut the rope into 4 x 3 metre lengths, middle each one and arrange them ready to bind together. Bunch the 8 leads together loosely, pulling the bight of the centre rope about 12cm above the others to form an eye. Secure the bunch near the top with a Constrictor Knot, then 30cm (or more for a longer fender) below this with another Constrictor Knot.

2

3

Hold the core with the eye downwards – select two opposite leads and lay them down along the core in your hand. Now crown the remaining six leads using the 'over two' method – each lead passes over the next two and the last one tucks under two, as shown above. Pull down taut.

SIDE FENDER | 213

4

5

Turn the work back so that the eye is at the top then proceed to crown all eight leads up around the core, also using the same 'over two' Crown Knot. Continue crowning, one on top of the other, pulling each one up taut until you reach the top Constrictor Knot. Take two opposite leads and securely bind them to the core just below the eye – cut the ends off short. Now tie another 'over two' Crown Knot with the remaining six leads so that it covers the two you have just cut off. Bind two more opposite leads to the core and cut those off short, before making the final Crown Knot with the remaining four leads. Pull this last Crown down tight and 'Super Glue' the top cross-over points on top of the Crown Knot (to ensure the knot does not come undone!) – allow the glue to dry then cut the ends off short.

6

Marlinespike Ropework

Disc Fender

Make good use of your old rope – don't throw it away.

This useful and decorative fender can be made in a variety of sizes, depending on the requirement and the rope available. This design is suitable for model boats too – so try making a model one first, it is well worth doing, just for the experience. The core for this fender is made up with a cheese coil, over which a layer of 'kackling' forms a protective outer layer.

TO MAKE THE CORE

You will need enough rope (old 3 strand is best) to form a cheese of 15 turns (3 layers of 5) around a suitable size cylindrical object (tin, pipe, jar, etc) the diameter of which should be about one third the diameter of the completed cheese. For example, if you are using 24mm diameter rope, five turns will be 120mm wide – thus you will need a cylinder 120mm diameter which will give you a final cheese of 360mm diameter, needing approximately 21 metres of rope.

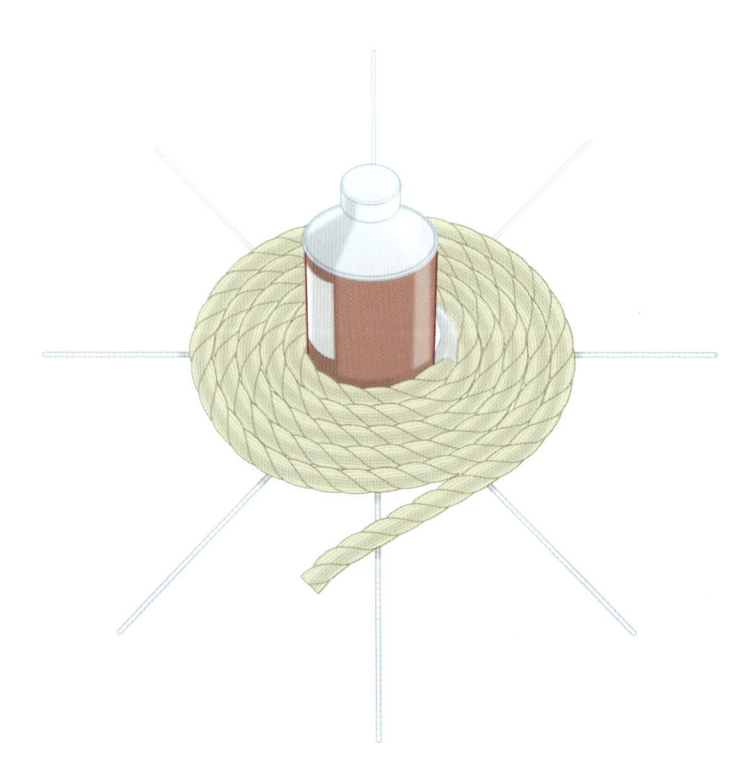

1

Start by tapering the end of the rope (about 100mm) and tape it to the standing part so that it fits tightly around the cylinder. Now cut 8 pieces of spun yarn, or small line to bind the cheese - lay these out at 45 degree angles on your table with one end in the centre. Place your cylinder on top of these lines and commence winding the cheese from inside to out for 5 complete turns.

2

Now lay on 5 turns from outside to in, on top of the first layer, then 5 turns from inside to out on top of that. Having completed the third layer of 5 turns, taper the end and tape it to the last turn. Alternatively, if you are using large diameter rope it might be easier to make three individual coils of 5 turns and lay one on top of the other.

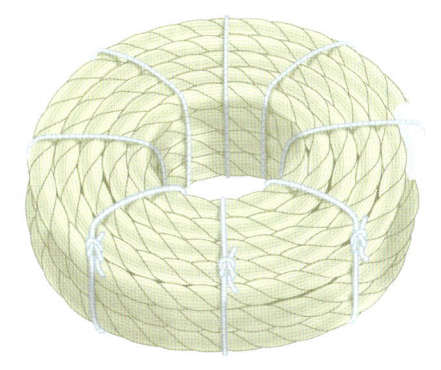

3

Remove the cylinder. Now take each of the eight binding lines and wrap them at one eighth intervals around the cheese (the Packer's Knot on p121 is a good knot to bind the first turn) with one or two turns and tie off with a Reef Knot. These ties not only hold the cheese together but they become a gauge for applying the 'kackling' in the next stage – so make sure that they are exactly 1/8th of the circumference apart. The completed core cheese should be firm and stable.

TO COVER THE FENDER

You need to do some estimating now - measure the circumference of the inside of the cheese, divide this by the diameter of the rope you will be using for the 'kackling' to give you the number of hitches. Pass the 'kackling' rope around the cheese and tie a Half Knot in it with an end about 25mm - mark the rope where it emerges from the knot, untie and measure from the mark to the end - this will give you the approximate length of each turn. Example: Inside circumference = 240mm, rope diameter = 6mm so the estimate is 40 hitches; multiply this by the hitch length 440mm - you will need approximately 17.6 metres of rope. You will probably not get 40 hitches on so reduce these by at least 4 leaving you with 36; divide this by 4 (the 4 quarters marked by the binding) and you will need to put 9 hitches in each quadrant - until you gain confidence in spacing the hitches, measure and mark the position of each hitch on the outside rim of the cheese with a marker pen. The spacing is important, otherwise you will end up with a large gap on the outer rim of the cheese, which can only be rectified by starting again.

A fender up to about 30cm diameter can be made by one person, anything larger, two people and some mechanical pulling power makes the job easier. Start with a Clove Hitch 'X' then take the lead going to the left and pass it to the right, through the centre of the cheese, up to the outer rim and make a half hitch, 'A'.

Pull up as tight as possible around the cheese – to stop it backing up on the previous hitch, stick a spike (a long bradawl is sufficient) into the cheese behind the hitch – when tight pin it with another spike through the 'kackling'. Now take the lead from the right of the Clove Hitch 'B' over the top of the first Half Hitch (hold the first end back over the Clove Hitch) then make a Half Hitch with this one also to the right. Half Hitch to the right all the way around the cheese. Pass A over B, insert spike into core hold B back to the left, Half Hitch A to the right, pull down tight back to the spike – pin to hold. Then – pass B over A, insert spike into core, hold A back to the left, Half Hitch B…et seq.

When you arrive back at the Clove Hitch, the two ends are now crossed and tucked under the Clove Hitch. The ends can now be tied off with a knob knot like a 3 strand Matthew Walker, a Figure of Eight Knot, dogged together with a whipping, or tucked under the 'kackling' along the ridge. You can now remove the binding cords if you wish.

Complete the job by splicing a suitable lanyard around the fender.

3

Bell Rope

This Bell Rope can be made with line between 2 and 8mm diameter to make a key fob or a rope for a bell from about 15 to 25cm. The knots used are all simple, except the Star Knot, and you do not have to follow the design religiously – use your imagination, bell ropes are a creation, your creation – this is just a sample starter.

Tools required: knife, whipping twine, tape, fid, (wire loop optional).

Materials: 10 metres of 6 or 8mm line (less for smaller line).

Cut 4 pieces of line, each 2.5 metres long.

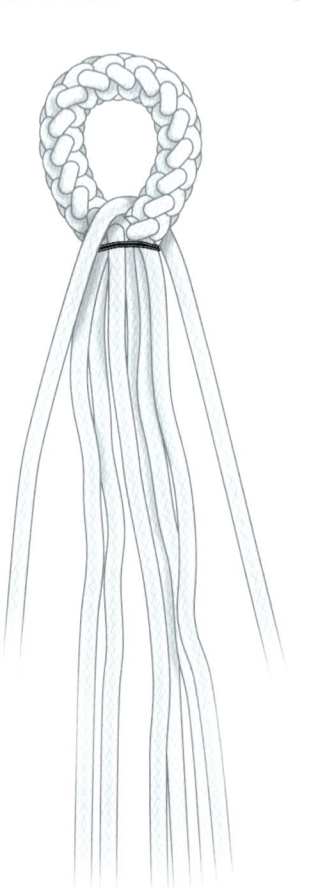

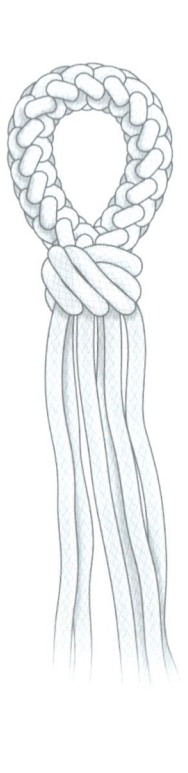

1

2

Middle 3 of the lines (apply a temporary stop) and starting at the centre, crown them to the right – make 8 Crown Knots one upon the other. Start at the middle again (remove the stop) and crown the three lines 8 times to the right also. Bend the work to make an eye and you should have enough room to put your finger through it – if not add crowns to each side as necessary. Tie a Constrictor Knot around the base of the eye and lay the 4th piece of line over it. Using all 8 lines, tie a Matthew Walker Knot (p64).

3

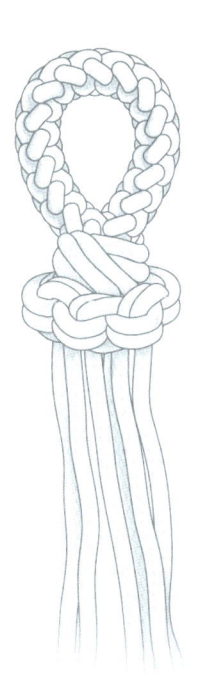

Tie a Star Knot (p190) using 7 or 8 of the cords.

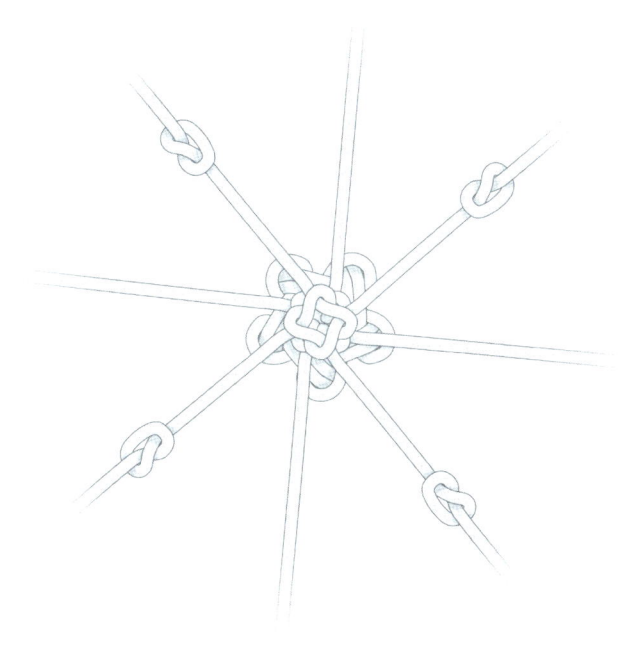

4

The shaft of the bell rope will be formed using a 4 upon 4 (8 cord) crowning – this is an effective way to use 8 cords without having to use a core. The resultant effect will look rather like hawser laid rope. Divide the 8 cords into 2 sets of 4 – tie an Overhand Knot in each alternate cord, as shown above so that you can be sure you are using each set in turn. Now crown one set to the right (or left) – ensure each cord of the second set is between the cords of the first set, then crown them on top of the first crown. Continue crowning alternate sets until you have a long enough shank. Even tension is very important, otherwise the knots will not lay neatly.

5

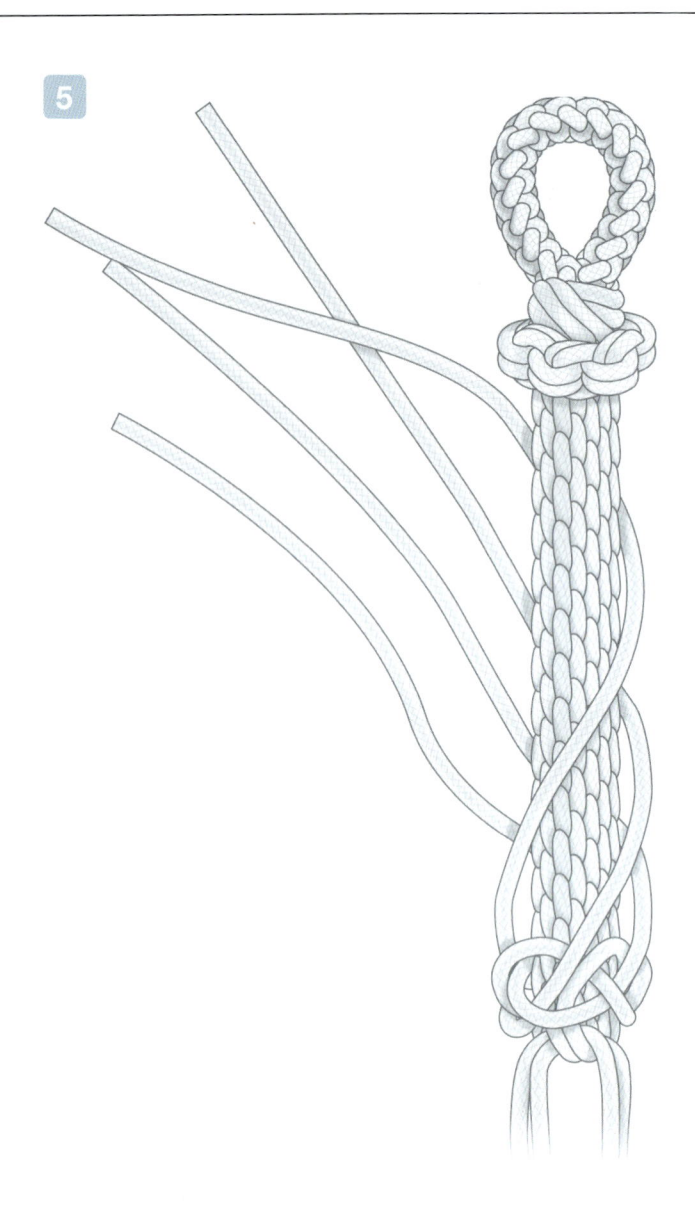

Next form a Diamond Knot on top of the shank using 4 of the 8 cords. First crown the cords, then make a Wall Knot above that – now follow the lead of each cord around the knot for 2 or 3 passes – the result will look like a Turk's Head. Pull up neatly and cut the ends off so that they shrink back under the knot.

BELL ROPE | 221

The four remaining cords are now crowned and pulled into the centre of the Diamond Knot and cut off.

Marlinespike Ropework

Baggy Wrinkle (Bag-o-Wrinkle)

Where sail cloth rubs on standing or running rigging it needs some protection from wear – this is resolved by applying Baggy Wrinkle to the rigging. The traditional way of making Baggy Wrinkle is to stretch out two lines, into which short pieces of cut up rope yarns are tied using the Lark's Head Knot. The method described here is adapted from the way wool was cut, to make hand woven rugs – and is quicker than the traditional method.

Tools required: Short length of wood approximately 30mm square (larger for longer pile), a nail or cup hook, 2 screw eyes. I use a large net mending needle but a simple coil can be used. Scissors or knife, whipping twine, vice or clamp to hold the wood at one end.

Materials: natural fibre rope yarns, large whipping twine or thin cord.

1

Middle a long length of large whipping twine or 1 – 1.5mm cord – tie an Overhand Loop in the bight. Place the knot over the nail or cup hook about 25mm from the end of the wood. Thread the two ends through the two screw eyes (this keeps them separated), about 25mm from the other end. Put the end of the wood into a vice or clamp it to a bench, pull the two cords VERY tight and secure them to the bench. Wind a convenient length of rope yarn on to a netting needle, or a figure 8 skein.

2

Stand at the end of the wood and thread the yarn from right to left – up through the middle, under both and down through the middle inside the turn. Pull tight and back to the previous knot.

3

Continue until you run out of yarn, then start another needle or skein, leaving enough end to reach the centre of the underside of the wood.

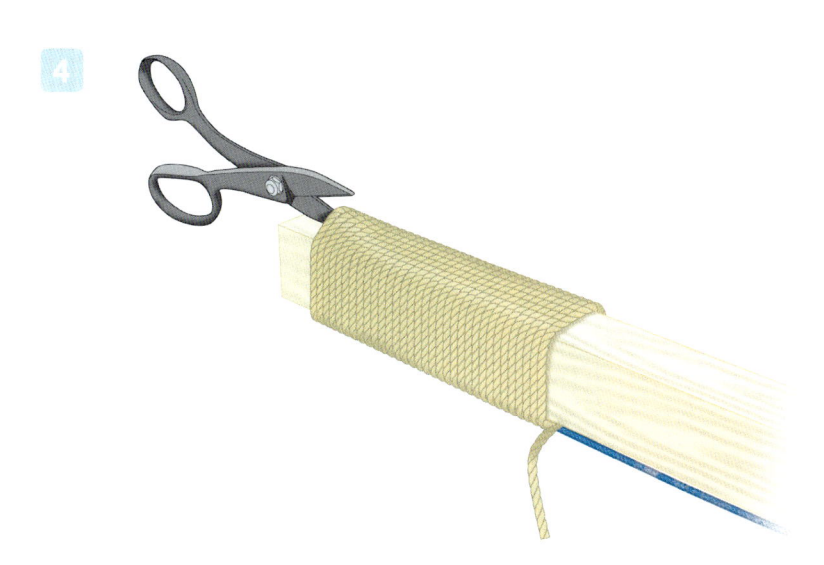

4

Having completed about two thirds of the way along the wood, stop, turn it over and cut the turns down the centre of the back (a groove in the wood helps).

5

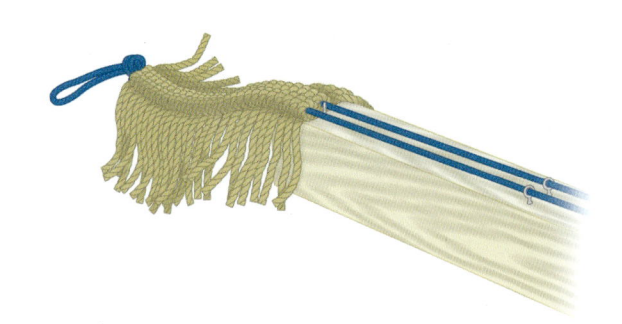

Now place the completed knotting over the nail or hook and continue knotting the next section in the same manner until you have as much as you can handle, or enough to complete the job.

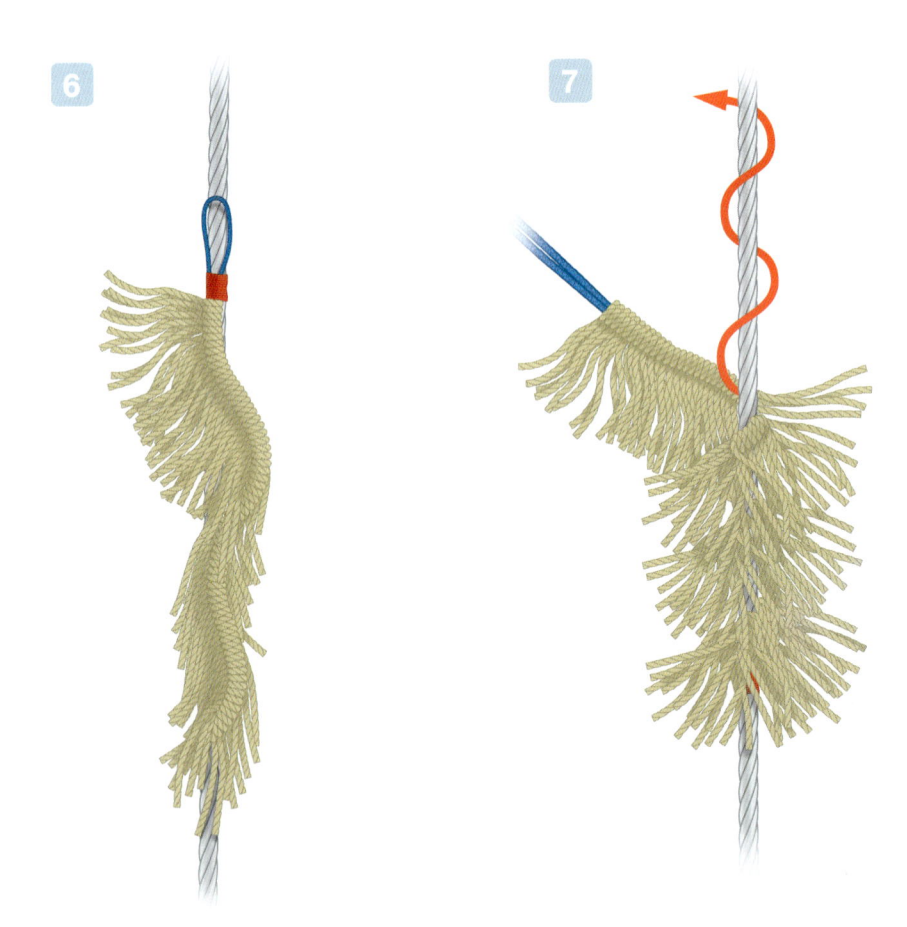

6

7

To apply the Baggy Wrinkle to the stay or runner – seize the centre cord of the Baggy Wrinkle to the lowest part of the stay to be covered – make sure it is VERY secure. Treat the wire with your usual anti-rust lanolin or suchlike and tape if required.

8

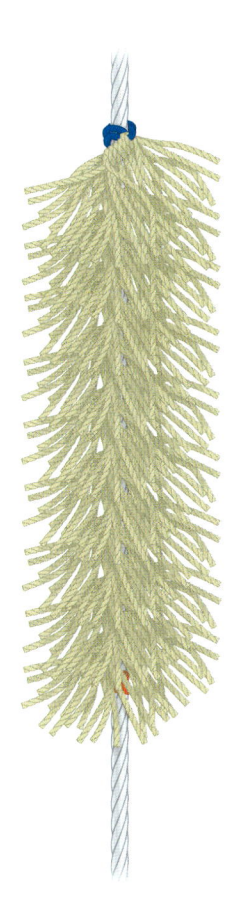

Now wind the Baggy Wrinkle tightly around the stay in an upward direction, finally securing the centre cord at the top. If another piece is to be added, seize the two pieces to the stay together.

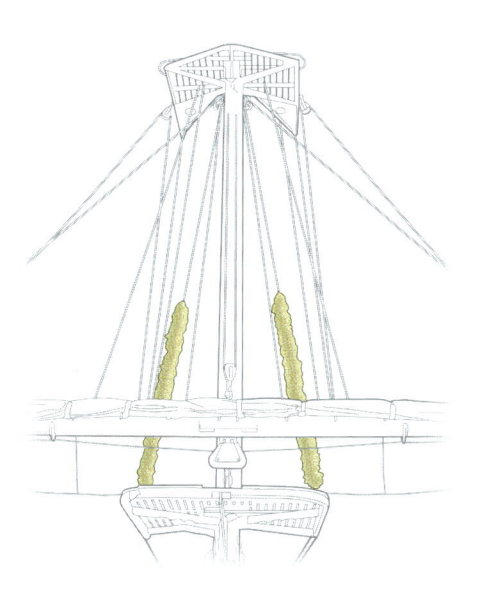

9

A Boat Hand Lead Line

A hand lead line is an essential tool if you do not have an echo sounder; even then, to have one in your locker in case of equipment failure is no bad thing.

Tools required: Swedish fid, needle and whipping twine.

Components: 25 metres of 8 to 10mm pre-stretched polyester three strand rope, 1 leg-of-mutton 3 kilogram lead, leather strips, 2mm line and coloured bunting/cloth.
Tallow to load the lead will also be needed, if the nature of the sea bed is required.

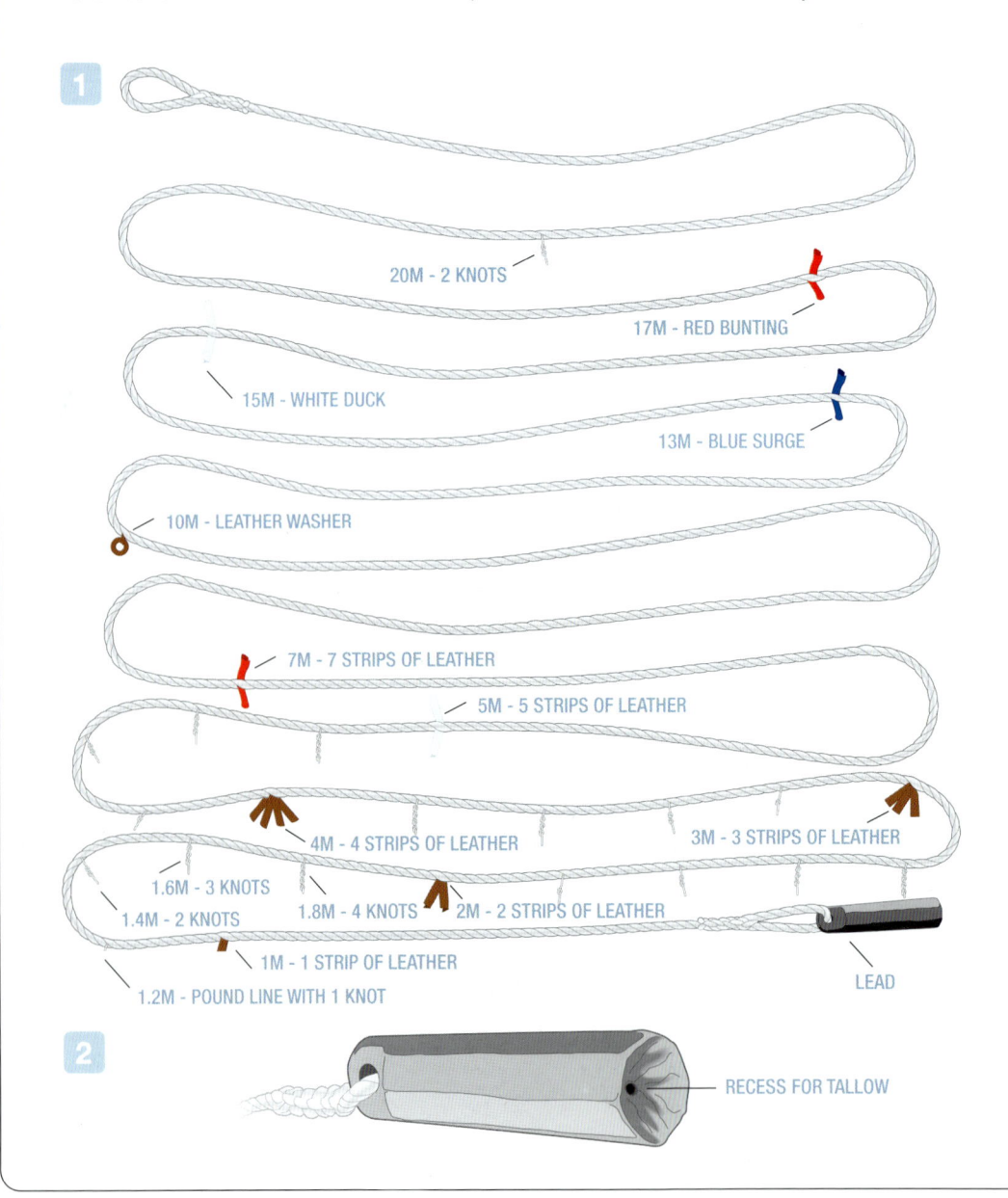

1

- 20M - 2 KNOTS
- 17M - RED BUNTING
- 15M - WHITE DUCK
- 13M - BLUE SURGE
- 10M - LEATHER WASHER
- 7M - 7 STRIPS OF LEATHER
- 5M - 5 STRIPS OF LEATHER
- 4M - 4 STRIPS OF LEATHER
- 3M - 3 STRIPS OF LEATHER
- 1.6M - 3 KNOTS
- 1.8M - 4 KNOTS
- 2M - 2 STRIPS OF LEATHER
- 1.4M - 2 KNOTS
- 1M - 1 STRIP OF LEATHER
- 1.2M - POUND LINE WITH 1 KNOT
- LEAD

2

- RECESS FOR TALLOW

Marlinespike Ropework

GLOSSARY & INDEX

Glossary

Bend	Verb used to describe the action of knotting two ropes together.
Bight	Any part of a rope between the two ends, especially when slack and bent back on itself to form a loop.
Binding	The tying with line around two or more objects to hold them tight together.
Braid	Yarns woven together to form a band, cover, or decoration.
To Braid	Is to form a braid with knotting normally in the hand or on a Maru Dai, or other specifically made formers.
Bungee	A line of elastic rubber yarns, bound and held by a man-made fibre stretchable cover – also known as 'shock cord'.
Cable	A large rope - anchor warp or chain.
Cable laid	Rope formed of three individual hawsers laid up to form a larger nine-strand rope or cable.
Capsize, a knot	Verb used to describe the change in the form of a knot. This can either be accidental – where stresses are applied to a loose or wrongly pulled up knot which cause the knot to become insecure; or deliberate - when forces are applied to parts of the knot to make it easier to untie.
Cleat	A wood or metal fitting having two horns, to which ropes are belayed.
Coachwhipping	The over/under/over pattern of knotting used for covering cylindrical objects.
Cord	The name given to several tightly twisted or plaited yarns to make a line with a diameter of less than 10mm (1/2 in).
Cordage	A collective general term when referring to ropes and cords.
Core or heart	The inner part or heart of a rope or sinnet of more than three strands and braided lines; it is formed from a loosely twisted strand or from a bundle of parallel yarns or plaited strands and runs the length of the rope. It may be just a filler or serve specifically as the main strength bearer in braided ropes.
Dog/Dogging	The act of whipping together the ends of two separate strands of rope to prevent them from pulling out.
Dress, a knot	To tighten, and arrange a loosely tied knot into its final shape.
End	Usually the end of a length of rope that is being knotted, but see Working end.
Eye	A closed loop formed in rope by knotting, seizing or splicing – see Hard eye. Also, an aperture in a hook, thimble or needle through which a line can be threaded.
Fender	Soft rope, rubber or plastic arrangement, used on the side of a vessel to prevent damage by dockside fittings or other vessels when alongside.
Fid	A tapered wooden pin or hollow metal spike, used to work or loosen strands of a rope, especially when splicing.
Frapping turns	Those turns around a lashing which serve to tighten it before securing the end.
Fray	Verb used to describe the unravelling, especially of the end, of a length of rope.
Grommet	A ring of rope, made up using one strand laid around itself three times.
Hard eye	A spliced eye which contains a thimble or round eye of metal or polymer construction so as to prevent undue wear on the rope from shackles and fittings.
Hard laid	Tightly laid up rope – tends to be stiff and difficult to knot or coil.
Hawser	A rope or cable large enough for towing or mooring.
Heart	See Core.
Heaving line	A light line, typically 8mm diameter about 30 metres long, with a Monkey's Fist, Heaving Line Knot or sandbag on the end as a weight.
Hitch	A knot that secures a rope to a post, ring, spar, etc. or to another rope.
Hot Knife	An electric (or gas) heated blade, used to cut and seal the ends of man-made fibre ropes.

GLOSSARY & INDEX

Karabiner	A metal coupling link with a safety closure – used as a Personal Protection Equipment link for roping activities.
Keckling (also Kackling)	Protective cover of rope to prevent wear.
Lanyard	A short rope or cord, usually three stranded but can be braided or ornamented, used to secure objects, rigging, or as a handle, safety line or hanging loop for tools and equipment.
Lash/Lashing	Term used when knotting over a loose article to hold it in place – bindings on poles etc to form frameworks.
Lay	The direction, either left or right-handed, of the twist of the strands forming a rope.
Lay Back	Term used to mean – putting all one's weight behind pulling a line or rope.
Lay up	The re-laying of the strands of a rope that have been un-laid, to restore the rope to its original form.
Lead	The direction taken by the working end through a knot.
Line	The generic name for cordage with no specific purpose, although it can be used to refer to rope with a definite use – e.g. fishing line, clothesline.
Loop	A part of a rope bent so that its parts come together.
Macramé	The art of knotting with simple knots to decorate or make clothing, hangings, bags, belts and coverings etc.
Mandrel	A cylindrical rod or tube around which hollow knotting, such as Turk's Head Knots and bracelets etc can be formed while in the tying process.
Marline	A thin line of two, often loosely twisted, strands, traditionally left hand laid. Used for seizing, marling, etc.
Marlinespike	A round pointed metal instrument for separating the strands of a rope (especially wire) when splicing or for use as a lever to tighten seizing.
Marling	The act of lashing or binding with marline (q.v.), taking a hitch at each turn.
Marry	To bring two ropes together so that they can be worked as one.
Messenger	A light line/rope used to haul the end of a larger heavier rope end from one point to another. Typically used between a heaving line and berthing hawser.
Monofilament	A single fibre of one of the polymers which has been extruded and thus has no joins.
Mooring	The term used for attaching a vessel to a fixed object – typically by anchor or to a buoy or berthing facilities.
Multiplait	Strong but flexible rope that does not kink largely because it is plaited using four or six pairs of strands, half of which are right-hand laid, the other half left-hand laid.
Nip	The binding pressure within a knot that prevents it from slipping.
Noose	A loop, formed by the working end being tied around the standing part of a rope, in such a way that it will open and close.
Nylon	Original common term for Polyamide.
Pass	To follow the path of a lead around a knot with the working end again.
Pick	Term used to denote one element of the weave in braided rope covers.
Prussik	Sliding knot used on a static climbing rope, commonly used as a generic term for any of the knots which have a 'slide and grip' function on a static rope.
Reeve	Verb used to describe the act of passing the end of a rope through a block, ring or cleat.
Riding turn	When the round turns of a line on a winch/capstan or bollard are entrapped by the standing part laying over them.
Rope	General term used for cordage that has a diameter of more than 10mm. Also used to specify a rope - as in Bell-rope, Bolt-rope etc.
Rove	When a rope is passed through the aperture in a block, eye or fairlead etc – it is said to be rove through the block etc.

GLOSSARY & INDEX

Safe working load (SWL)	The estimated load that can be placed on a rope without it breaking, given its age, condition, the knots used and any shock loading. NB: safe working load may be as little as one-sixth of the manufacturer's quoted breaking strength.
Secure	To belay a line such that it will not move – a knot is said to be secure if, when tied, no manner of shaking or use will inadvertently untie it.
Seizing	Binding with turns of small stuff which secures two parts of the same rope together or one rope parallel to another rope.
Sennit or sinnet	A flat, round or square form of knotting which forms a braid, normally using three or more strands.
Serving	A binding in small stuff, or fine wire etc. Used particularly over wire rope splices.
Sinnet	See Sennit.
S-laid rope	Left hand laid stranded rope.
Sling	A rope or tape joined at the ends to form a loop which can be attached to a fixed point or static line to act as a suspension loop.
Slipped	The passing of a bight, rather than an end, to complete a knot – whereby the knot can be untied by pulling the bight free.
Small stuff	Twine, string, line or cord with a diameter of less than 10mm ($^{1}/_{2}$in).
Soft laid	Loosely laid up rope – making it soft and supple.
Spill	A knot is said to have spilled if, by accident or deliberate pulling of an end the knot changes its form, such that it will no longer be secure and is likely to come apart with any further movement.
Splice	Verb used to describe the act of joining the ends, or the end and the standing part, of a rope or ropes, by interweaving strands or braids.
Standing part	The part of a rope that is fixed, under tension or dormant, as opposed to the end that is free (the working end) with which the knot is tied.
Stop	A binding knot or whipping used as a temporary measure to stop a rope or bundle from unravelling.
Stopper	A short length of rope or chain, secured at one end - used to control the running or securing another rope.
Strand	Yarns twisted together in the opposite direction to the yarn itself; rope made with twisted strands (not braided) is known as laid line.
Stretch	Recoverable stretch – stretch created by a load, but when the load is removed the rope resumes its original form and length.
Non-Recoverable Stretch	Often called 'Creep' as the elongation is gradual and does not recover.
Temporary Whipping	The use of tape or a binding knot to form a 'Stop'.
Turn	One 360 degree path taken by a rope around an object or when coiled. To 'take a turn' is to make a single round with the rope around an object such as a cleat or bollard.
Unlay	To separate the strands or yarns of a rope.
Weave	The in/out or under/over pattern formed by interlacing strands or cords.
Webbing	Woven strapping – often used for slings or strops.
Whipping	The act of tightly wrapping small stuff around the end of a length of rope to prevent it unlaying and fraying.
Working end	The part of the rope used in tying a knot - the opposite of standing part.
Yarn	A number of fibres twisted together.
Z-laid	Right-hand laid rope.

Index

Page numbers in **bold** type indicate major references where appropriate.

alpine butterfly bend	80
alpine butterfly loop	**113**, 135, 145
anchor bend	54, **103**
angler's loop	56-58
artilleryman's knot/loop	**112**, 145
Asher, Harry	96
'Ashley Book of Knots'	81
Ashley's bend	81
backsplice	160
backsplice, three strand	146-147
baggy wrinkle (bag-o-wrinkle)	96, **222-225**
balls of 'small stuff'	14
becket, halyard	160
becket bend	73
belaying pin	33
belays	30-36
bollard, single and double	30
cleat	32
ground stake	34
ring	35, 49
staghorn	31
T-Bar	31
winches	36
bell rope	190, **218-221**
bends	44-45, 72-92
alpine butterfly bend	80
anchor bend	54, **103**
Ashley's bend	81
becket bend	73
blood knot bend	88-89
bowline bend	92
carrick bend	90-91
fisherman's bend	35, **54**
harness bend	86-87
heaving line bend	76
Hunter's bend	82-83
racking bend	75, **77**
rigger's bend	82-83

seizing bend	75, **78-79**
sheet bend	**45**, 75
double	74
one way	75
variants	73
binding knots	**46-47**, 51, 127
bindings	126-142
see also seizing; serving	
binoculars lanyard	200-201
Blake's hitch	99
blocks	24-27
blood knot bend	88-89
boat hand lead line	226
bobbins of 'small stuff'	15
bollards, belaying to	30
bottle knot	122
bowlines	114-119
bowline bend	92
bowline on a bight	117
climber's method bowline	115
common bowline	30, 55, 105, **114**
'flying' bowline	56, **57-58**
running bowline	119
tucked bowline	116
water bowline	118
braided rope	**12**, 17, 18
brummel, McDonald	168-169
brummel splice	166, 169
bungee cord	**13**, 83
buntline hitch	106
Butane back splice or end seal	145
butcher's knot	121
cabin strings with three drops	206-207
care of rope	16
carrick bend	90-91
chain lashing	132-133
chain shortening	18, 19, 202
chain stopper	142

Chatham ropemasters	13	multiplait	154-155
check knot	90, **91**	one tuck	170-171
cheese (coil)	19, 214-217	three strand	148-149
cleat, belaying to	32		
clove hitch	49, 51, **97**, 127, 130, 131,	fake (or flake) rope stowage	19
	133, 136, 139, 193, 216	fender, disc	214-217
clove hitch, slipped	**50**, 97	fender, side	212-213
clove hitch over a post	50	fid, hollow	**21**, 161, 162, 163, 166, 168, 169
clove hitch to rail or ring	49	fid, Swedish	**21**, 144, 154, 155, 172, 173
coiling ropes	17-19	figure of eight knot	**42-43**, 60, 85, 121, 217
see also cheese		figure of eight loop	120
coils of rope	16	fisherman's bend	35, **54**
constrictor knot	**51**, 127, 145, 156,	fisherman's eight knot	85
	190, 199, 212, 218	fisherman's knot	44, 84
coverings, decorative rail,		fisherman's loop, double	123
spar and stanchion	192-193	flake (or fake) rope stowage	19
cow hitches	96	French hitching	192
crown knot	**66**, 146, 147, 198, 205,		
	212, 213, 218, 219	granny knot	46, **47**
crown sinnet lanyard	198	grommet, three strand rope	175-176
		ground stake, belaying to	34
deck coiling ropes	19	gun tackle	26
decorative rail, spar and		guyline hitch	107
stanchion coverings	192-193	gyn tackle	27
diagonal lashing	138-139		
diamond knot	**199**, 200, 207, 220	half hitch	**48**, 86-87, 95, 97, 103,
disc fender	214-217		129, 135, 142, 193
dispensing rope etc.	14-16	half hitch, slipped	20, **49**, 50, 95, 135
double fisherman's loop	123	half hitching	130
double luff	26	half knot	**46**, 176, 208, 210
double overhand knot	**40**, 60, 84, 111	halyard becket	160
double overhand loop	111	halyard knot	108
double overhand noose	**123**, 203	hand coiling	17, 18
double sheet bend	74	handy billy	26
drums of rope	15	hanks of rope	14
Du Pont	10	harness bend	86-87
		harness hitch	112
end knots	39-43, 60-66	harness loop	112
see also whipping		heaving line bend	76
ends, 'dogged'	**149**, 155	heaving line knot	**61**, 76
eye splices		heaving line weight	60, 61-63, 76
braid on braid	161-163	high post hitch	100
braid with core	164-165	hitches	48-54, 94-108
hollow braid	168-169	Blake's hitch	99

GLOSSARY & INDEX

buntline hitch	106
clove hitch	49, 51, **97**, 127, 130, 131, 133, 136, 139, 193, 216
clove hitch, slipped	**50**, 97
clove hitch over a post	50
clove hitch to rail or ring	49
cow hitches	96
guyline hitch	107
half hitch	**48**, 86-87, 95, 97, 103, 129, 135, 142, 193
half hitch, slipped	20, **49**, 50, 95, 135
harness hitch	112
high post hitch	100
icicle hitch	102
killick hitch	104
lighterman's hitch	30, 34
magnus hitch	52
marling hitch	48
mooring hitch	30, 34
pedigree cow hitch	96
pile hitch	101
prusik hitch	98
ring hitch	73, **96**, 197
rolling hitch	**52-53**, 141
round turn and two half hitches	35, **54**, 95
scaffold hitch	**105**, 127
timber hitch	**104**, 127, 138
trucker's hitch	134-135
waggoner's hitch	134-135
hitching	
French	192
half	130
marling	131
moku	193
St Mary's	193
hooks, mousing	128
Hunter, Dr	82
Hunter's bend	82-83
icicle hitch	102
inspecting rope	16-17
jigger	26
Josephine knot	90, **91**

jury mast knot	124
'kackling'	214, 215, **216**
killick hitch	104
king-spoke Turk's head knot	194-195
knife lanyard	199
'Knotting Matters'	107
lanyards	196-203
binoculars	200-201
crown sinnet	198
knife	199
Solomon bar	196-197
spectacles	202-203
lark's head knot	**96**, 128, 222
lashings	126-142
chain	132-133
diagonal	138-139
knots used	127
square	136-137
lead line, boat hand	226
light gyn	27
lighterman's hitch	30, 34
loops	55-58, 110, 124
see also bowlines	
alpine butterfly loop	**113**, 135, 145
angler's loop	56-58
artilleryman's loop	**112**, 145
figure of eight loop	120
fisherman's loop, double	123
harness loop	112
overhand loop	**41**, 111
overhand loop, double	111
perfection loop	56
luff tackle	26
'lump' knots	60, **61-63**
magnus hitch	52
maintenance of rope	16
manrope knot	66
marlinespike ropework	182-226
marling hitch(ing)	48, 131
Marlow Ropes Ltd	13
mast dropper	205

GLOSSARY & INDEX

mat, ocean plait	208-209
mat, square	210-211
mat, thump	204
Matthew Walker knot	**64-65**, 217, 218
McDonald, Margie	168
McDonald brummel	168-169
moku hitching	193
monkey's fist	**62-63**, 76
monofilament line, tying	88-89, 111
mooring hitch	30, 34
mousing	128, 129
multiplait rope	11
Nelson, Ken	206
nooses	110, 119, 123
overhand noose	41
overhand noose, double	**123**, 203
poacher's noose	123
ocean plait mat	208-209
overhand knot	**39**, 44, 60, 82, 84, 107, 111
overhand knot, double	**40**, 60, 84, 111
overhand knot, slipped	**39**, 41, 60
overhand loop	**41**, 111
overhand loop, double	111
overhand noose	41
overhand noose, double	**123**, 203
packer's knot	**121**, 215
palm and needle whipping	69-70
parbuckle	27
pedigree cow hitch	96
perfection loop	56
pile hitch	101
poacher's noose	123
prusik hitch	98
quoit, three strand rope	175-176
racking bend	75, **77**
rail coverings, decorative	192-193
reef bow	47
reef knot	**46**, 72, 92, 105, 127, 128, 197
reels of rope	15

rigger's bend	82-83
ring, belaying to	35, 49
ring hitch	73, **96**, 197
rinsing ropes	19
rogue's yarn	13
rolling hitch	**52-53**, 141
rope, new, form supplied in	14-16
rope construction	
braided	12
man-made fibres	**10**, 13, 168
multiplait	11
natural fibres	9
stranded	11
rope markings	13
rope stopper	141
round turn and two half hitches	35, **54**, 95
round turns	**53**, 54
runner	25
sailmaker's tools	21
sailmaker's whipping	68
St Mary's hitching	193
scaffold hitch	**105**, 127
scaffold knot	123
seizing	144, **179-180**
seizing bend	75, **78-79**
serving	144, **177-178**, 192
shackle, mousing	129
sheet bend	**45**, 75
sheet bend, double	74
sheet bend, one way	75
sheet bend variants	73
shock cord	**13**, 83
side fender	212-213
slipped clove hitch	**50**, 97
slipped half hitch	20, **49**, 50, 95, 135
slipped overhand knot	**39**, 41, 60
Smith, John	102
Solomon bar lanyard	196-197
Spanish windlass	28
spar coverings, decorative	192-193
spectacles lanyard	202-203
splicing	144-176
back splice	160

GLOSSARY & INDEX

braid on braid eye splice	161-163
braid with core eye splice	164-165
braided rope	144, 160-169, 172-174
brummel splice	166, 169
hollow braid eye splice	168-169
knots used	145
multiplait eye splice	154-155
multiplait rope	144, 154-159
multiplait rope to chain splice	158-159
multiplait short splice	156-157
one tuck eye splice	170-171
reduction splice	166-167
rope to wire splice	172-174
stranded rope	144, 146-153, 175-176
taper splice	166-167
three strand back splice	146-147
three strand eye splice	148-149
three strand long splice	152-153
three strand short splice	150-151
three strand to chain splice	147
tools	**21**, 144, 149, 154, 155, 161, 162, 163, 166, 168, 169, 173
with wire	170-174
yachtsman's roll splice	170-171
spools of 'small stuff'	15
square knot	196, 197
square lashing	136-137
square mat	210-211
staghorn, belaying to	31
stanchion coverings, decorative	192-193
star knot	**190-191**, 219
stopper, chain	142
stopper, rope	141
stopper knots	39-43, 60-66
see also whipping	
stowing ropes	17-19
stranded rope	**11**, 17
strings, cabin, with three drops	206-207
T-Bar, belaying to	31
tackles	24-27
tape	13, 86-87
taped ends	145
terms used in knotting and ropework	20

throwing line weight	60, 61-63, 76
thumb knot	39
thump mat	204
timber hitch	**104**, 127, 138
tools	**21-22**, 144, 149, 154, 155, 161, 162, 163, 166, 168, 169, 173
Toss, Brion	168, 193
transom knot	137, **140**
tricing	25
trucker's dolly/hitch	134-135
Turk's head knots	183-189
king-spoke	194-195
six lead five bight	**188-189**, 194, 205
three lead five bight	186-187
three lead four bight	**184-185**, 204
waggoner's hitch	134-135
wall knot	66, 220
whipping	67-70
common	**67**, 145, 174
palm and needle	69-70
sailmaker's	68
winch, belaying to	36
windlass, belaying to	36
windlass, Spanish	28
wire, splicing with	170-174

RYA Protecting and Promoting Boating

15% discount on all RYA books for RYA members

The RYA is the UK governing body of motor and sail cruising, dinghy and yacht racing, powerboating, windsurfing and personal watercraft. We are committed to publishing high quality books that you can trust on all aspects of boating.

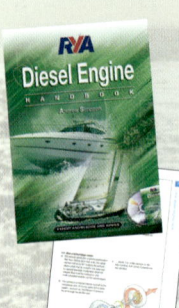

RYA Diesel Engine Handbook

From one of the UK's most respected journalists, Andrew Simpson, with an accompanying CD-Rom by Nick Eales of Sea Start, the RYA Diesel Engine Handbook provides the expert instruction required by any diesel engine boater. 
G25
Available now!

RYA Start Powerboating

Official book of Levels 1 and 2 of the National Powerboating Scheme and ideal for day boaters, anglers and divers. Written by expert powerboater Jon Mendez.
G48
Available now!

RYA Crew to Win

Packed with full colour photographs and diagrams, and written by Olympic medallist Joe Glanfield, RYA Crew to Win covers all the technical essentials needed to succeed in crewed boats.
G39
Available now!

RYA Go Cruising!

The long-awaited follow-up to Claudia Myatt's Go Sailing books, this beautifully illustrated, fun and informative title covers all the essentials required to help young people become valuable members of crew on both sail and power yachts.
G42
Available now!

RYA VHF Handbook

From the author of the RYA Navigation Handbook a brand new addition to the best selling RYA Handbook series. Details everything that sailors need to know about using VHF radios and simplifies a sometimes daunting subject.
G31
Available now!

To find out more about RYA Publications, or to place an order, please visit
www.rya.org.uk/shop
or call **0845 345 0372**

LOOKING FOR THE PERFECT GIFT?

We now sell RYA Vouchers that can be used to purchase RYA training courses at over 250 participating centres in the UK and abroad.

For further information, call **0845 345 0400** or visit **www.rya.org.uk/vouchers**

RYA

MEMBERSHIP

Promoting and Protecting Boating

www.rya.org.uk

JOIN NOW online at www.rya.org.uk

RYA

MEMBERSHIP

Promoting and Protecting Boating

The RYA is the national organisation which represents the interests of everyone who goes boating for pleasure. The greater the membership, the louder our voice when it comes to protecting members' interests. Apply for membership today, and support the RYA, to help the RYA support you.

Benefits of Membership

- Access to expert advice on all aspects of boating from legal wrangles to training matters
- Special members' discounts on a range of products and services including boat insurance, books, videos and class certificates
- Free issue of certificates of competence, increasingly asked for by everyone from overseas governments to holiday companies, insurance underwriters to boat hirers
- Access to the wide range of RYA publications, including the quarterly magazine
- Third Party insurance for windsurfing members
- Free Internet access with RYA-Online
- Special discounts on AA membership
- Regular offers in RYA Magazine

... and much more

JOIN NOW online at www.rya.org.uk

JOIN NOW - membership form opposite

Join online at **www.rya.org.uk**

Visit our website for information, advice, members' services and web shop

Instructions to your Bank or Building Society to pay by Direct Debit

Please complete this form and return it to:
Royal Yachting Association, RYA House, Ensign Way, Hamble, Southampton, Hampshire SO31 4YA

To The Manager: _____ Bank/Building Society

Address: _____

Post Code: _____

1. Name(s) of account holder(s)

2. Branch Sort Code

3. Bank or Building Society account number

4. Cash, Cheque, Postal Order enclosed £ _____
Made payable to the Royal Yachting Association

Office use only: Membership Number Allocated **077**

Originators Identification Number

| 9 | 5 | 5 | 2 | 1 | 3 |

5. RYA Membership Number (For office use only)

6. Instruction to pay your Bank or Building Society
Please pay Royal Yachting Association Direct Debits from the account detailed in this instruction subject to the safeguards assured by The Direct Debit Guarantee.
I understand that this instruction may remain with the Royal Yachting Association and, if so, details will be passed electronically to my Bank/Building Society.

Signature(s) _____

Date _____

Office use / Centre Stamp

Banks and Building Societies may not accept Direct Debit instructions for some types of account

① Important To help us comply with Data Protection legislation, please tick *either* Box A or Box B (you must tick Box A to ensure you receive the full benefits of RYA membership). The RYA will not pass your data to third parties.

☐ **A.** I wish to join the RYA and receive future information on member services, benefits (as listed in RYA Magazine and website) and offers.
☐ **B.** I wish to join the RYA but do not wish to receive future information on member services, benefits (as listed in RYA Magazine and website) and offers.

When completed, please send this form to: RYA, RYA House, Ensign Way, Hamble, Southampton, SO31 4YA

②

	Title	Forename	Surname	Date of Birth	Male	Female
1.				D D / M M / Y Y	☐	☐
2.				D D / M M / Y Y	☐	☐
3.				D D / M M / Y Y	☐	☐
4.				D D / M M / Y Y	☐	☐

Address

Town   County   Post Code

Evening Telephone   Daytime Telephone

email

Signature: _____ Date: _____

③ Type of membership required: *(Tick Box)*

☐ **Personal** *Annual rate £39 or £36 by Direct Debit*
☐ **Under 21** *Annual rate £13 (no reduction for Direct Debit)*
☐ **Family*** *Annual rate £58 or £55 by Direct Debit*

* Family Membership: 2 adults plus any under 21s all living at the same address

④ Please tick ONE box to show your main boating interest.

☐ Yacht Racing   ☐ Yacht Cruising
☐ Dinghy Racing   ☐ Dinghy Cruising
☐ Personal Watercraft   ☐ Inland Waterways
☐ Powerboat Racing   ☐ Windsurfing
☐ Motor Boating   ☐ Sportsboats and RIBs

Please see Direct Debit form overleaf